Another Big Book of American Trivia

D0106729

Another BIG BOOK OF
American Trivia

★ ★ ★

J. STEPHEN LANG

Tyndale House Publishers, Inc.
WHEATON, ILLINOIS

Library of Congress Cataloging-in-Publication Data

Lang, J. Stephen.
    Another big book of American trivia / J. Stephen Lang.
        p.   cm.
    Sequel to: The big book of American trivia.
    ISBN 0-8423-0155-0 (sc)
    1. United States—Miscellanea.   2. Popular culture—United States—
Miscellanea. I. Title.
    E156.L35   1997
    973'.076—dc21   97-7009

Printed in the United States of America

03   02   01   00   99   98   97
8   7   6   5   4   3   2   1

CONTENTS

INTRODUCTION

With so many people fascinated with trivia, and with such a great subject as America, why not publish a book of *American Trivia*? We did. And we called it *The Big Book of American Trivia*.

The problem: One volume couldn't possibly do justice to such a *big* subject. The possibilities for topics and questions seemed endless. That's why we humbly present this second volume, since *The Big Book of American Trivia* just couldn't cover all the material provided by this huge, quirky, inspiring, puzzling, and fascinating thing we call the U.S.A.

Entertainment, the way we amuse ourselves, is a huge category—the Grammy Awards, TV, dance, musicals, Oscar-winning songs, rock group members, and more. We also amuse ourselves with *literature,* covered in the section Write On, which concentrates on best-sellers and notable biographies. And, of course, related to amusing ourselves is *sports.*

How about *everyday life?* The section Clothed and Fed looks at things we eat, drink, and wear. Related to this is The Mighty Dollar, with some intriguing questions about American advertising and some truly lavish spenders.

What about *places?* Geography need not be dull, not if you're curious about American place-names and the great tourist attractions across the nation, including some of the older ones. You'll love the questions in the sections Tourists Forever and A Sense of Place. (If your family is on a road trip, these questions are a great place to start.)

Knowing how most people love their home turf, a section of *state* questions seemed essential—ten questions about each state (and D.C., too) to be exact.

Then there is *history.* A boring topic? No way! There's an entire section on *the decades of the nineteenth century* called Breezing through History—a few questions on each decade, hitting the high points and bringing up a few oddities too.

Above all, there are *people*—The Famous and Infamous, from Pat Sajak to Thomas Edison to Joan Rivers to Stonewall Jackson to Cal Ripken Jr. to Erma Bombeck to Billy Graham. Our American family portrait includes millions of faces—not all pretty, but always intriguing.

Under these broad categories are more than 150 topical sections. Included are Notable Nicknames; TV History; The Great American Musical; Sports Firsts; Criminals Great and Small; The Well-Dressed American; Sister Acts (and Other Family Acts); The Bible on the American Map; Business, American Style; Unusual Museums; A Day at the Beach; and so on. I couldn't include every subject, but the range is wide—inventors, advertising, famous women, national parks, best-sellers, food and drink, Civil War sites, and many, many others.

The topics are organized in fifteen sections. But despite the organization, the book is for browsing. It was made to fill up your family's time on a car or plane trip ("Are we there yet?"), your daily commute on the train, the hour you spend waiting at the dentist's office, the times when you and other folks in your car pool are in the mood for a game of "quiz me." In other words, the book is designed to be read randomly, anywhere, and with no preparation of any kind. It is designed to entertain the person who unashamedly likes to be entertained—and challenged.

As the writing of this book progressed, it became, truly, a labor of love. After traveling abroad a number of times, I still find that my home country is the most fascinating, the one that lends itself most readily to the kind of book you are now holding.

If you find yourself able to answer every question in this book correctly, give yourself an A+ in American Studies. If not, then after reading this you may consider yourself a little wiser, and maybe even a little more appreciative of this vast, enchanting land.

PART ONE
The Famous & the Infamous

☆ Notable Nicknames

1. What recent president's nicknames include "Dutch," "the Great Communicator," and "the Teflon President"?
2. The founder of Wal-Mart preferred that his employees call him "Mr. Sam." Who was he?
3. What great inventor was "the Wizard of Menlo Park"?
4. What pop idol, who died in 1977, was "the King"?
5. What lanky president from Illinois was "the Rail Splitter"?
6. The First Battle of Manassas in 1861 saw the bestowing of the Civil War's most famous nickname. What became the permanent nickname of Confederate general Thomas Jackson?
7. What pop singer, famous for "The Night They Drove Old Dixie Down," was known as "the Queen of Protest"?
8. Apple orchard planter and folk hero John Chapman was better known by what name?
9. What big band leader was known as "the King of Jazz"?
10. What early president was nicknamed "the Father of American Independence"?
11. What famous senator, known as "Mr. Republican," has a memorial bell tower in D.C.?
12. The home of the cranky journalist called "the Sage of Baltimore" is open as a museum. Who was he?
13. What Nebraska city was named for a great American explorer known as "the Pathfinder"?
14. Colonial New Yorkers called them "the Bennington Mob," but in Vermont they were known as what?
15. Oakland, California, has a park named for its most famous poet, known as "the Poet of the Sierras." Who was he?
16. What great statesman and presidential candidate was known as "the Great Commoner"?

Notable Nicknames *(answers)*

1. Ronald Reagan
2. Sam Walton
3. Thomas Edison
4. Elvis Presley, of course
5. Abraham Lincoln
6. "Stonewall," after one of Jackson's fellow generals said, "Look, there is Jackson standing like a stone wall."
7. Joan Baez
8. Johnny Appleseed
9. Paul Whiteman
10. John Adams, the second president
11. Robert Taft
12. H. L. Mencken
13. Fremont, named for John C. Frémont, who was also a Union general and presidential candidate
14. The Green Mountain Boys, the Revolutionary War band led by Ethan Allen
15. Joaquin Miller; an eccentric character, Miller's house (in the park) reflects its owner's quirkiness.
16. William Jennings Bryan

17. What early president, who succeeded to the office after President Harrison died, was referred to as "His Accidency"?
18. At least ten cities or towns, including ones in Illinois and Indiana, share what name, after a "Swamp Fox"?
19. Front Royal, Virginia, contains the home of the Confederacy's most famous female spy, "the Confederate Cleopatra." Who was she?
20. During the Civil War, Confederate general Leonidas Polk was given a nickname based on his prewar profession. What was it?
21. What patriotic songwriter known as "the Yankee Doodle Dandy" played in one movie, *The Phantom President*, in 1932?
22. What Kentucky politician of the 1800s was known as "the Great Compromiser"?
23. TV chef Graham Kerr was what kind of "Gourmet"?
24. What world-famous pirate is said to have buried his loot on one of Georgia's islands?
25. What infamous Union general in the Civil War was nicknamed "Cump"?

☆ What's My Line? Common Bonds

If you hear the names Ronald Reagan, Abraham Lincoln, and Thomas Jefferson, you say (probably), "Ah! They're all U.S. presidents!" Test your knowledge of famous Americans of today and yesterday as you detect the common bond of each of the following groups. Remember, these include *everything*—comics, authors, politicians, artists, writers—a cast of thousands.

1. Rush Limbaugh, G. Gordon Liddy, Oliver North
2. Edgar Allan Poe, Robert Lowell, Edgar Lee Masters
3. Joan Rivers, Rosie O'Donnell, Lily Tomlin
4. Bil Keane, Gary Larson, Jeff MacNelly
5. Pat Sajak, Groucho Marx, Peter Marshall

17. John Tyler, first vice president to become president upon the president's death
18. Marion, named for Francis Marion, the Revolutionary War's "Swamp Fox"
19. Belle Boyd, who had several colorful nicknames
20. He was an Episcopal bishop, and he became known as the Confederacy's "Fighting Bishop"—an odd combination of careers.
21. George M. Cohan
22. Henry Clay
23. "The Galloping Gourmet"
24. Edward Teach, better known as "Blackbeard"; the alleged burial place is known (naturally) as Blackbeard Island.
25. William T. Sherman, whose middle name was Tecumseh—"Cump," for short

What's My Line? Common Bonds *(answers)*

1. Conservative radio talk show hosts
2. Poets
3. Comediennes
4. Cartoonists
5. Game show hosts

6. Grandma Moses, Edward Hicks, George Inness
7. William F. Buckley, Cal Thomas, Paul Greenberg
8. Robert Schuller, Billy Graham, Oral Roberts
9. Burt Bacharach, Irving Berlin, George M. Cohan
10. Philip C. Johnson, Benjamin Latrobe, Albert Kahn
11. Robert Fulton, Elias Howe, Cyrus McCormick
12. Flip Wilson, George Carlin, John Byner
13. Millard Fillmore, Rutherford Hayes, John Tyler
14. James Fenimore Cooper, Nathaniel Hawthorne, Ernest Hemingway
15. Buckminster Fuller, Cass Gilbert, James Hoban
16. Michael Medved, Gene Siskel, Rex Reed
17. John James Audubon, Mary Cassatt, Frederic Remington
18. Ursula LeGuin, Ray Bradbury, Isaac Asimov
19. David Brinkley, Walter Cronkite, Tom Brokaw
20. Henry Wadsworth Longfellow, Ogden Nash, Stephen Vincent Benét
21. Lee Meriwether, Bess Myerson, Terry Meuwsen
22. Hulk Hogan, Gorgeous George, Sgt. Slaughter
23. Frank Capra, Tim Burton, Oliver Stone
24. Dave Barry, Erma Bombeck, Mike Royko
25. Neil Simon, Thornton Wilder, Eugene O'Neill
26. Gerald Ford, Ronald Reagan, Dwight Eisenhower
27. Cathy Guisewite, Johnny Hart, Bob Thaves
28. Jesse Helms, Phil Gramm, Orrin Hatch
29. August Saint-Gaudens, David Smith, John Bernard Flannagan
30. Jerry Falwell, Fulton Sheen, Pat Robertson

☆ Three Suicides

1. What Nobel Prize–winning novelist, famed for *A Farewell to Arms* and other classics, shot himself in 1961?
2. George Eastman, who committed suicide in 1932, founded what famous company?

6. Painters
7. Syndicated newspaper columnists
8. TV preachers
9. Songwriters
10. Architects
11. Inventors
12. Comedians
13. U.S. presidents
14. Novelists
15. Architects
16. Film critics
17. Painters
18. Science fiction writers
19. TV network anchormen
20. Poets
21. Miss America winners
22. Wrestlers
23. Movie directors
24. Syndicated humor columnists
25. Playwrights
26. Republican presidents
27. Cartoonists
28. Senators
29. Sculptors
30. TV preachers

Three Suicides *(answers)*

1. Ernest Hemingway
2. Eastman Kodak, maker of film, cameras, etc.; Eastman himself was the inventor of flexible film, making photography practical for everyone instead of just professionals.

3. What glamorous blonde star died in 1962, supposedly by overdosing on sleeping pills?

✩ Notable Women, and Some Less Notable

1. What famous Indian woman of colonial times died in England after being baptized as a Christian?
2. The first female guest host on *The Tonight Show* was what comedienne?
3. What generic name was given in World War II to American women who worked in factories?
4. What Wild West legend did Calamity Jane request to be buried beside?
5. What old and respected women's organization has a museum in Washington, D.C.?
6. Which was the first U.S. service academy to admit women?
7. What Indian woman, nicknamed "Bird Woman," was a guide on the Lewis and Clark expedition of 1804?
8. What notable antialcohol group has its headquarters in Evanston, Illinois?
9. Rochester, New York, has a memorial to what women's rights leader of the 1800s?
10. Barbara Fritchie House in Frederick, Maryland, commemorates a ninety-five-year-old woman who supposedly defied a Confederate general. Who was he?
11. Wells, Maine, has a wildlife refuge named for what popular twentieth-century science writer?
12. Glen Echo, Maryland, has a museum devoted to the founder of the Red Cross. Who was she?
13. Ponca City, Oklahoma's Pioneer Museum, is devoted to what type of person?

3. Marilyn Monroe

Notable Women, and Some Less Notable *(answers)*

1. Pocahontas
2. Joan Rivers
3. Rosie the Riveter
4. Wild Bill Hickok; both are buried at Mount Moriah Cemetery in Deadwood, South Dakota.
5. The Daughters of the American Revolution (DAR)
6. The Coast Guard Academy
7. Sacajawea
8. The Women's Christian Temperance Union (WCTU); the home of its founder, Frances Willard, is also in Evanston.
9. Susan B. Anthony
10. Thomas "Stonewall" Jackson, who marched through town in 1862; according to legend, Fritchie waved her Union flag, against Jackson's orders.
11. Rachel Carson, author of *The Sea around Us* and *Silent Spring*
12. Clara Barton
13. Pioneer women; the museum memorializes the courage of women on the frontier.

14. What name was given to navy women in World War I?
15. Lenox, Massachusetts, has the estate of which noted woman author of the twentieth century?
16. Charlotte, North Carolina, and Charlottesville, Virginia, were named for a very important woman in Britain. Who was she?
17. The Whirly Girls are women pilots of what type of vehicles?

☆ Also Known As . . .

The name a person is born with is *not* necessarily the name the public knows. This is true not only of entertainers but also of criminals, politicians, sports figures, authors, and practically anyone in the public eye. The clues here list the *real* names of famous people, with a little hint for each one. Try to determine the name that each one is known by.

1. Newton Leroy McPherson (Republican leader in the late twentieth century)
2. Gary Keillor (radio variety show host)
3. Marion Gordon Robertson (TV evangelist)
4. William Bonney (gangster of the 1800s)
5. Jacob Cohen (stand-up comic who "don't get no respect")
6. Dino Crocetti (crooner, former movie partner of Jerry Lewis)
7. Mary Jean Tomlin (comedienne)
8. Edward Albert Heimberger (actor, remembered for *Green Acres)*
9. Alphonso D'Abruzzo (sitcom and movie actor, famous for *M*A*S*H)*
10. Thomas Mapother (handsome movie idol of the 1980s and 1990s)
11. John Sanford (comic and sitcom actor, noted for *Sanford and Son)*

14. The Yeomanettes
15. Edith Wharton, author of *The Age of Innocence* and other classics
16. Queen Charlotte, the wife of King George III
17. Helicopters

Also Known As . . . *(answers)*
1. Newt Gingrich
2. Garrison Keillor
3. Pat Robertson
4. Billy the Kid
5. Rodney Dangerfield
6. Dean Martin
7. Lily Tomlin
8. Eddie Albert
9. Alan Alda
10. Tom Cruise
11. Redd Foxx

12. Allen Konigsberg (bespectacled comic and movie director-writer)
13. Bernice Frankel (comic actress, noted for *The Golden Girls*)
14. Lucille Le Sueur (movie queen of the 1930s and 1940s)
15. Doris von Kappelhoff (blonde singer and actress)
16. Frederick Austerlitz (dancer, actor, singer)
17. Betty Joan Perske (actress, wife of Humphrey Bogart)
18. Robert Edward Turner (Atlanta-based TV executive)
19. Jack Eichelbaum (early movie studio head)
20. Gloria Svensson (silent movie star)
21. Anne Maria Italiano (actress, wife of Mel Brooks)
22. Charles Buchinski (tough action-film hero)
23. Albert Einstein (comic and movie director)
24. Anthony Benedetto (romantic singer)
25. John Florence Sullivan (radio comic)
26. Greta Gustafsson (movie queen of the 1930s)
27. Frances Gumm (singer and actress, noted for *Oz*)
28. Benjamin Kubelsky (violin-playing comic)
29. David Kotkin (magician)
30. Henry John Deutschendorf Jr. (Rocky Mountain singer)
31. Thomas Lanier Williams (twentieth-century playwright)
32. Isaiah Edwin Leopold (zany comic of film and TV)
33. Denton True Young (phenomenal baseball pitcher)
34. Borge Rosenbaum (piano-playing comic)
35. James Bumgarner (actor, noted especially for *Maverick*)
36. Robert Williams (black comic actor, noted for *Benson*)
37. Paul Rubenfeld (comic and former kids' show host)
38. Ehrich Weiss (famous escape artist)
39. Moses Horowitz (one of a famous comic trio—nyuk, nyuk)
40. Larry Zeigler (TV interviewer, glasses)

12. Woody Allen
13. Beatrice Arthur
14. Joan Crawford
15. Doris Day
16. Fred Astaire
17. Lauren Bacall
18. Ted Turner
19. Jack Warner (of Warner Brothers)
20. Gloria Swanson
21. Anne Bancroft
22. Charles Bronson
23. Albert Brooks
24. Tony Bennett
25. Fred Allen
26. Greta Garbo
27. Judy Garland
28. Jack Benny
29. David Copperfield
30. John Denver
31. Tennessee Williams
32. Ed Wynn
33. Cy Young
34. Victor Borge
35. James Garner
36. Robert Guillaume
37. Pee-Wee Herman
38. Harry Houdini
39. Moe Howard (one of the Three Stooges)
40. Larry King

☆ Bigger than Life: Folklore Figures

Americans have always loved a tall tale. Maybe because it's such a big country, it has to have folktales (and folk heroes) to match. Some of these folklore figures were real human beings whose exploits got "stretched" as time passed. And some were just plain *mythical.*

1. What lumberjack was said to have lived between the Winter of the Blue Snow and the Spring That the Rain Came Up from China?
2. What huge (and oddly colored) animal was the pet of the lumberjack in question 1?
3. What frontiersman and Indian fighter wore a coonskin cap and had a rifle he fondly called "Old Betsy"?
4. What mythical New England sea captain was supposed to be as tall as a ship's mast?
5. The legendary Indian hero Manabozho was transformed by poet Henry Wadsworth Longfellow into what figure?
6. Washington Irving took a German folktale about a goatherd who meets some gnomes and turned it into what classic American short story about a man who took a *long* nap?
7. Parson Mason Weems invented what legend about George Washington's boyhood?
8. What Wild West legend was supposedly raised by a coyote, rode a cougar, used a snake as a lariat, and could ride a tornado?
9. What real-life frontiersman supposedly described himself as "half-horse, half-alligator, a little touched with the snapping turtle"?
10. John Chapman, known for traveling on foot and planting apple trees throughout America, was transformed into a folk hero with what name?

Bigger than Life: Folklore Figures *(answers)*

1. Paul Bunyan, whose tales were told in lumber camps all over the northern U.S.
2. Paul's fabulous blue ox, Babe.
3. Daniel Boone; the coonskin cap may be legend, but he definitely did own Old Betsy.
4. Alfred Stormalong, usually just called by his last name.
5. Hiawatha, whose story is told in Longfellow's *Song of Hiawatha*
6. Rip Van Winkle; Irving took pains to hide the fact that he hadn't invented the tale out of his own head.
7. The story of George Washington chopping down a cherry tree ("Father, I cannot tell a lie."); a legend, but still a nice story.
8. Pecos Bill, the Superman of cowboy tales. Walt Disney did a delightful animated film of ol' Bill.
9. Davy Crockett; since he actually died fighting at the Alamo, his animal ancestry did not make him invincible.
10. Johnny Appleseed; the real John was a missionary for the religious sect called Swedenborgians.

11. Mike Fink, the red-haired "king bully" of the Mississippi River boatmen, was said to drink a full gallon of what liquid every day?

12. Jim Bowie, inventor of the famed Bowie knife and known as a slave trader and ferocious fighter, died at what notorious Texas location?

13. Barbara Fritchie was, in legend, a ninety-five-year-old Maryland woman who defiantly waved the Union flag at what invading Confederate general?

14. In 1906 Daniel Carter Beard started a boys organization called The Society of the Sons of _____. Which American frontiersman was the group named for?

15. The French Canadian woman Emmeline Labiche, separated by the English from her fiancé, was transformed by Longfellow into what poetic heroine?

16. "Brethren of the Coast" was a polite name for what feared group of sea captains of the 1700s?

17. What color was the creature called "the Steed of the Prairies" or "the Ghost Horse of the Plains"?

18. What ghastly creature was supposedly sighted in the 1810s near Boston and Long Island?

19. Gambler Steve Brodie claimed in 1886 that he had jumped off a famous New York bridge and survived. What bridge?

☆ Eureka! Famous Discoveries

1. In the 1600s a priest discovered a "thick water which ignited like brandy" in New York state. What was it?

2. What no-stick substance did Roy Plunkett discover in 1938?

3. In 1540 Lopez de Cardenas discovered what natural wonder, more than twenty miles long?

11. Whiskey; Fink was such a wild man that every red-haired child along the river was referred to as "Mike Fink's brat."
12. The Alamo; he was partially disabled at that time, but fought like a tiger anyway.
13. Thomas "Stonewall" Jackson; in poet John Greenleaf Whittier's version of the tale, Jackson had ordered that anyone displaying the flag would be shot. Barbara defied him, which deeply impressed Jackson.
14. Daniel Boone; the society was eventually incorporated into the Boy Scouts.
15. *Evangeline,* a lovely story that ends with the aged heroine meeting her fiancé many years later in Louisiana
16. Pirates; actually, Brethren of the Coast was their own name, and they had their own code of ethics.
17. White, of course (What other color would a ghost horse be?)
18. A sea serpent, generally referred to as the Gloucester sea serpent
19. The Brooklyn Bridge; Brodie was an actual person, and somehow his preposterous tale has made him a folk hero.

Eureka! Famous Discoveries *(answers)*

1. Petroleum; it was known by the Indians years before anyone realized the fluid had some uses.
2. Teflon (which is easier than its scientific name, tetrafluorethylene polymers)
3. The Grand Canyon

4. Sunflower Landing in Mississippi is important because the first European saw the Mississippi River at that site. Who was he?

5. What mineral was discovered in Arizona's Vulture Mine in the 1800s?

6. What important passageway through the Appalachian Mountains was discovered in 1750?

7. What valuable substance was discovered in Louisiana in 1901?

8. What radioactive ore, much of it in the Southwest, was discovered by a Navajo Indian in 1950?

9. What mineral discovery of 1859 transformed Virginia City, Nevada, into one of the wealthiest cities in the country?

10. What process for giving durability to rubber was accidentally discovered by Charles Goodyear?

11. What type of field was discovered in Kilgore, Texas?

12. What event in January 1848 transformed sparsely settled California into a booming Golden State?

13. San Diego's main city park is named for what Spanish explorer (best known for discovering the Pacific Ocean)?

14. What energy source, discovered in 1857, dealt the deathblow to America's whaling industry?

☆ Favorite Sons (and Daughters)

People and places go together, and some celebrities have definite _place_ connections—like Walt Disney and California, Will Rogers and Oklahoma, etc. Match each set of people here with the state they're connected with—and remember, these are Americans from every period of history. (Note: If you see someone's name listed more than once, attribute that to our mobile society. Ronald Reagan, for example, is associated with California, although he was born and educated in Illinois.)

4. Spanish explorer Hernando de Soto, who discovered the river in 1541
5. Gold; the mine was the richest gold find in Arizona.
6. The Cumberland Gap
7. Petroleum, which became a major part of the state's economy
8. Uranium
9. The Comstock Lode, which yielded both gold and silver
10. Vulcanizing, which made durable auto tires a possibility
11. An oil field—the largest in the U.S.
12. The discovery of gold at Sutter's mill, leading to the gold rush of 1849
13. Balboa
14. Petroleum; afterward people no longer had the need for the whale oil, which had been used as lamp fuel.

1. Robert E. Lee, Edgar Allen Poe, Pat Robertson, John Tyler
2. Helen Keller, "Bear" Bryant, George Wallace, Booker T. Washington
3. Newt Gingrich, Gladys Knight, Crawford Long, Alexander Stephens
4. Benjamin Franklin, Stephen Foster, James Buchanan, Robert Fulton
5. Sam Houston, Phil Gramm, Sam Rayburn, Carol Burnett
6. Clark Gable, John Glenn, Pete Rose, Robert A. Taft
7. Tom Bodett, Susan Butcher, E. L. "Bob" Bartlett, Sydney Laurence
8. Woodrow Wilson, Bruce Springsteen, Thomas Paine, Albert Einstein
9. Linda Ronstadt, Cochise, Wyatt Earp, William Rehnquist
10. P. T. Barnum, Katharine Hepburn, Mark Twain, Eli Whitney
11. King Kamehamaha, Father Damien, Queen Liliuokalani, Daniel Inouye
12. Glen Campbell, Dizzy Dean, Dick Powell, Orval Farbus
13. Abraham Lincoln, Cyrus McCormick, Carl Sandburg, Frank Lloyd Wright
14. Harlan Sanders, Muhammad Ali, John James Audubon, Henry Clay
15. Henry Wadsworth Longfellow, Hannibal Hamlin, Edna St. Vincent Millay, James G. Blaine
16. Brigham Young, Orrin Hatch, Donny Osmond, Merlin Olsen
17. John Steinbeck, Earl Warren, Bret Harte, Richard Nixon
18. Ty Cobb, Ray Charles, Joel Chandler Harris, Margaret Mitchell
19. Bob Dole, Dwight Eisenhower, Wild Bill Hickok, Alf Landon
20. Paul Revere, John F. Kennedy, Henry David Thoreau, Louisa May Alcott

Favorite Sons (and Daughters) *(answers)*

1. Virginia
2. Alabama
3. Georgia
4. Pennsylvania
5. Texas
6. Ohio
7. Alaska
8. New Jersey
9. Arizona
10. Connecticut
11. Hawaii
12. Arkansas
13. Illinois
14. Kentucky
15. Maine
16. Utah
17. California
18. Georgia
19. Kansas
20. Massachusetts

21. Robert Frost, Daniel Webster, Franklin Pierce, Mary Baker Eddy
22. David Letterman, Red Skelton, Lew Wallace, Larry Bird
23. Calvin Coolidge, Ethan Allen, James Fisk, John Dewey
24. Henry Ford, Lee Iacocca, Will Kellogg, Chief Pontiac
25. Alan Simpson, Buffalo Bill Cody, Nellie Tayloe Ross, James Bridger
26. Dave Barry, Joseph Stilwell, Edmund Kirby Smith, Marjorie Kinnan Rawlings
27. Chief Joseph, William E. Borah, Frank Church, Sacajawea
28. Al Hirt, Pierre Beauregard, Huey Long, Louis Armstrong
29. E. I. du Pont, John P. Marquand, Howard Pyle, Caesar Rodney
30. Orson Welles, Robert LaFollette, Jacques Marquette, Harry Houdini
31. John Deere, Stephen Douglas, Marshall Field, Benny Goodman
32. Barry Goldwater, Francisco Kino, Morris Udall, Carl Hayden
33. Minnie Pearl, Alvin York, Andrew Jackson, James K. Polk
34. Will Rogers, Johnny Bench, Sequoyah, Oral Roberts
35. Molly Brown, M. Scott Carpenter, Mamie Eisenhower, Ben Nighthorse Campbell
36. George Gallup, Meredith Willson, Grant Wood, Henry Wallace
37. Amelia Earhart, Walter Chrysler, William Inge, Carry Nation
38. Johnny Cash, Brooks Robinson, William Fulbright, C. Vann Woodward
39. Luther Burbank, William Randolph Hearst, Ronald Reagan, Jack London
40. Francis Scott Key, Charles Carroll, Upton Sinclair, H. L. Mencken

21. New Hampshire
22. Indiana
23. Vermont
24. Michigan
25. Wyoming
26. Florida
27. Idaho
28. Louisiana
29. Delaware
30. Wisconsin
31. Illinois
32. Arizona
33. Tennessee
34. Oklahoma
35. Colorado
36. Iowa
37. Kansas
38. Arkansas
39. California
40. Maryland

☆ What's My Line? Common Bonds (Part 2)

What do Natalie Cole, Amy Grant, and Kate Smith have in common? They are (or were) all pop singers. Find the common bond that unites the groups below. Keep in mind that the names are from both past and present.

1. Meryl Streep, Katharine Hepburn, Sissy Spacek
2. Andrew Wyeth, Georgia O'Keefe, Jackson Pollack
3. Ira Gershwin, Lorenz Hart, Alan Lerner
4. Robert Frost, Carl Sandburg, James Russell Lowell
5. William McKinley, John F. Kennedy, James Garfield
6. Francis Marion, George Washington, Light-Horse Harry Lee
7. Cochise, Crazy Horse, Geronimo
8. Herbie Mann, Artie Shaw, Jack Teagarden
9. Jonathan Edwards, Reinhold Niebuhr, Robert Dabney
10. Steve Allen, Johnny Carson, Jack Paar
11. Jackie Vernon, Jack Carter, Red Skelton
12. Herman Melville, Joan Didion, Pat Conroy
13. T. S. Eliot, Conrad Aiken, Sara Teasdale
14. Lee Harvey Oswald, Leon Czolgosz, Charles Guiteau
15. George Catlin, Winslow Homer, Hans Hofmann
16. Sam Houston, Winfield Scott, Zachary Taylor
17. Ross Perot, Theodore Roosevelt, George Wallace
18. Harold Arlen, Richard Rodgers, Harry Warren
19. James Oglethorpe, William Penn, Lord Baltimore
20. Stan Kenton, Roy Haynes, Keith Jarrett
21. Pat Paulsen, Steven Wright, Richard Pryor
22. John Hinckley Jr., Sara Jane Moore, Squeaky Fromme
23. U. S. Grant, William Sherman, George Meade
24. Rembrandt Peale, Gilbert Stuart, Thomas Sully
25. Fats Waller, Herbie Hancock, Art Pepper
26. Tim Conway, Don Knotts, Jim Backus

What's My Line? Common Bonds (Part 2) *(answers)*

1. Movie actresses
2. Painters
3. Song lyricists
4. Poets
5. Presidents who were assassinated
6. Military leaders in the American Revolution
7. Native American leaders against white expansion
8. Jazz musicians
9. Theologians
10. Former *Tonight Show* hosts
11. Comedians
12. Novelists
13. Poets
14. Presidential assassins
15. Painters
16. Leaders in the Mexican War
17. Third-party presidential candidates
18. Songwriters
19. Theologians
20. Jazz musicians
21. Comedians
22. People attempting (unsuccessfully) to assassinate presidents
23. Union generals in the Civil War
24. Painters
25. Jazz musicians
26. Comics

27. Isaac Hull, Stephen Decatur, Oliver Perry
28. Elvis Presley, the Everly Brothers, Bobby Darin
29. Benjamin West, John Singer Sargent, Archibald Willard

☆ Inventive Types

Europeans used to talk about "Yankee ingenuity" (back when *Yankee* meant "American," not "Northerner"). Rumor has it that the U.S. is lagging behind in cleverness and technology, but you'd never guess that from our history. The phonograph, motion pictures, plastics . . . the list goes on and on.

1. What great inventor had only three months of formal schooling?
2. What popular office machine, now becoming obsolete, was invented by Latham Sholes in 1867?
3. What welcome innovation did Benjamin Franklin make in eyeglasses?
4. What synthetic fabric, still commonly used, did Wallace Carothers invent in 1934?
5. What label did Thomas Edison put on his chemical bottles so no one would bother them?
6. Eli Whitney is famed for inventing the cotton gin in 1793. Just what did the gin *do?*
7. Inventor Elisha Graves Otis is associated with what item found in every tall building?
8. What prickly item, used by farmers (and prisons), was invented by Joseph Glidden in 1874?
9. What telegraph inventor also made the first daguerreotype in America?
10. Thomas Edison invented his kinetoscope in 1887. What world-changing form of entertainment evolved from it?
11. The clothespin, the circular saw, and the metal-tipped pen were invented by what unique American religious group?

27. Military leaders in the War of 1812
28. Pop singers
29. Painters

Inventive Types *(answers)*

1. Thomas Edison; he was self-educated, having acquired the habit of reading every library book he could.
2. The typewriter; Sholes also invented the keyboard layout of letters and numbers, which is now used on all computer keyboards.
3. Bifocals
4. Nylon, first marketed in 1938
5. "Poison"
6. Separated cotton fibers from its seeds, a painstaking job that had been done by hand for many years
7. The elevator; he didn't invent it, but he did make it safer.
8. Barbed wire
9. Samuel Morse; the daguerreotype was an early form of photography.
10. Motion pictures
11. The Shakers, who advocated a simple lifestyle and timesaving devices

12. What new type of weapon did Samuel Colt invent in 1835?
13. What great inventor perfected flexible rolls of film?
14. Who invented and marketed a lightweight sewing machine for use in the home?
15. What invention, developed in 1878, did Thomas Edison say was his favorite? (Hint: disk)
16. Who invented a type of submarine before he invented his more famous steamboat?
17. What new type of weapon was introduced by Richard Gatling in 1886?
18. What useful household item did H. C. Booth invent in 1901? (Hint: air and hoses)
19. What president introduced such novelties as dumbwaiters and calendar clocks to his home at Monticello?

☆ More Notable Nicknames

1. What deep-voiced country singer is "the Man in Black"?
2. Painter Anna Mary Robertson was better known by what nickname?
3. What pop idol has been called "Ol' Blue Eyes" and "the Voice"?
4. What universally loved lariat-swinging comic was known as "Oklahoma's Favorite Son"?
5. What pop singer, who was "born in the U.S.A.," is "the Boss"?
6. What great hero of Texas history was known both as "the Raven" and as "Big Drunk"?
7. What well-tanned TV and radio host is "America's Oldest Teenager"?
8. The Indian girl Matoaka of colonial times is better known by what name?

12. The revolver, which enabled a man to fire without reloading
13. George Eastman, of Eastman Kodak fame
14. Isaac Singer, whose Singer company is still operating
15. The phonograph
16. Robert Fulton
17. A six-barrel gun, the first workable machine gun; the U.S. army later added four more barrels.
18. The vacuum cleaner
19. Thomas Jefferson, a scientist and inventor as well as a politician

More Notable Nicknames *(answers)*

1. Johnny Cash
2. Grandma Moses
3. Frank Sinatra
4. Will Rogers
5. Bruce Springsteen
6. Sam Houston; "Raven" had been bestowed by his Indian friends, and "Big Drunk" came from his favorite form of recreation, though he finally kicked the habit.
7. Dick Clark
8. Pocahontas, which was actually her nickname, meaning "playful"

9. What colorful and domineering Louisiana politician of the 1930s had the nickname "Kingfish"?

10. What president was dubbed "Tippecanoe" for defeating the Shawnee Indians at the Battle of Tippecanoe?

11. What elderly nickname began to be used for country singer Louis Marshall Jones when he was only 23?

12. What early president's chubbiness led to his nickname "His Rotundity"?

13. What renowned Louisiana French rogue had the nickname of "the Gentleman Pirate"?

14. What great actor, from a family of great actors, was known as "the Great Profile"?

15. What early president was such a smooth lawyer and politician that he was nicknamed "the Little Magician"?

16. What early secretary of the treasury was called "Alexander the Coppersmith" because he introduced the copper penny?

17. What political opponent of Abraham Lincoln was known as "the Little Giant"?

18. Gangster George Kelly was better known by what ballistic nickname?

19. What Christian author was known as "Queen of the West" in her movie days?

20. What president had been a Mexican War general nicknamed "Old Rough and Ready"?

21. What strong-willed president's strong-willed daughter was known as "Princess Alice"?

22. What Indian woman, famous for aiding the Lewis and Clark expedition, was nicknamed "Bird Woman"?

23. Nicknamed "Handsome Frank," what president was a Mexican War veteran and a New Hampshire native?

24. "The Father of Country Music" was also called "the Singing Brakeman." Who was he?

9. Huey Long, who was assassinated in 1935
10. William Henry Harrison, who ran with vice presidential candidate John Tyler using the slogan "Tippecanoe and Tyler too"
11. "Grandpa" (Later the name became more appropriate.)
12. John Adams, second president
13. The colorful Jean Lafitte
14. John Barrymore
15. Martin Van Buren, eighth president
16. Alexander Hamilton (Alexander the coppersmith is a Bible character. See 2 Timothy 4:14.)
17. Stephen Douglas, a small man with a large head and a large ego
18. "Machine Gun" Kelly
19. Dale Evans, wife of Roy Rogers
20. Zachary Taylor, twelfth president
21. Teddy Roosevelt's; he stated that Alice was the one person he couldn't dominate.
22. Sacajawea
23. Franklin Pierce
24. Jimmy Rogers

25. What president, called "Old Hickory," was also given the nickname "Sharp Knife" by Indians he had conquered?
26. What president nicknamed his son Thomas "Tad" because he thought he looked like a tadpole?
27. What "Queen of Country Comedy" always made her entrance with a boisterous "Howdeee!"?

☆ By Any Other Name . . .

So many celebrities choose (for whatever reason) to change the name they were born with. Try to identify the celebrities whose *birth names* are listed here, along with a hint for each one.

1. Cherilyn Sarkisian (singer, actress)
2. Harold Lipschitz (sitcom actor, known for *Barney Miller*)
3. Sara Ophelia Cannon (country comic, "Howdeeee!")
4. Robert Zimmerman (folk-rock singer of the 1960s and beyond)
5. Madonna Louise Ciccone (can't you guess?)
6. William Claude Dukenfield (hard-drinking film comic of the 1940s)
7. Roy Scherer Jr. (handsome movie idol of the 1960s, paired with Doris Day)
8. David Meyer (TV actor, famed for *The Fugitive*)
9. David Kaminsky (redheaded comic, movie actor of the 1950s)
10. Michael Douglas (comic movie actor, twice as Batman)
11. Roberta Jean Anderson (pop singer with a "Big Yellow Taxi")
12. Norma Jean Mortenson (blonde movie idol of the 1950s)
13. Carlos Ray (martial arts champ and actor)
14. Walter Palanuik (western movie actor, able to do one-handed push-ups)

25. Andrew Jackson
26. Abraham Lincoln
27. Minnie Pearl, who died in 1996

By Any Other Name . . . *(answers)*

1. Cher
2. Hal Linden
3. Minnie Pearl
4. Bob Dylan
5. Madonna
6. W. C. Fields
7. Rock Hudson
8. David Janssen
9. Danny Kaye
10. Michael Keaton
11. Joni Mitchell
12. Marilyn Monroe
13. Chuck Norris
14. Jack Palance

15. Jane Peters (blonde movie queen of the 1930s, married to Clark Gable)
16. Prince Rogers Nelson (rock star, formerly known as . . .)
17. Spangler Arlington Brugh (handsome movie idol of the 1930s and 1940s)
18. Randy Traywick (tight-lipped country singer)
19. Leonard Rosenberg (comedian, known for *The Odd Couple*)
20. Joan Sandra Molinsky (comedienne and talk show host—can we talk?)
21. Emmanuel Goldenberg (movie actor, often a gangster)
22. Virginia McMath (actress, dancer, Fred Astaire's partner)
23. Leonard Slye (movie cowboy and singer, with a fast-food chain)
24. Joe Yule Jr. (short movie actor, beginning as a child)
25. Winona Horowitz (young movie actress of the 1990s)
26. Milton Hines (comic and kids' show host)
27. Ramon Estevez (movie actor, father of another Estevez)
28. Belle Silverman (New York opera queen)
29. Philip Silversmith (TV comic, known for Sergeant Bilko)
30. Robert Modini (actor, known for *The Untouchables*)
31. Annie Mae Bullock (pop singer, formerly part of a husband-and-wife act)
32. Harold Lloyd Jenkins (country singer)
33. Rudolpho D'Antonguolia (handsome movie idol of the silent era)
34. Marion Morrison (macho movie man for forty years, particularly in westerns)
35. Jerome Silberman (comic movie actor, married to Gilda Radner)
36. Cornelius McGillicuddy (baseball great)
37. Hyman Arluck (songwriter, noted for "Over the Rainbow")
38. Leon Bismarck Beiderbecke (jazz musician)
39. Stevland Morris (blind pop singer)
40. Sarah Jane Fulks (actress and former wife of a president)

15. Carole Lombard
16. Prince
17. Robert Taylor
18. Randy Travis
19. Tony Randall
20. Joan Rivers
21. Edward G. Robinson
22. Ginger Rogers
23. Roy Rogers
24. Mickey Rooney
25. Winona Ryder
26. Soupy Sales
27. Martin Sheen
28. Beverly Sills
29. Phil Silvers
30. Robert Stack
31. Tina Turner
32. Conway Twitty
33. Rudolf Valentino
34. John Wayne
35. Gene Wilder
36. Connie Mack
37. Harold Arlen
38. Bix Beiderbecke
39. Stevie Wonder
40. Jane Wyman

☆ More Favorite Sons (and Daughters)

Think of Abraham Lincoln, and what place do you think of? Illinois, probably. We connect famous people with certain places. Given the names of four very famous Americans, could you connect them with a particular state?

1. John Hancock, Clara Barton, John Quincy Adams, Oliver Wendell Holmes
2. Gerald Ford, Aretha Franklin, Tom Selleck, Edna Ferber
3. Zachary Taylor, Daniel Boone, Kit Carson, Abraham Lincoln
4. John Adams, Emily Dickinson, Nathaniel Hawthorne, Alexander Graham Bell
5. Spencer Tracy, Edna Ferber, Thornton Wilder, Alfred Lunt
6. Willie Mays, Talullah Bankhead, Wernher von Braun, John Hunt Morgan
7. Ansel Adams, Shirley Temple, Levi Strauss, Paul Masson
8. Samuel Colt, Harriet Beecher Stowe, Noah Webster, Jonathan Edwards
9. Ernest Hemingway, Oscar Mayer, Adlai Stevenson, William Jennings Bryan
10. James Earl Jones, Tammy Wynette, Shelby Foote, Leontyne Price
11. James Dean, Ernie Pyle, Hoagy Carmichael, Theodore Dreiser
12. Omar Bradley, Harry Truman, T. S. Eliot, Walter Cronkite
13. Gary Cooper, Chet Huntley, Brent Musberger, Myrna Loy
14. Herbert Hoover, Buffalo Bill, Billy Sunday, John Wayne
15. Hubert Humphrey, Sinclair Lewis, Charles Schulz, William Mayo
16. William Jennings Bryan, Fred Astaire, Gen. John J. Pershing, Harold Lloyd

More Favorite Sons (and Daughters) *(answers)*

1. Massachusetts
2. Michigan
3. Kentucky
4. Massachusetts
5. Wisconsin
6. Alabama
7. California
8. Connecticut
9. Illinois
10. Mississippi
11. Indiana
12. Missouri
13. Montana
14. Iowa
15. Minnesota
16. Nebraska

17. George Gershwin, Henry James, Franklin Roosevelt, Martin Van Buren
18. Louis L'Amour, Angie Dickinson, Lawrence Welk, Eric Sevareid
19. James Thurber, William Howard Taft, U. S. Grant, Neil Armstrong
20. William Faulkner, Elvis Presley, Oprah Winfrey, Jefferson Davis
21. Billy the Kid, Georgia O'Keefe, Al Unser, Kit Carson
22. Theodore Roosevelt, Susan B. Anthony, Herman Melville, Millard Fillmore
23. Mark Twain, Walt Disney, Jesse James, J. C. Penney
24. Pearl Buck, Don Knotts, Chuck Yeager, Nick Nolte
25. Sandra Day O'Connor, Zane Grey, Geronimo, Frank Lloyd Wright
26. Johnny Carson, Willa Cather, Henry Fonda, Chief Red Cloud
27. Stephen Austin, George Bush, James Bowie, Howard Hughes
28. Thomas Jefferson, Patrick Henry, Thomas "Stonewall" Jackson, George Washington
29. Paul Laxalt, Walter Van Tilburg Clark, Pat McCarran, John William McKay
30. Aaron Burr, Grover Cleveland, Thomas Edison, Frank Sinatra
31. Billy Graham, Edward R. Murrow, Thomas Wolfe, Jesse Helms
32. Woody Guthrie, Jim Thorpe, Carl Albert, Wiley Post
33. Andrew Carnegie, Betsy Ross, Maxwell Anderson, George C. Marshall
34. James A. Garfield, Jack Nicklaus, Sherwood Anderson, Eddie Rickenbacker
35. Strom Thurmond, Wade Hampton, John C. Calhoun, Andrew Jackson

17. New York
18. North Dakota
19. Ohio
20. Mississippi
21. New Mexico
22. New York
23. Missouri
24. West Virginia
25. Arizona
26. Nebraska
27. Texas
28. Virginia
29. Nevada
30. New Jersey
31. North Carolina
32. Oklahoma
33. Pennsylvania
34. Ohio
35. South Carolina

36. Bing Crosby, Marcus Whitman, Gary Larson, Mary McCarthy
37. James Monroe, Jerry Falwell, William Henry Harrison, John Marshall
38. Roger Williams, Gilbert Stuart, Nelson Eddy, Nathanael Greene
39. Calamity Jane, Tom Brokaw, Crazy Horse, George McGovern
40. Davy Crockett, Roy Acuff, Cordell Hull, Ernie Ford
41. William F. Buckley, Ed Koch, Paul Simon (the singer, not the politician), Barbara Bush

☆ More Inventive Types

1. What face-saving personal item did King Camp Gillette introduce to the world in 1901?
2. Polytetrafluoroethylene, invented by Du Pont labs, is better known by what household name? (Hint: no-stick)
3. The clothing item known as a "slide fastener" is better known by what trademarked name?
4. What familiar word did Thomas Edison invent for people to use when answering the telephone?
5. In 1937 Chester Carlson invented xerography, the first method of doing what?
6. Bakelite, invented in 1909 by Leo Baekeland, was the first of what type of world-changing material?
7. George Eastman made photography available to the average person by his invention of what type of camera?
8. What all-American drink was invented by Englishman Richard Blechynden at the 1904 St. Louis World's Fair?
9. The Pageant of Light Festival in Fort Myers, Florida, commemorates a great inventor who lived in the town. Who? (Hint: light)

36. Washington
37. Virginia
38. Rhode Island
39. South Dakota
40. Tennessee
41. New York

More Inventive Types *(answers)*

1. The safety razor (Every morning, millions of men are grateful.)
2. Teflon
3. Zipper
4. *Hello*
5. Photocopying (Doesn't *xerography* sound a lot like *Xerox?*)
6. Plastic
7. The Kodak, a workable box camera that did not require a professional photographer
8. Iced tea; finding that his *hot* tea wasn't selling well in the sweltering heat of summer, Blechynden tried something shockingly new.
9. Thomas Edison; the festival is held on Edison's birthday.

10. The inventor of the Cherokee Indian alphabet has a birthplace museum in Vonore, Tennessee. Who was he?
11. What noted inventor of farm equipment (who has a company named for him) lived in Grand Detour, Illinois?
12. If you are visiting the World of Rubber in Akron, Ohio, what inventor will you learn about?
13. In 1868 what inventor formed a company in Connecticut to produce cylinder locks?
14. What great inventor took his "working vacations" in a Florida home known as Seminole Lodge?
15. Laurens Hammond invented what type of electric musical instrument? (Hint: Hammond)
16. Betty Nesmith invented what bottled product designed to "cover" for secretaries?
17. William Lear not only manufactured jets but also invented what type of now defunct audio format?
18. When Robert Fulton went from New York to Albany in 32 hours in 1807, how did he travel?
19. What great inventor's laboratory in Boston includes the world's first telephone switchboard?

☆ Alias . . .

Many of the famous are known by . . . an alias. Given the person's birth name (along with a helpful hint), you will no doubt quickly identify each of the following celebrities.

1. Joseph Levitch (movie comic and Labor Day telethon host)
2. Eugene Orowitz (TV actor, *Bonanza*, and *Little House on the Prairie*)
3. Hugh Cregg (rock singer, with the News)
4. Nathan Birnbaum (cigar-chomping comedian, turned 100 and died in 1996)
5. Nicholas Coppola (comic movie actor)

10. Sequoyah; his was the first attempt to commit an Indian language to written form.
11. John Deere
12. Charles Goodyear, who developed the process for vulcanizing, which made rubber durable enough for auto tires
13. Linus Yale
14. Thomas Edison; his workshops and laboratory are now open to the public.
15. The electric organ
16. Liquid Paper
17. Eight-track tapes
18. By the first practical steamboat, which he'd invented
19. Alexander Graham Bell's

Alias . . . *(answers)*

1. Jerry Lewis
2. Michael Landon
3. Huey Lewis
4. George Burns
5. Nicholas Cage

6. Leslie Townes Hope (movie actor and stand-up comic)
7. Bela Ferenc Blasko (horror movie idol, with bite)
8. Ray Charles Robinson (pop singer, "What'd I Say")
9. Norma Egstrom (sultry singer, with a "fever")
10. Mary Kaumeyer (movie actress, working with Bob Hope and Bing Crosby)
11. Melvin Kaminsky (comic and movie director, remembered for *Young Frankenstein*)
12. Milton Berlinger (TV comic in the 1950s)
13. Edward Iskowitz (singer, noted for "Whoopee")
14. Alfred Caplin (cartoonist, known for "Li'l Abner")
15. Israel Baline (one of the greatest American songwriters)
16. Frances Octavia Smith (queen of Western movies)
17. John Birks Gillespie (jazz trumpeter)
18. Harlean Carpenter (blonde movie idol of the 1930s)
19. Harry Bouton (magician)
20. Charles Eugene Boone (wholesome pop singer, milk drinker)
21. Samuel Cohen (songwriter, famous for "High Hopes")
22. Nathaniel Coles (singer, known for "Mona Lisa")
23. Asa Yoelson (singer, famous for "Mammy" and "Toot Toot Tootsie")
24. Harriet Stratemeyer Adams (author of novel series for boys and girls)
25. Frank James Cooper (movie idol, known especially for westerns)
26. Howard William Cohen (caustic sportscaster)
27. Ruth Elizabeth Davis (movie queen from the 1930s on)
28. Joseph Keaton (stone-faced silent movie comic)
29. Esther Pauline Friedman (advice columnist)
30. Leslie King (Republican president)
31. Sidney Leibowitz (singer, married to Eydie Gorme)
32. Salvatore Lucania (gangster of the Roaring '20s and '30s)
33. Kenneth Millar (popular detective novelist of the 1960s)

6. Bob Hope
7. Bela Lugosi
8. Ray Charles
9. Peggy Lee
10. Dorothy Lamour
11. Mel Brooks
12. Milton Berle
13. Eddie Cantor
14. Al Capp
15. Irving Berlin
16. Dale Evans
17. Dizzy Gillespie
18. Jean Harlow
19. Harry Blackstone
20. Pat Boone
21. Sammy Cahn
22. Nat "King" Cole
23. Al Jolson
24. Carolyn Keene (author of the Nancy Drew series) and Franklin W. Dixon (author of the Hardy Boys series)
25. Gary Cooper
26. Howard Cosell
27. Bette Davis
28. Buster Keaton
29. Ann Landers
30. Gerald R. Ford
31. Steve Lawrence
32. Lucky Luciano
33. Ross MacDonald

34. Frederick Bickel (film actor, two-time Oscar-winner)
35. Edla Furry (Hollywood gossip columnist)
36. Ethel Zimmerman (belting queen of Broadway)
37. Michael Peschowsky (comic and movie director, famed for *The Graduate*)
38. Gladys Smith (queen of silent movies)
39. Barnet David Rosofsky (champion boxer of the 1930s)
40. Avrom Goldbogen (movie producer and one husband of Elizabeth Taylor)
41. Edward Chester Babcock (songwriter, famous for "Call Me Irresponsible")
42. Andrew Warhola (pop artist, popular in the 1960s)
43. Glenn Scobey Warner (football coach)
44. Salvatore Guaragna (songwriter, famous for "I Only Have Eyes for You")
45. Manfred Lee and Frederic Dannay (authors of popular mystery novels)

☆ What's My Line? Common Bonds (Part 3)

What do Tom Brokaw, Walter Cronkite, and Dan Rather have in common? They are (or were) all TV news anchormen. Find the common bond that unites the groups below. Keep in mind that the names are from both past and present.

1. Kelsey Grammer, Andy Griffith, Ted Danson
2. O. Henry, Edgar Allan Poe, Bret Harte
3. Jeff MacNelly, Herblock, Doug Marlette, Rube Goldberg
4. Grant Wood, John Trumbull, Andy Warhol
5. Hal David, Johnny Mercer, Oscar Hammerstein II
6. William Brewster, William Bradford, John Alden
7. George Will, Cal Thomas, Dave Broder, Paul Greenberg
8. Gus Kahn, Gerry Goffin, Carole King, Howard Dietz

34. Frederic March
35. Hedda Hopper
36. Ethel Merman
37. Mike Nichols
38. Mary Pickford
39. Barney Ross
40. Mike Todd
41. Jimmy Van Heusen
42. Andy Warhol
43. Pop Warner
44. Harry Warren
45. Ellery Queen

What's My Line? Common Bonds (Part 3)
(answers)

1. TV sitcom actors
2. Short story authors
3. Editorial cartoonists
4. Painters
5. Song lyricists
6. Pilgrims
7. Syndicated editorial columnists
8. Song lyricists

9. Alan Jackson, George Jones, Conway Twitty
10. J. E. B. Stuart, Edmund Kirby Smith, Joseph E. Johnston
11. James Whistler, John Steuart Curry, John Singleton Copley
12. Jimmy Van Heusen, Jimmy Webb, Jimmy McHugh
13. Anthony Wayne, Daniel Morgan, John Paul Jones
14. Bix Beiderbecke, Gene Krupa, Wes Montgomery
15. Sir Walter Raleigh, John Smith, William Bradford
16. William Safire, Florence King, Vermont Royster
17. Ricky Nelson, Roy Orbison, Buddy Holly
18. Mell Lazarus, Mike Peters, Charles Schulz
19. Thomas Hart Benton, Thomas Eakins, George Bellows
20. Billy Sunday, D. L. Moody, George Whitefield
21. Cole Porter, George Gershwin, Gus Edwards
22. Dik Brown, Chester Gould, Jim Davis
23. Emily Dickinson, Richard Wilbur, Edward Taylor
24. Al Gore, Dan Quayle, Hannibal Hamlin
25. Roger Williams, Jonathan Edwards, Cotton Mather
26. Alexander Graham Bell, Thomas Edison, Lee De Forest
27. Charles Ives, Aaron Copland, Howard Hanson
28. Frank Sinatra Jr., Patricia Hearst, Charles Lindbergh Jr.
29. Robert E. Lee, Stonewall Jackson, James Longstreet

☆ Notable Women, and Some Less Notable (Part 2)

1. Candy Lightner founded what organization after her young daughter was killed by a drunk driver?
2. In Tuscumbia, Alabama, you can tour the home of a world-famous author noted for overcoming her handicaps of blindness and deafness. Who was she?
3. In a 1945 poll, what fictional woman ranked as the best-known woman after the president's wife? (Hint: cakes)
4. What wild-haired comedienne always griped about her husband, "Fang"?

9. Country singers
10. Confederate generals in the Civil War
11. Painters
12. Songwriters
13. Military leaders in the American Revolution
14. Jazz musicians
15. English colonists
16. Syndicated newspaper columnists
17. Pop singers
18. Cartoonists
19. Painters
20. Evangelists
21. Songwriters
22. Cartoonists
23. Poets
24. Vice presidents
25. Colonial preachers
26. Inventors
27. Composers
28. Famous people who were kidnapped
29. Confederate generals in the Civil War

Notable Women, and Some Less Notable (Part 2)
(answers)

1. MADD, Mothers Against Drunk Drivers
2. Helen Keller
3. Betty Crocker
4. Phyllis Diller

5. The WAVES of World War II were women in which branch of service?
6. What western sharpshooter was a star in Buffalo Bill's Wild West Show and was nicknamed "Little Sure Shot"?
7. The top-selling nonfiction book of 1974 was a Christian marriage manual by Marabel Morgan. What was it?
8. The view from what famous Colorado mountain inspired Katherine Bates to write "America the Beautiful"?
9. One of the most famous murder trials took place in Fall River, Massachusetts, in 1892. Who was accused of murdering her father with an ax?
10. What parental group was founded by Phoebe Hearst and Alice Birney in 1897? (Hint: school)
11. What name was given to Marine women serving in World War I?
12. When President John Quincy Adams was skinny-dipping in the Potomac River, how did journalist Anne Royall obtain an interview with him?
13. The classic 1896 *Boston Cooking School Cook Book* was authored by what cooking queen?
14. Haverhill, Massachusetts, has a statue of Hannah Dustin, who was captured by Indians in 1697. According to tradition, she returned carrying what prize?
15. What denomination was started in the 1860s by Ellen White? (Hint: Saturday)
16. What famed author of Maine stories has a home in the town of Kittery?
17. Which branch of the military had women serving as SPARs?
18. In what southwestern Indian tribe did the men do weaving while the women constructed the buildings?
19. Boston's Longyear Museum honors the founder of Boston's most famous religious sect. Who was she?

5. The navy; WAVES stands for Woman Accepted for Volunteer Emergency Services, in case you wondered.
6. Annie Oakley; Indian chief Sitting Bull bestowed her nickname "Little Sure Shot."
7. *The Total Woman*
8. Pikes Peak
9. Lizzie Borden, accused of murdering her father and stepmother with an ax; she was acquitted.
10. The PTA, Parent-Teacher Association
11. Marinettes, believe it or not
12. She sat on his clothes on the riverbank and refused to leave until he consented to an interview. (Presumably he was still immersed in the river while she asked him questions.) The story is probably legendary, but she was an actual person and a friend of Adams.
13. Fannie Farmer
14. The scalps of ten of her captors
15. The Seventh-day Adventists
16. Sarah Orne Jewett, who died in 1909
17. The Coast Guard
18. The Pueblos
19. Mary Baker Eddy, founder of Christian Science

20. Florence Martus is memorialized in the "Waving Girl" statue on the waterfront of a famous Georgia port. Which port?
21. What antibooze crusader spent her last years in a Eureka Springs, Arkansas, boardinghouse called Hatchet Hall?

20. Savannah; Florence was noted, during the early 1900s, for waving at every ship that passed through Savannah's port.
21. Carrie Nation, famous for her "hatchetation" of saloons; people talked about the "Carrie Nation nonintoxication hatchetation."

PART TWO

Clothed & Fed
Everyday
Matters

☆ The Well-Dressed American

1. A "boater," which many men wore in the early 1900s, was what article of clothing?
2. The early Virginia laws regulating "excess" in clothing were known by what colorful name?
3. The men of New England adorned their shoes with fake roses made of what fabric?
4. In the 1660s what article of adornment became as popular in America as in England? (Hint: powdered)
5. What woman's fashion innovation, introduced in 1711, changed the shape (literally) of women for many years?
6. What was the most common color of hose for both men and women throughout the 1700s?
7. What item, useful on a rainy day, was introduced around 1738 (and opposed by some religious groups)?
8. In the 1750s women often wore "bosom bottles" on their dresses. What did the bottles hold?
9. In the 1770s people began using umbrellas for what other purpose than keeping off rain?
10. In the 1770s women of all ages began wearing those uncomfortable items known as "stays." By what better name do we know them?
11. *Plocacosmos* was a 1782 handbook for what crucial part of one's appearance? (Hint: mousse)
12. If a man of the 1700s wore a "false tail," what was he wearing?
13. Shoes of the 1700s used what kind of fastener?
14. What item used on both men's and women's hair throughout the 1700s finally went out of style by 1800?
15. In 1804 patents were issued for "galluses," an important part of menswear. What do we call them today?
16. The earliest women's boots, debuting around 1830, were fastened in what way?

The Well-Dressed American *(answers)*

1. A flat-topped straw hat, still popular with barbershop quartet singers
2. Blue laws; only later did "blue laws" come to refer to closing businesses on Sundays. The Virginia blue laws were passed in 1619.
3. Silk (No synthetics were available in those days.)
4. Wigs, also known as periwigs, which were often powdered white or other colors; some locales tried (and failed) to prohibit wearing wigs.
5. The hoop skirt
6. White; sometimes, though, the hose were embroidered in colored threads with the person's name.
7. Umbrellas; Quakers and other "simple living" addicts though umbrellas were pretentious.
8. Fresh flowers with their stems immersed in water, held in tiny vases; they were the equivalent of today's corsages.
9. As parasols, for protection against the sun (Well, after all, they didn't have sunscreen.)
10. Corsets
11. Hairdressing; the book's subtitle was *The Whole Art of Hair Dressing,* and it was extremely popular.
12. A fake queue—that is, a fake pigtail (or ponytail) at the base of his natural hair; the connecting point was usually concealed with ribbon.
13. Buckles
14. Powder
15. Suspenders, or braces; the idea in those days was to keep a man's pant cuffs high and dry.
16. Laces up the sides

17. Novelist Nathaniel Hawthorne observed around 1837 that young American men had starting doing what to their faces?
18. Author Amelia Bloomer introduced what article of female clothing?
19. The articles of clothing collectively called "white work" or "white sewing" or "the under wardrobe" are now called what?
20. As seen in pictures of Abe Lincoln, what change in men's facial hair occurred in the 1860s?
21. What native item of footwear became popular in the 1860s because of stories of Wild Bill Hickok?
22. The first baseball uniforms, sported by the Cincinnati Red Stockings in 1868, featured what type of pants?
23. What item was introduced, unpadded, into baseball in 1875?
24. What item became an accepted part of men's (but not women's) accessories in the 1890s?
25. What popular form of exercise in the 1890s was a key factor in women's skirts becoming shorter?
26. What type of hosiery, which reappeared in the 1960s, made a fashion splash around 1908?
27. Around 1910, women were told to cure "automobile wrinkles" on their faces by applying what chilled vegetables?
28. As automobiles became popular, what did women wear to hold their hats in place?
29. By 1920, what scandalous length of skirt were women wearing?
30. Long, one-button jackets with padded shoulders were part of what distinctive men's suits of the 1940s? (Hint: rhymes)
31. What new abbreviated item of men's clothing became respectable in the early 1950s?

17. Growing mustaches, a practice introduced from England; throughout the 1700s almost all men (and women) had been clean shaven.
18. Bloomers, naturally; introduced around 1850, they struck some men and women as "immodest."
19. Lingerie, a term that came into use around 1850
20. Beards; Lincoln was the first president to wear one. Thanks to the disruption of life caused by the Civil War, many soldiers let their facial hair grow and kept it after the war ended.
21. Moccasins
22. Knickerbockers, or knickers; they were widely ridiculed at first.
23. A glove
24. A cigarette, which gradually became chic at social functions; it was not acceptable for women, as the Virginia Slims advertisements have reminded us.
25. Bicycling, which took the country by storm in the 1880s and 1890s; women's skirts were gradually shortened by at least two inches.
26. Fishnet
27. Cucumbers
28. Veils; remember that all the early automobiles were roofless and windshieldless.
29. Knee-length, considered quite shocking at the time
30. Zoot suits
31. Bermuda shorts; hitherto, shorts had been considered strictly for athletic competition.

32. What type of dance shoes became briefly popular in the 1950s?
33. Disney's 1955 film *Davy Crockett* made what type of cap popular among boys?
34. What British hairdresser (whose name now appears on a line of hair products) sprung the "mod" look on America in the 1960s?
35. What was *the* color for go-go boots?
36. What skimpy piece of female attire made its U.S. appearance in 1966?
37. What aptly named garment was the follow-up to the miniskirt?
38. What willowy British model became the U.S. fashion ideal in the mid-1960s?
39. What drastic change was made in the legs of both men's and women's pants beginning in 1969?
40. What tieless (and usually 100 percent polyester) men's suits were briefly popular in the 1970s?

☆ Munchables: Things to Eat

"As American as . . ." what? Apple pie, of course. We Americans love our food, no matter what the diet fanatics may say. The world has learned to love our food, too. Around the world, American culture is largely identified (for better or worse) with things we eat.

1. What new color was introduced into M&M's in 1995?
2. What food spread was introduced by George J. French in 1904? (Hint: yellow)
3. What colorful candy did E.T. eat in the 1983 movie?
4. New England and Manhattan are two types of what all-American seafood soups?
5. The "pine of the Indies" that Christopher Columbus found so delicious was what tropical fruit?

32. Ballet shoes
33. A coonskin, like ole Dave himself wore (In fact, Crockett did *not* wear one, but does anyone want to argue with a Disney movie?)
34. Vidal Sassoon
35. White
36. The miniskirt, considered quite shocking at that time
37. The maxi-coat, introduced in 1967; it was often worn *with* a miniskirt.
38. Leslie Hornsby, better known as Twiggy
39. They flared out, becoming the infamous bell-bottoms.
40. Leisure suits; no one misses them much.

Munchables: Things to Eat *(answers)*

1. Blue
2. Mustard
3. Reese's Pieces
4. Clam chowder
5. Pineapple

6. What very rich chocolate disc is one you'll "go ga-ga" for?
7. The soft-shell crab, which can be eaten shell and all, is what species of Atlantic coast crab?
8. What popular southern vegetable adds the gumminess to gumbos?
9. Ventura, California, is the center of production of what citrus fruit? (Hint: ade)
10. What candy bar, named for heroes of a French adventure, was introduced by Mars Candy in 1932?
11. Hominy, a staple of southern cooking, is a form of what vegetable?
12. What popular American food is named from the Italian word for pie?
13. What important liquid did Gail Borden begin to can in 1856?
14. What type of berry did New England sea captains use to prevent the disease scurvy? (Hint: turkey)
15. What is the popular rhyming name in restaurants for a seafood and beef dinner?
16. What animal became the mascot of the Borden company in the 1930s?
17. Avery Island, Louisiana, is home of the famous McIlhenny Company, which produces what notorious liquid seasoning?
18. The hot dogs at Nathan's Famous can be had at what New York amusement section?
19. A *crevette* is what type of southern seafood?
20. If you wanted to eat the pecan-and-chocolate Derby pie, where would you go?
21. What famous breakfast food maker has a museum in Akron, Ohio? (Hint: man with a hat)
22. Burgoo, popular in Kentucky and other southern locales, is what type of food?
23. Chili made with chocolate and cinnamon is a specialty of what southern Ohio city?

6. Goo-Goo Clusters ("You'll go ga-ga for Goo-Goo.")
7. The blue crab; the soft-shell type is a blue that has just molted its old (hard) shell. Before the new shell has hardened, the blues are soft-shells.
8. Okra
9. Lemons
10. Three Musketeers
11. Corn
12. Pizza, of course
13. Evaporated milk; it was important because it allowed milk to be stored for long periods. When the Civil War began, Borden's product became crucial.
14. Cranberries, which are high in vitamin C
15. Surf and turf
16. Elsie the cow
17. Tabasco sauce, which the company has been making since 1868
18. Coney Island; *Coney Island* or *Coney* used to be synonyms for hot dog.
19. A shrimp, the typical gulf coast shrimp used in most American seafood dishes
20. Louisville, Kentucky, which named the dessert for the famous horse race
21. Quaker Oats, which operates Quaker Square in Akron, its former headquarters
22. A stew, similar to Brunswick stew, which includes beef, chicken, and whatever other creature is available at the time
23. Cincinnati

24. What colorful and jiggly dessert was supposedly invented by Peter Cooper in 1845?
25. What first lady is sometimes credited with inventing ice cream?
26. What popular southern fruit dish uses orange slices, bananas, and shredded coconut?
27. What colorful vegetable makes Manhattan clam chowder differ from New England clam chowder?
28. What type of food did Clarence Birdseye begin to package in 1921?
29. Ray Kroc, a fifty-two-year-old malt machine salesman, started the franchising of what fast-food chain?
30. What widely marketed Nabisco cracker had as its symbol a small boy in a yellow slicker and boots?
31. If you are eating a thick, hearty soup made of okra, seafood, chicken, and vegetables, what Louisiana dish are you eating?
32. If you buy *perros calientes* in Miami, what familiar American food are you eating?
33. Corbin, Kentucky, was the site of the first of a popular chain of fast-food restaurants. Which chain?
34. What food fest is held each February in Hershey, Pennsylvania?
35. What very German snack food could you see being made at Pennsylvania's Sturgis House?
36. What popular dessert item (which requires no silverware) was introduced at the 1904 St. Louis World's Fair?
37. What food became popular at the turn of the century under the name *dachshund sausage*?
38. What popular Mexican food's name is the Spanish word for "plug"?
39. Chincoteague, Virginia, has a museum devoted to what edible shellfish?

24. Gelatin
25. Dolley Madison, wife of James Madison
26. Ambrosia
27. Tomatoes, which give the Manhattan type its distinctive reddishness
28. Frozen food; it was the first to be sold for home use. He got the idea after he had been ice fishing and had seen fish freeze as soon as they were taken out of the water.
29. McDonald's
30. Uneeda Biscuit
31. Gumbo
32. Hot dogs; the many Spanish-speaking residents use their words for hot dog.
33. Kentucky Fried Chicken, now known simply as KFC
34. The Chocolate Lovers' Extravaganza (What other food do you associate with "Hershey"?)
35. Pretzels; it was the U.S.'s first commercial pretzel bakery.
36. The ice-cream cone
37. Hot dogs
38. The taco
39. The Oyster

☆ All around the House

We take everyday products for granted, but sometimes there's a story behind their name or the company that produces them. And when we vacation, we often find companies that throw their doors open to people eager for that great American freebie, the factory tour.

1. What home products company—known especially for soaps and toothpastes—could you tour in Cincinnati, Ohio?
2. The Brooklyn Flint Glass Works eventually became what well-known glass company? (Hint: blue flower)
3. On what familiar product will you see a little girl carrying an umbrella?
4. What new computer software was introduced in a great media blitz by Microsoft in 1995?
5. Bradley, Vorhees, and Day, a brand of underwear, is better known by what name?
6. What company, noted for making floor wax, can be toured in Racine, Wisconsin?
7. If you are in Richmond, Virginia, looking at an exhibit on the history of tobacco, what company are you touring?
8. Wolverine World Wide Corporation is the maker of what noted line of shoes? (Hint: woof)
9. In Ada, Michigan, you can tour the headquarters of what famous door-to-door products company?
10. The Blue Diamond company in Sacramento, California, offers company tours. What edible product is Blue Diamond noted for?
11. Besides bubble gum, what collectible item is the Fleer Corporation known for?
12. If you tour the Imperial Holly Corporation in Houston, what product will you see being made?

All around the House *(answers)*

1. Procter & Gamble
2. Corning Glass
3. Morton Salt (Did anyone miss this?)
4. Windows 95
5. B.V.D., naturally
6. Johnson Wax
7. Philip Morris, one of the largest tobacco companies in the world
8. Hush Puppies
9. Amway
10. Nuts
11. Sports trading cards
12. Sugar

13. What corporate giant, whose products are found in every household in America, was founded in 1883 in Lynn, Massachusetts? (Hint: light)
14. Minute Maid, Hi-C, and Ramblin' Root Beer are all marketed by what world-famous cola maker of Atlanta, Georgia?
15. The Great Atlantic and Pacific Tea Company is better known by what name?
16. Redlands, California, has the stunning Kimberly Crest House and Gardens, named for the founder of what paper company?
17. If you are touring the Boise Cascade Company in International Falls, Minnesota, what product do you see being made?
18. The "World of Oil" exhibit in San Francisco is the property of what petroleum company?
19. Weight Watchers, 9-Lives, and Star-Kist are all owned by what ketchup maker?
20. Sohio is a major company headquartered in Cleveland, Ohio. What is the company's key product?
21. What soap brand, still sold today, was first marketed in the 1890s as an antiseptic remedy for cuts and injuries?
22. What remarkable sewing item, still in use today, was introduced in 1892?
23. Weightlifting equipment is a key industry in what Pennsylvania city?
24. What household items do we associate with Oneida, New York?

☆ Three Sweet Treats

1. What former western movie star markets Happy Trails Chocolates?

13. General Electric
14. Coca-Cola
15. A & P
16. Kimberly-Clark, known for Kleenex and other products
17. Paper, the chief product of this heavily forested region
18. Chevron
19. H. J. Heinz
20. Oil; Sohio is Standard Oil of Ohio.
21. Lifebuoy, which was sold "for preservation of health"
22. Thread on spools
23. York; if you have any experience with free weights, you've seen the familiar York name.
24. Silverware

Three Sweet Treats *(answers)*

1. Roy Rogers, whose theme song was "Happy Trails"

2. What insect is pictured on Bit-O-Honey wrappers?
3. What pricey department store chain, based in Dallas, sells Texas Brag chocolates?

☆ Mail Call

1. What beloved pop singer's face finally appeared on a stamp after people voted about which portrait to use?
2. What was new about the U.S. postage stamps issued in July 1847?
3. What does the postal abbreviation RFD stand for?
4. The nation's first postmaster general also appeared on the first five-cent stamp in 1847. Who? (Hint: lightning)
5. Who (as if you couldn't guess) was the first president to appear on a postage stamp?
6. In what D.C. building could you visit the Hall of Stamps?
7. What famous mail service ran a route from St. Joseph, Missouri, to Sacramento, California?
8. What popular items went on sale in 1873 for one penny each?
9. The postal code VI applies to what U.S. possession in the Caribbean?
10. "Second-class mail" applies to what items?
11. Commemorative stamps issued in 1995 honored key people in what major American war?
12. What was new about the adhesive on some stamps issued in 1992?
13. The *zip* in zip code stands for what?
14. What president's face appeared on the first Confederate postage stamp?
15. In 1887 the U.S. policy was that mail delivery was free to every community having how many residents?
16. Richard Fairbanks was, in 1639, the first person to hold what position?

2. Honeybees, naturally
3. Neiman-Marcus

Mail Call *(answers)*

1. Elvis Presley; people could vote for the younger or older Elvis image. They opted for the younger.
2. They had adhesive.
3. Rural Free Delivery
4. Benjamin Franklin
5. George Washington, naturally
6. The Postal Service headquarters, of course
7. The Pony Express
8. Postcards
9. The Virgin Islands
10. Newspapers and magazines
11. The Civil War; the set had an equal number of Confederate and Union figures.
12. They were self-adhesive—the first of the famous "non-lickers."
13. Zone Improvement Plan; ZIP has been used for so long that few people remember what it originally meant.
14. Jefferson Davis, president of the Confederacy
15. Ten thousand
16. Postmaster; Fairbanks, who lived in Boston, handled mail for one penny per letter.

17. The year 1857 saw the introduction of a machine that did what to envelopes?
18. How many full days did it take Pony Express men to ride from St. Joseph, Missouri, to Sacramento, California?
19. In 1918 the U.S. Post Office issued the first of what type of stamps? (Hint: wings)

☆ Thirsty Americans

1. Druggist Caleb Brabham invented what popular soft drink in 1893? (Hint: *not* Coke)
2. What red juice is the state beverage of Ohio?
3. What popular clear drink was named Bib-Label Light-hearted Lemon-Lime Soda when introduced in 1929?
4. What all-American drink was introduced at the (very hot) St. Louis World's Fair in 1904?
5. Charles Elmer Hires introduced what new type of soft drink in 1869?
6. What did the 7 in 7UP originally stand for?
7. The sports drink Gatorade was named for what school's mascot?
8. What popular drink's formula is kept in a safe in Atlanta, Georgia, under the name 7X?
9. What drinkable product was unleashed on the world in Georgetown, Kentucky, in 1789?
10. Snapple beverages were first advertised by what portly radio talk show host?
11. If you're eating Doritos, Ruffles, or Lay's potato chips, you could quench your thirst with the drink made by their parent company. What company?
12. The Starbucks and Gloria Jean's chains can serve you several varieties of what beverage?
13. What new type of soft drink of the 1870s was called "a tonic to purify the blood and make rosy cheeks"? (Hint: Hires)

17. Postmarked them
18. Seven days, plus about seventeen hours
19. Airmail stamps; the first airmail flight was from New York to Washington.

Thirsty Americans *(answers)*

1. Pepsi
2. Tomato juice
3. 7UP (Aren't you glad the name changed?)
4. Iced tea
5. Root beer
6. The number of ounces in the bottle
7. The University of Florida
8. Coca-Cola
9. Bourbon whiskey, invented by Rev. Elijah Craig
10. Rush Limbaugh
11. Pepsi, which also owns Pizza Hut, KFC, and Taco Bell
12. Coffee
13. Root beer

14. Sipping on café au lait while munching on beignets is a tradition in what southern metropolis?
15. During the Prohibition era, what potent drink was supposed to have been made in bathtubs?
16. What soft drink has its own special museum in Atlanta, Georgia?
17. What beverage was advertised in the 1990s with celebrities who wore "mustaches" of it?
18. What convenience store chain can sell you a Big Gulp or a Super Gulp?
19. In 1961 Coca-Cola introduced the drink that became the world's most popular lemon-lime soda. What was it?
20. What is the only state that grows coffee? (Hint: tropical)
21. Who is the mustachioed man whose face appears on boxes of Lipton tea?
22. Swiss Miss is what type of hot beverage?

☆ All around the House (Part 2)

1. What popular treat did William Breyer hand-churn in his Philadelphia home?
2. Maxwell House, Tang, Jell-O, and Velveeta are all marketed by what company (better known for its tobacco)?
3. What decorative product is associated with Sandwich, Massachusetts?
4. What Delaware-based chemical company introduced nylon to the world?
5. What huge food corporation bought the Jolly Green Giant line? (Hint: dough boy)
6. Kannapolis, North Carolina, takes its name from the town's chief industry, a certain textile manufacturer. What is the company's name?

14. New Orleans
15. Gin
16. Coca-Cola; The World of Coca-Cola reminds visitors that Coke originated in Atlanta.
17. Milk
18. 7-Eleven
19. Sprite
20. Hawaii
21. Mr. Lipton himself, Thomas Lipton, the British tea merchant who made a fortune in England and the U.S.; he's wearing a captain's cap because he was also a noted yachtsman.
22. Hot cocoa

All around the House (Part 2) *(answers)*

1. Ice cream—as in Breyer's Ice Cream; it's no longer hand-churned, of course.
2. Philip Morris
3. Glass; the famous Sandwich pressed glass is considered America's greatest contribution to the glass industry.
4. Du Pont
5. Pillsbury, which then shut down the original Jolly Green Giant plant in Minnesota
6. Cannon, maker of towels, sheets, etc.

7. Allstate insurance, Dean Witter finances, and Coldwell Banker realty are all owned by what huge department store chain?
8. Battle Creek, Michigan, is the center of what food industry?
9. The huge clock with a fifty-foot dial in Jersey City, New Jersey, is owned by what noted toiletries company?
10. What well-known first-aid company has its headquarters in New Brunswick, New Jersey?
11. The Red Lobster seafood restaurants are owned by what famous cereal maker? (Hint: *not* Kellogg's)
12. What department store chain was originally named Golden Rule by its devout Christian founder?
13. Midland, Michigan, is home to what famous chemical company? (Hint: oven cleaner)
14. If you feel sneezy, you could visit Marinette, Wisconsin, and tour what noted paper company?
15. What company's headquarters in Oakland, California, is made of aluminum?
16. Krazy Glue, Cracker Jack, and Classico sauces are all marketed by what famous food company? (Hint: moo)
17. In Kalamazoo, Michigan, what noted drug company could you tour?
18. What famous meatpacking company is headquartered in Austin, Minnesota?
19. What typical Cuban product is manufactured in Ybor City in Tampa, Florida?
20. What notable earthmoving company has its headquarters in Peoria, Illinois?
21. What Scottish-born furnituremaker set up his plant in New York City, producing some of the most famous American furniture?
22. If you wanted to see Crisco being manufactured, what Ohio city would you visit?

7. Sears
8. Breakfast cereals; Kellogg's, Post, and Ralston Purina all have facilities there.
9. Colgate-Palmolive
10. Johnson & Johnson
11. General Mills, maker of Total, Wheaties, and Cheerios
12. J. C. Penney
13. The Dow Chemical Company
14. The Scott Paper Company
15. The Kaiser Aluminum Company
16. Borden, Inc. (famous for Elsie the cow)
17. Upjohn
18. Hormel
19. Cigars; Ybor City has a large Cuban community.
20. Caterpillar (It's unlikely you would have Caterpillar "around the house," but it's at least likely that some of their equipment was used while your house was being built.)
21. Duncan Phyfe
22. Cincinnati; the Procter & Gamble factory can be toured.

☆ More Munchables

1. What toaster pastries did Kellogg's first market in 1964?
2. What fast-food entrepreneur has his own museum in Louisville, Kentucky?
3. Frank Perdue and his son Jim pitch what food in the Perdue commercials?
4. Hostess snacks and Wonder bread are all marketed by what noted pet food company?
5. What nuts, popular in pies, were often called "Mississippi nuts" in colonial times?
6. Campbell's thought about calling this line "Fork Soups." What are they called?
7. Norman, home of the University of Oklahoma, hosts an annual festival honoring what addictive food?
8. What food is at the center of the Republic of Texas Chilympiad?
9. What tropical fruit was a symbol of hospitality in southern households?
10. Chubby, gray-haired, smiling Dave Thomas is founder and TV spokesman for what fast-food chain?
11. Hanes underwear, L'eggs stockings, and Kiwi shoe polish are all owned by what maker of rich snack cakes?
12. What candy maker introduced his bar in 1899 and his kiss in 1907?
13. Clarence Crane created what multicolored (and "holey") roll candy?
14. What popular pan food did Shakey Johnson begin selling in Sacramento, California, in 1956?
15. What fast-food mogul claimed his product contained a "secret recipe of eleven herbs and spices"?
16. In 1802 President Thomas Jefferson received a 1,235-pound block of what food, as a gift from dairy farmers?
17. What brand of candy bar did David L. Clark introduce in 1886?

More Munchables *(answers)*

1. Pop-Tarts
2. The late Harlan B. Sanders of Kentucky Fried Chicken fame
3. Chicken
4. Ralston Purina, headquartered in St. Louis
5. Pecans, which is the name the Indians used for them
6. Chunky Soups
7. Chocolate; the festival features artwork with a chocolate theme.
8. Chili, naturally; it is the men's state championship chili cook-off.
9. The pineapple, which was often carved in woodwork and embroidered on linens
10. Wendy's
11. Sara Lee
12. Hershey
13. Life Savers
14. Pizza (Remember Shakey's Pizza?)
15. Harlan Sanders of Kentucky Fried Chicken
16. Cheese, about four feet across and fifteen inches thick. It was still being served in 1805.
17. The Clark Bar (surprise!)

18. Candy makers Mars and Murray have what popular bite-size candy named for them?
19. Hamburger University is a manager training school operated by what fast-food chain?
20. What popular crunchy, salty snack was (probably) invented by George Crum in 1853?
21. What type of cooking, made famous in Louisiana, swept the country beginning in the 1980s?
22. What Pennsylvania theme park belongs to a candy company?
23. What popular flat food was popularized by World War I GIs returning from Italy?
24. What great American sandwich was supposedly created at a New Haven, Connecticut, diner in 1900?
25. What food, sometimes called "America's most famous dessert," was named by May Wait, wife of the patent holder? (Hint: jiggle)
26. What flower did E. A. Stuart name his canned condensed milk for?
27. What tropical fruit is the most popular breakfast fruit in America?
28. What Texas singer is now better known as a sausage entrepreneur?
29. What fast-food chain is (after the U.S. Army) the nation's biggest supplier of food each day?
30. The world-famous K-Paul's restaurant in New Orleans is famous for what type of cooking?
31. What lunch meat is the center of an annual festival in Lebanon, Pennsylvania?
32. If a New Orleans diner asks for some "debris" on his po'boy sandwich, what will he get?
33. What famous chocolate company was founded in Pennsylvania in 1903?

18. M&M's
19. McDonald's
20. Potato chips
21. Cajun cooking, which is now available in every part of the country
22. Hersheypark
23. Pizza
24. The hamburger
25. Jell-O
26. The carnation
27. The banana, according to a 1995 survey
28. Jimmy Dean
29. McDonald's
30. Cajun; K-Paul's is probably the most famous Cajun cookery in the world.
31. Bologna, which is manufactured locally
32. Roast beef pan drippings and gravy
33. Hershey

34. Bellevue, Ohio, has an annual festival honoring what popular pie fruit?
35. What fruit, used mostly in baking, is supplied by California's fertile Coachella Valley?
36. In Athens, Texas, what much-loved southern vegetable is the center of a festival every July?
37. Gilroy, California, has a festival celebrating what pungent vegetable?
38. They're brambleberries in England, but what are they in the U.S.?
39. Farming of what fish is a rapidly growing business in the southern U.S.? (Hint: whiskers)

34. Cherries; the Cherry Festival is held in late June.
35. The date; about 95 percent of dates produced in the U.S. come from this valley.
36. The black-eyed pea; the Black-eyed Pea Jamboree features pea-popping and pea-shelling races.
37. Garlic, a major crop in California
38. Blackberries
39. Catfish

PART THREE
Amusing Ourselves Silly

☆ Grasping for a Grammy

Officially, they're the National Academy of Recording Arts and Sciences Awards—but it's much easier to say Grammys. Whatever the name, they're considered the highest awards in the music industry, and the Grammy awards show is one of TV's most-watched programs every year.

Incidentally, the name Grammy comes from the shape of the award: a gilded miniature version of an old-time record player, a gramophone.

1. In 1960, Album of the Year was *Button Down Mind*, a spoken comedy album by what low-key sitcom actor?
2. Songwriter Carole King's huge-selling Album of the Year (in 1971) had what textile name?
3. Elton John's 1994 Grammy-winning "Can You Feel the Love Tonight?" was from what Disney cartoon feature? (Hint: Africa)
4. "I Will Always Love You," which won a Grammy for Whitney Houston in 1993, was actually written by which platinum blonde country music queen?
5. Kim Carnes won in 1981 for a song about the eyes of which Hollywood actress?
6. What reclusive megastar won in 1983 both for the single "Beat It" and the album *Thriller*?
7. According to Tony Bennett's 1962 Record of the Year, where did he leave his heart?
8. What blind Puerto Rican singer-guitarist won in 1968 for his version of the Doors' song "Light My Fire"?
9. What group won in 1969 for the album *Blood, Sweat, and Tears*?
10. Carole King won in 1971 for writing the song "You've Got a Friend." What fellow songwriter won for singing it?

Grasping for a Grammy (*answers*)

1. Bob Newhart; at the time he recorded the album, Newhart was only a stand-up comic, not a sitcom actor.
2. *Tapestry*
3. *The Lion King*
4. Dolly Parton
5. Bette Davis; the song was "Bette Davis Eyes."
6. Michael Jackson, of course
7. "I Left My Heart in San Francisco"
8. José Feliciano
9. Blood, Sweat, and Tears
10. James Taylor

11. Paul Simon's Grammy-winning 1986 album *Graceland* aroused some controversy because he had recorded it in what *very* controversial country?
12. What disco movie soundtrack won Album of the Year in 1978? (Hint: white suits)
13. What husband-and-wife team won in 1975 for "Love Will Keep Us Together"?
14. What singer, best known for his comedy songs like "The Streak," won a 1970 Grammy for the gentle song "Everything Is Beautiful"?
15. What pop-soul quintet won for "Up, Up and Away"?
16. What popular California band won in 1977 for the single "Hotel California"?
17. Ray Charles won in 1960 for his recording of the Georgia state song, which is what?
18. The song that became Bobby Darin's theme song won in 1959. What was the song?
19. Bobbie Gentry won in 1967 for a song about a boy who "jumped off the Tallahatchie Bridge." What was the song?
20. What songstress, the daughter of a famous crooner, won in 1991 for "Unforgettable," which her father had also recorded?
21. What mariachi-brass band won for Record of the Year in 1965 for "A Taste of Honey"?
22. What pop duo won for "Mrs. Robinson" in 1968 and "Bridge Over Troubled Water" in 1970?
23. What composer and bandleader won in 1961 for "Moon River" and in 1963 for "The Days of Wine and Roses"?
24. *September of My Years* and *A Man and His Music* won Album of the Year in 1965 and 1966 for what crooner?
25. Who won Grammys for the single and album both titled *By the Time I Get to Phoenix*?

11. South Africa, which at that time was under an unofficial ban; American singers weren't supposed to perform or record there.
12. *Saturday Night Fever*
13. The Captain and Tennille
14. Ray Stevens
15. The Fifth Dimension
16. The Eagles
17. "Georgia on My Mind"
18. "Mack the Knife"
19. "Ode to Billie Joe"
20. Natalie Cole, daughter of Nat "King" Cole
21. Herb Alpert and the Tijuana Brass
22. Simon and Garfunkel
23. Henry Mancini
24. Frank Sinatra
25. Glen Campbell

26. What comedienne won Comedy Album of the Year for playing obnoxious telephone operator Ernestine in *This Is a Recording*?

☆ Emmy Time

Trying to get away from TV in America would be like trying to get away from air. The tube has its unpleasant side, but most of us have fond memories of a favorite show or character. The TV people themselves honor their own favorites each year with the Emmy awards. Some of the winners you'll know, and some may really surprise you.

1. What still-popular comedy (with a red-haired star) won Emmys for Best Situation Comedy in 1952 and 1953?
2. What comedy, a spinoff from *Cheers*, won several times for Best Comedy Series in the 1990s?
3. Robert Young and Jane Wyatt both won Emmys in the 1950s for their dad and mom roles on what warmhearted family comedy?
4. Raymond Burr won an Emmy in 1961 for his portrayal of what tough-minded attorney-detective?
5. What Saturday night favorite of the 1970s won several Emmys for Best Comedy-Variety Series? (Hint: "I'm so glad we had this time together. . . .")
6. Ted Danson and Kirstie Alley won for their roles in what Boston pub comedy in the 1990s?
7. What thriller series (remade as a movie in 1996) was Best Drama Series in 1968? (Hint: self-destruct)
8. What famous movie actress of the 1940s won an Emmy in 1966 for playing a ranch matriarch on *The Big Valley*?
9. A 1963 award went to "Julie and Carol at Carnegie Hall," which starred what two beloved performers?
10. What series starring a rock group was Best Comedy Series of 1967? (Hint: train to Clarksville)

26. Lily Tomlin

Emmy Time *(answers)*

1. *I Love Lucy*
2. *Frasier*
3. *Father Knows Best,* which is still popular in reruns
4. *Perry Mason*
5. *The Carol Burnett Show*
6. *Cheers*
7. *Mission: Impossible*
8. Barbara Stanwyck
9. Julie Andrews and Carol Burnett
10. *The Monkees*

11. What wacky detective comedy (whose star had a telephone in his shoe) was Best Comedy Series in 1968 and 1969?

12. Betty White and Beatrice Arthur both won for their roles in what comedy series set in a Florida retirement center?

13. What pudgy actor won for his roles in *All in the Family* and *In the Heat of the Night*?

14. Tony Randall and Jack Klugman both won (in different years) for their roles on what comedy about two bickering roommates?

15. Robert Young played a compassionate doctor in what Emmy-winning series of the late 1960s?

16. What beloved family drama, set in the Appalachians, won Best Drama Series in 1973?

17. Lucille Ball won not only won for *I Love Lucy*, but for what series in the 1960s?

18. What macho, hirsute movie actor won for his role in the comedy series *Evening Shade*?

19. Peter Falk won in two different decades for the same role, a bumbling detective. Who?

20. What comedy series, which won three years in a row, was set in a Minnesota TV station?

21. Beatrice Arthur won in 1977 for playing a character who first appeared on *All in the Family*. What character?

22. What zany comic, famous for playing Geraldine Jones, had a show that won Best Variety Series in 1971?

23. Isabel Sanford won an Emmy for another character spun off from *All in the Family*. What was the series?

24. Ed Asner, who won more than once for his role in *Lou Grant*, had played the same role in what comedy series?

25. What beloved Western series (with Matt, Doc, and Miss Kitty) won Best Drama Series in 1957?

26. What variety show, which ran on Sunday nights for decades, won an Emmy in 1955?

11. *Get Smart*
12. *The Golden Girls*
13. Carroll O'Connor
14. *The Odd Couple*
15. *Marcus Welby, M.D.*
16. *The Waltons* (good night, John-Boy)
17. *The Lucy Show* (You'd think they could have been more creative with the titles. . . .)
18. Burt Reynolds, who won in 1991
19. *Columbo;* Falk won in 1972 and 1990.
20. *The Mary Tyler Moore Show;* Best Comedy Series, 1975–77
21. *Maude,* who began as Edith Bunker's opinionated cousin
22. Flip Wilson
23. *The Jeffersons,* who had originally been neighbors of the Bunkers
24. *The Mary Tyler Moore Show*
25. *Gunsmoke*
26. *The Ed Sullivan Show*

27. *Truth or Consequences* won an Emmy in 1950 in what category?
28. Barbara Bel Geddes won for her role as the matriarch in what phenomenally popular nighttime soap opera?
29. What chase series (which became a popular movie in 1993) was Best Drama Series in 1966?
30. What show, centered on a TV comedy writer, won Best Comedy Series four years in a row in the 1960s? (Hint: Rob and Laura)
31. What zany comedy show, which introduced such stars as Lily Tomlin and Goldie Hawn to the world, won an Emmy in 1968?

☆ The Great American Musical

The musical may be one of America's greatest contributions to the world of entertainment. Certainly some of the most popular plays and movies are musicals. And some of the best songs ever written were originally part of a musical production. Below are sets of songs, each from a particular musical. See if you can name the play or movie that each set came from.

1. "Climb Every Mountain," "My Favorite Things," "Do Re Mi"
2. "Surrey with the Fringe on Top," "A Girl Who Can't Say No," "People Will Say We're in Love"
3. "Maria," "Cool," "I Feel Pretty"
4. "Getting to Know You," "Hello, Young Lovers," "I Have Dreamed"
5. "You Can't Get a Man with a Gun," "Doin' What Comes Naturally," "There's No Business Like Show Business"
6. "Some Enchanted Evening," "Happy Talk," "Bali Hai"
7. "Day by Day," "Prepare Ye the Way of the Lord," "We Beseech Thee"

27. Best Game Show; this award is no longer awarded since there are now so few game shows.
28. *Dallas*
29. *The Fugitive*
30. *The Dick Van Dyke Show*, winning 1963–66, a record for consecutive wins
31. *Rowan and Martin's Laugh-In* (which won for Best Variety Series, not Best Comedy)

The Great American Musical *(answers)*

1. *The Sound of Music*
2. *Oklahoma!*
3. *West Side Story*
4. *The King and I*
5. *Annie Get Your Gun*
6. *South Pacific*
7. *Godspell*

8. "I Could Have Danced All Night," "Wouldn't It Be Loverly?" "Get Me to the Church on Time"
9. "Greased Lightning," "Beauty School Dropout," "Look at Me, I'm Sandra Dee"
10. "If Ever I Would Leave You," "I Wonder What the King Is Doing Tonight?" "What Do the Simple Folk Do?"
11. "Ol' Man River," "Can't Help Lovin' Dat Man," "Life Upon the Wicked Stage"
12. "Tradition," "Matchmaker, Matchmaker," "If I Were a Rich Man"
13. "Seventy-six Trombones," "Marian the Librarian," "Wells Fargo Wagon"
14. "Thank Heaven for Little Girls," "The Parisians," "I Remember It Well"
15. "Wilkommen," "Maybe This Time," "Mein Herr"
16. "Let Me Entertain You," "Small World," "If Mama Was Married"
17. "People," "Don't Rain on My Parade," "I'm the Greatest Star"
18. "Put on a Happy Face," "Kids," "Honestly Sincere"
19. "Smoke Gets in Your Eyes," "Lovely to Look At," "The Touch of Your Hand"
20. "Try to Remember," "Soon It's Gonna Rain," "It Depends on What You Pay"
21. "Indian Love Call," "Song of the Mounties," "Totem Tom Toms"
22. "Ease on Down the Road," "Don't Nobody Bring Me No Bad News," "Slide a Little Oil to Me"
23. "Luck, Be a Lady Tonight," "Sit Down, You're Rockin' the Boat," "Take Back Your Mink"
24. "Aquarius," "Let the Sunshine In," "Good Morning, Starshine"
25. "The Heather on the Hill," "Go Home with Bonnie Jean," "Almost Like Being in Love"

8. *My Fair Lady*
9. *Grease*
10. *Camelot*
11. *Show Boat*
12. *Fiddler on the Roof*
13. *The Music Man*
14. *Gigi*
15. *Cabaret*
16. *Gypsy*
17. *Funny Girl*
18. *Bye Bye Birdie*
19. *Roberta*
20. *The Fantasticks*
21. *Rose Marie*
22. *The Wiz*
23. *Guys and Dolls*
24. *Hair*
25. *Brigadoon*

26. "The Night Dolly Parton Was Almost Mine," "Fisherman's Prayer," "Highway 57"

☆ Shall We Dance? America on Its Legs

Dancing is as universal and as human as breathing. Once in a while someone describes a particular dance as scandalous or immoral. (In fact, people used to describe the waltz in those terms . . . long ago.) But, regardless, dancing goes on, and America has spawned more than its share of fads and crazes . . . and even a few dances that endure.

1. What Latin-rock dance craze swept America in 1996?
2. What phenomenally popular 1977 John Travolta movie helped launch the disco craze?
3. America's longest-surviving folk dance is a "reel" named for what southern state?
4. What country line dance of the 1990s was based on Billy Ray Cyrus's song "Achy Breaky Heart"?
5. Who was the most famous movie dance partner for Ginger Rogers and Eleanor Powell?
6. ABBA, probably the world's top group of the disco era, was from what country in Europe?
7. What mop-topped weight-loss guru sold dance videos called *Sweatin' to the Oldies*?
8. *Club Dance*, a popular program of country dancing, is a feature of what cable network?
9. What popular dance of the 1960s had a "nautical" touch?
10. What was, and still is, America's biggest chain of dance studios?
11. What agile movie dancer did a famous dance with Jerry, the cartoon mouse?

26. *Pump Boys and Dinettes*

Shall We Dance? America on Its Legs *(answers)*

1. The Macarena
2. *Saturday Night Fever*
3. Virginia; until you've danced the Virginia reel, you ain't never really danced.
4. The Achy Breaky Dance (surprise!)
5. Fred Astaire, who else?
6. Sweden; the name ABBA, by the way, came from the group members' initials.
7. Richard Simmons
8. The Nashville Network, or TNN
9. The Swim
10. Arthur Murray
11. Gene Kelly

12. The Bump, which was slightly scandalous, was popular in what decade?
13. America's most popular dance in time was, and is, what?
14. What *very* simple dance did Chubby Checker introduce on *American Bandstand* in 1960?
15. What sassy Latin dance swept America after being introduced from Cuba in the mid-1950s?
16. After Chubby Checker coaxed Americans on with "Let's Do the Twist," who coaxed them on with "Let's Twist Again"?
17. What popular sliding ragtime dance of the early 1900s was named after a large American game bird?
18. The very athletic form known as break dancing was popular in what decade?
19. Weird Al Yankovic is famous for setting rock songs to what old-fashioned type of dance music?
20. What "star search" TV dance show of the 1980s was hosted by Denny Terrio?
21. What group party dance of the 1960s took its name from a jumpy woodland creature?
22. What married couple made ballroom dancing extremely popular in the early 1900s?
23. What bandleader, killed in a plane crash in 1944, was probably the most popular supplier of dance music of his day?
24. What dance, involving leaning backward under a stick, is always done to a Caribbean beat?
25. What religious sect, famous for its simplicity and its well-made furniture, was also famous for its spirited dancing?
26. What world-famous jazz clarinetist and bandleader was known as "the King of Swing"?
27. What pop diva, who claimed to be a born-again Christian, was the reigning queen of disco in the 1980s?

12. The 1970s—beginning about 1974, to be exact
13. The waltz (When was the last time you waltzed?)
14. The twist
15. The cha-cha
16. Chubby Checker
17. The turkey; the dance was the turkey trot.
18. The 1980s
19. Polkas
20. *Dance Fever*
21. The bunny hop
22. Vernon and Irene Castle, who popularized the tango, the hesitation waltz, and many other dances
23. Glenn Miller
24. The limbo (Whether it's actually considered a dance is debatable.)
25. The Shakers (No, it's no accident that they "danced for the Lord" and were named "Shakers" by their detractors.)
26. Benny Goodman
27. Donna Summer

28. By congressional proclamation, what type of dance is the official folk dance of the U.S.?
29. What famous dance of the Hopi Indians can never be viewed by visitors?
30. What famous tap dancer is commemorated by a statue in Richmond, Virginia?
31. Clogging is a style of dance from what part of the country?
32. What bouncy dance of the 1920s was named for a port city in South Carolina?
33. What popular ballroom dance is named for a bushy-tailed forest creature?
34. What dance do we associate with Hawaii?
35. What jitterbug-like dance of the 1930s was named for pilot Charles Lindbergh?
36. What country variation of the two-step became popular in the 1980s?

☆ Three Crossover Superstars

1. The lead singer with the rock group First Edition later became what country superstar? (Hint: silver beard)
2. What blonde country-pop star made a splash in movies and has her own theme park near her Tennessee hometown?
3. What star of Christian contemporary music made a successful crossover in the 1990s with songs like "Baby, Baby" and "House of Love"?

☆ Sister Acts (and Other Family Acts)

The world of pop music has always had its sister acts—as well as brother acts, husband-and-wife acts, and so forth. Maybe talent runs in families . . . or maybe talented people marry

28. Square dancing
29. The snake dance, using live rattlesnakes
30. Bill "Bojangles" Robinson; the statue shows him in midstep.
31. The Appalachian Mountains; supposedly it has roots in dances brought from Ireland.
32. The Charleston
33. The fox-trot
34. The hula, of course
35. The lindy
36. The Texas two-step

Three Crossover Superstars *(answers)*

1. Kenny Rogers
2. Dolly Parton; the park is Dollywood.
3. Amy Grant

other talented people. In any case, test your knowledge of some musical families.

1. What Mormon brother act got its start singing as a barbershop quartet at Disneyland?
2. What singer, who became a Republican Congressman in the 1990s, had a popular variety show in the 1970s with his long-haired wife?
3. Phil and Don are the first names of what rock duo, most famous for "Bye Bye Love"?
4. Carly Simon was married for a while to (and recorded with) what "Fire and Rain" singer?
5. The Judds, a favorite family act in country music, were what relation?
6. June Carter, herself part of the famous Carter country music clan, is married to what "Man in Black"?
7. How many members of Van Halen are actually *named* Van Halen?
8. Dennis, Carl, and Brian Wilson were (and still are) members of what California megagroup?
9. What pop music legend recorded "Somethin' Stupid" with his daughter Nancy?
10. Rita Coolidge was briefly married to (and recorded with) what gravelly voiced singer-songwriter?
11. John and Tom Fogerty were members of what "bayou rock" supergroup of the 1970s?
12. What very talented family, based in Gary, Indiana, had its first hit in 1970 with "ABC"?
13. Plaintive-voiced country singer Jessie Colter was married to what deep-voiced "outlaw" country legend?
14. Gerry Goffin, one of pop music's best songwriters of the 1960s, had a notable singer-songwriter as wife and writing partner. Who? (Hint: *Tapestry*)

Sister Acts (and Other Family Acts) *(answers)*

1. The Osmonds
2. Sonny Bono, married to (of course) Cher at the time
3. The Everly Brothers
4. James Taylor; they had a hit with "Mockingbird."
5. Mother (Naomi) and daughter (Wynona)
6. Johnny Cash
7. Two—Eddie and Alex
8. The Beach Boys
9. Frank Sinatra
10. Kris Kristofferson
11. Creedence Clearwater Revival
12. The Jacksons, or (as they were first known) the Jackson 5, brother Michael being the most famous, of course
13. Waylon Jennings
14. Carole King

15. Whose back-up group, the Pips, consisted of her brother, sister, and two cousins?
16. Which of the Mamas and Papas actually were related?
17. Bonnie, Ruth, and June, who had hits with "He's So Shy" and "Neutron Dance," are what sister act?
18. Eydie Gorme has long been married to what crooner?
19. What brother-sister duo's career ended in 1982 when sister Karen died of anorexia?
20. When Annie Mae Bullock performed with her husband Ike, what was her stage name?
21. The country singer nicknamed "Bocephus" is the son of what country legend?
22. Tammy Wynette, one of country music's megastars, recorded songs with what husband, also a megastar?

☆ Singing for Oscar

Some of our best songs make their debuts in movies. Every year the Motion Picture Academy awards an Oscar to the best (in the Academy's opinion) song from a movie. A lot of these have become fixtures in America's song repertoire. A few have been completely forgotten, and a few will surprise you in a big way.

1. The first Oscar-winning song was a dance number, "The Continental," in a 1934 film starring what famous dance pair?
2. The winner for 1966 had the same title as its movie, a story about an African lion. What was the title?
3. "Sooner or Later" was sung by what sultry blonde diva in the 1990 movie *Dick Tracy*?
4. Debbie Boone's popular song "You Light Up My Life" was from what 1977 movie?
5. "Under the Sea" won in 1989. What underwater cartoon movie was it from?

15. Gladys Knight's
16. John and Michelle Phillips, who were married
17. The Pointer Sisters
18. Steve Lawrence
19. The Carpenters, Karen and Richard
20. Tina Turner, of the Ike and Tina Turner Revue
21. Hank Williams; Bocephus is Hank Williams Jr.
22. George Jones

Singing for Oscar *(answers)*

1. Fred Astaire and Ginger Rogers; the movie was *The Gay Divorcee.*
2. "Born Free," in the movie *Born Free*
3. Madonna
4. *You Light Up My Life*—a case where the song was much better known (and just plain better) than the movie
5. Disney's *The Little Mermaid*

6. "The Morning After," winner for 1972, was from what movie about an overturned cruise ship?

7. "Chim-Chim-Cheree" was from what Disney film about a "practically perfect" English nanny?

8. *Butch Cassidy and the Sundance Kid* featured what Oscar-winning (and phenomenally popular) song sung by B. J. Thomas?

9. "A Whole New World" was from a Disney film based on the Arabian Nights. What was the film?

10. What blonde star sang the award-winning "Que Sera Sera" in the movie *The Man Who Knew Too Much*?

11. What beloved comedian sang the Oscar-winning song "Buttons and Bows" in the Western spoof *The Paleface*?

12. Bing Crosby, playing a singing priest, sang the award-winning "Swinging on a Star" in what warmhearted 1944 movie?

13. "When You Wish Upon a Star," one of the best-loved songs from a Disney movie, was from what 1940 favorite?

14. Plantation slave Uncle Remus sang what jolly song in the Disney film *Song of the South*?

15. Who (as if you couldn't guess) sang "Over the Rainbow" in *The Wizard of Oz*?

16. The song that became Bob Hope's theme song was an Oscar winner, sung by him in the movie *The Big Broadcast of 1938*. What was the song?

17. What ever-popular Irving Berlin Christmas song from the film *Holiday Inn* won in 1942?

18. The song "Talk to the Animals" was from what movie about an Englishman who could literally converse with animals?

19. One of the least-known Oscar winners was "It Goes Like It Goes," from what 1979 film showing Sally Field as a union activist?

6. *The Poseidon Adventure*
7. *Mary Poppins,* 1964
8. "Raindrops Keep Fallin' on My Head," winner for 1969
9. *Aladdin,* 1992
10. Doris Day; the song won for 1956 and became Day's theme song.
11. Bob Hope; the song was the winner for 1948.
12. *Going My Way*
13. *Pinocchio*
14. "Zip-a-Dee-Doo-Dah," which won in 1947
15. Judy Garland, who played Dorothy
16. "Thanks for the Memories"
17. "White Christmas"
18. *Dr. Doolittle,* 1967
19. *Norma Rae*

20. "We May Never Love Like This Again" was from what 1974 movie about a burning skyscraper?
21. Tex Ritter sang the Oscar-winning song "Do Not Forsake Me, O My Darling" in what popular 1952 Gary Cooper cowboy film?
22. What blonde star played the lead in *Calamity Jane* and crooned its Oscar-winning song, "Secret Love"?
23. What song, which will always be connected with Nat "King" Cole, won in 1950, sung in the forgotten movie *Captain Carey, USA*?
24. What ex-wife of a president and later a star of TV's *Falcon Crest* sang the winner "In the Cool, Cool, Cool of the Evening" in *Here Comes the Groom*?
25. Audrey Hepburn played Holly Golightly and sang "Moon River" in what wacky 1961 comedy?
26. What appropriately titled song from the 1980 movie *Fame* won an Oscar?
27. "What a Feeling" was from what popular 1983 movie about a female welder who's also a dancer?
28. Christopher Cross sang "The Best You Can Do" in what 1981 movie about a hard-drinking millionaire?
29. The 1982 movie *An Officer and a Gentleman* contained what romantic and inspiring hit song?
30. The 1971 winner was Isaac Hayes's theme song from a movie about a tough-talking black detective. What was the movie?

20. *The Towering Inferno*
21. *High Noon*
22. Doris Day; the song won for 1953.
23. "Mona Lisa"
24. Jane Wyman, former wife of Ronald Reagan; the song won for 1951.
25. *Breakfast at Tiffany's*
26. "Fame"
27. *Flashdance*
28. *Arthur;* the song is also called "Arthur's Theme."
29. "Up Where We Belong"; it was a big hit for Jennifer Warnes and Joe Cocker.
30. *Shaft;* the song was (surprise!) "Theme from *Shaft.*"

☆ All in Fun . . .

Ask foreigners what American sights they wish to see, and attractions like Disney World usually top their lists. Yankee ingenuity is admired, but so is Yankee tomfoolery. The questions here are a sort of "potpourri" of amusement—from the mildly amusing to the amazingly amusing.

1. The ever-popular yellow smiley face was drawn by Harvey Ball in what decade?
2. What holiday temporarily changes Knott's Berry Farm park into Knott's Scary Farm?
3. What fast-food chain's headquarters in Oak Brook, Illinois, is called Hamburger Central?
4. By what better name was twenty-eight-inch-tall Charles S. Stratton known? (Hint: Barnum's circus)
5. What New Jersey resort town opened its first casino in 1978?
6. What cable network has its headquarters at Opryland USA in Nashville?
7. What brand of vitamins was named after a popular video game of the 1980s?
8. What vanilla-and-chocolate treat was created by Christian Nelson of Iowa in 1921?
9. What new type of movie theater first appeared in 1933 in Camden, New Jersey?
10. What type of wrestling has its world championship meet in Petaluma, California?
11. If you wanted to engage in crab racing, what state would you visit?
12. What escape artist was especially famous for his "Water Torture Cell" escape?
13. With a capacity of 63,000, what San Francisco ballpark is the National League's largest?

All in Fun . . . *(answers)*

1. The 1960s—1963, to be specific; it has never completely gone out of style.
2. Halloween
3. McDonald's
4. General Tom Thumb
5. Atlantic City
6. The Nashville Network, of course
7. Pac-Man
8. The Eskimo Pie
9. The drive-in
10. Wrist wrestling (still known in some quarters as Indian wrestling or arm wrestling)
11. Maryland; the town of Crisfield has the National Hard Crab Derby each September.
12. Harry Houdini, probably America's best-known escape artist
13. Candlestick Park

14. "Eve with a lid on" is what type of dessert, in lunch counter slang?
15. What beloved Oklahoma comic and rope-slinger claimed "All politics is applesauce"?
16. What did New England whale hunters in the 1800s refer to as a "Nantucket sleigh ride"?
17. Athens, Georgia, has an inanimate object that legally owns itself. What is it?
18. What bandleader was sometimes called "the Liberace of the Accordion"?
19. What Republican presidential candidate of the 1960s identified himself as AuH_2O?
20. Louisiana has the Live Oak Society, dedicated to preserve live oak trees at least one hundred years old. What distinctive payment is used for membership dues?
21. What world-famous author bequeathed his many cats to the town of Key West, Florida?
22. Tufts University received the remains of Jumbo, belonging to P. T. Barnum. What type of animal was it?
23. Six Flags Over Mid-America is in what mid-American state?
24. What Texas metropolis is known for having a city bridge that houses more than a million bats?
25. During its wild gold rush days, what was the popular alternative name for Los Angeles?
26. What Atlantic resort island, a haven for Civil War blockade runners, has a Confederate museum?
27. According to Old West lore, how did cowboys keep their eyes open when driving their herds all night?
28. In Nebraska what is the meaning of the Indian word *Ak-Sar-Ben*?
29. What game did movie theaters play during the Great Depression to help earn extra money?

14. Apple pie with a topping; "Eve" always refers to apples in lunch counter lingo.
15. Will Rogers; since he "never met a man he didn't like," he must have even liked applesauce peddlers.
16. The whaleboat being towed along on the line behind the harpooned whale—an adventure, no doubt, but surely rather frightening
17. An old oak tree; the owner deeded the tree and the surrounding land to . . . the tree.
18. Lawrence Welk
19. Barry Goldwater; AuH_2O is the chemical formula for gold and water.
20. Twenty-five acorns per year
21. Ernest Hemingway; his home in Key West is home to more than forty cats, descendants of the cats he owned in the 1930s.
22. An elephant
23. Missouri, not far from St. Louis
24. Austin; the bat flight every day at dusk has become a tourist attraction.
25. Los Diablos—meaning "the devils," as opposed to the city's real name, "the angels"
26. Bermuda
27. They pasted them open with tobacco. (If you're skeptical, join the crowd.)
28. It isn't an Indian word; it's *Nebraska* spelled backward, and several spots in Omaha, Nebraska, have the Ak-Sar-Ben name.
29. Bingo

30. What hobby reached a peak of popularity after the publication of the book *Roots*?
31. If you are dining at the Palace Court or the Empress Court, what renowned Las Vegas hotel and pleasure palace are you in?

☆ TV History

This set of questions is referring not to history on TV but to *the history of TV itself*. We're so TV-saturated that we forget that TV wasn't always around (not to mention color, cable, VCRs, satellite dishes, etc.).

1. What astounding event (showing a man walking on bare ground) was broadcast around the world on July 20, 1969?
2. The first televised presidential debates were in September 1960 between John F. Kennedy and what challenger?
3. WGY of Schenectady, New York, was the first station to schedule commercial broadcasts in the U.S. Do you know (or can you guess) the year this occurred?
4. In 1945 the Federal Communications Commission allotted how many channels for commercial broadcasts?
5. What popular TV fright-show host is honored with the exhibit "Day of a Playwright" in Binghamton, New York?
6. Which cable TV network awards the annual Video Music Awards?
7. What was new and shocking about the CBS broadcast from New York on June 25, 1951?
8. That same year, the first nationwide broadcast was an address by what president?
9. Just before Christmas 1951, NBC broadcast a new opera it had commissioned by noted composer Gian Carlo Menotti. It is still popular at Christmas. What is the title?

30. Genealogy—that is, tracing one's family tree
31. Caesar's Palace

TV History *(answers)*

1. The first moon landing, with astronauts Neil Armstrong and Buzz Aldrin
2. The Republican candidate, Richard Nixon
3. 1928—May 11, 1928, to be precise
4. Thirteen; which is still the number of VHF channels. UHF was added later as more channels were needed. (And then came cable. . . .)
5. Rod Serling, host of *The Twilight Zone* and *Night Gallery*; he grew up in Binghamton.
6. MTV, naturally, the pioneer in music videos
7. It was in color—the first commercial broadcast in color.
8. Harry Truman, addressing a conference in California. The address was carried by ninety-four stations across the country.
9. *Amahl and the Night Visitors*; it has the distinction of being the first opera written strictly for television.

10. What phenomenally popular TV police series of the 1980s resulted from the NBC president's two-word memo, "MTV cops"?

11. UHF channels on your TV begin with what number?

12. In what remote location was Vice President Richard Nixon when he broadcast in August 1959?

13. What famous house did TV viewers get to see on February 14, 1962, with Jackie Kennedy as tour guide?

14. On December 17, 1969, Herbert Buckingham Khaury married Victoria May Budinger on *The Tonight Show*. By what name was he better known?

15. In 1963 a televised White House ceremony honored a famous British statesman by making him an honorary U.S. citizen. Who was he?

16. In April 1969 what brother act had its show canceled by CBS for its controversial humor?

17. What Republican vice president in 1969 referred to TV newsmen as an "unelected elite" who tried to control people's thoughts?

18. In a Jets-Raiders game in 1968, NBC cut away from the game at the last minute to broadcast what children's movie?

19. In 1996 ABC was acquired by what entertainment giant? (Hint: Florida)

20. On February 11, 1960, what *Tonight Show* host walked off his show because NBC had censored one of his jokes the night before?

21. What high-ranking federal group had its first televised meeting on October 25, 1954?

22. What large object could TV viewers see up close for the first time in June 1966, courtesy of *Surveyor I?*

10. *Miami Vice*
11. Fourteen; the VHF channels end at thirteen.
12. Moscow, Russia
13. The White House, of course; the TV tour was seen by forty-six million viewers.
14. Tiny Tim, a (briefly) popular novelty singer at the time; his seventeen-year-old bride was known as "Miss Vicki."
15. Winston Churchill
16. *The Smothers Brothers Comedy Hour;* they sued CBS for $31 million in damages.
17. Spiro Agnew, vice president under Richard Nixon
18. *Heidi;* people at the time referred to it as "the Heidi game." The Raiders scored twice in nine (unbroadcasted) seconds and won the game.
19. The Disney Company
20. Jack Paar; he was back to work by March 7.
21. The Cabinet, along with President Eisenhower
22. The moon; it televised some (very grainy) pictures. This was three years before a man walked on the moon.

☆ Band Boys: Members of Rock Groups

When you hear the names Paul McCartney, John Lennon, George Harrison, and Ringo Starr, you say, "Ah, the Beatles." And if you don't say this, the following questions probably won't be your favorites in this book. Anyway, see if you can name the group by reading the list of members in the group. Keep in mind that rock groups have a high turnover rate. Also keep in mind that the groups here are from every period of pop music, not just the present. (These are all *American* groups, by the way, so you won't find the Rolling Stones, Dire Straits, etc.)

1. Brian Wilson, Dennis Wilson, Carl Wilson, Mike Love, Al Jardine
2. David Crosby, Stephen Stills, Graham Nash, Neil Young
3. David Lee Roth, Eddie Van Halen, Mike Anthony, Alex Van Halen
4. Jim Morrison, Ray Manzarek, Robby Krieger
5. Frankie Valli, Bob Gaudio, Nick Massi, Tommy De Vito
6. Glenn Frey, Don Henley, Don Felder, Joe Walsh
7. Sly Stone, Freddie Stone, Cynthia Robinson, Jerry Martini
8. Bill Medley, Bobby Hatfield
9. John Fogerty, Tom Fogerty, Stu Cook, Cosmo Clifford
10. Bill Golden, Joe Bonsall, Richard Sterban, Duane Allen
11. Davy Jones, Mickey Dolenz, Mike Nesmith, Peter Tork
12. John Phillips, Michelle Phillips, Cass Elliott, Denny Doherty
13. John Sebastian, Joe Butler, Steve Boone
14. Ronnie Van Zant, Gary Rossington, Allen Collins, Billy Powell
15. Steve Perry, Neal Schon, Ross Valory
16. Steve Tyler, Joe Perry, Tom Hamilton, Joey Kramer

Band Boys: Members of Rock Groups *(answers)*

1. The Beach Boys
2. Crosby, Stills, Nash, and Young (surprise!)
3. Van Halen
4. The Doors
5. The Four Seasons
6. The Eagles
7. Sly and the Family Stone
8. The Righteous Brothers
9. Creedence Clearwater Revival
10. The Oak Ridge Boys
11. The Monkees
12. The Mamas and the Papas
13. The Lovin' Spoonful
14. Lynyrd Skynyrd
15. Journey
16. Aerosmith

17. Robbie Robertson, Garth Hudson, Levon Helm, Rick Danko
18. David Clayton-Thomas, Bruce Cassidy, Robert Pitch, Richard Martinez
19. David Gates, James Griffin, Mike Botts
20. Rick Nielsen, Robin Zander, Bun E. Carlos
21. Lionel Richie, William King, Thomas McClary
22. Tom Petty, Mike Campbell, Stan Lynch, Benmont Tench
23. Howard Kaplan, Mark Volman, Al Nichol, Jim Tucker
24. John Kay, Jerry Edmonton, Michael Monarch
25. David Byrne, Chris Frantz, Tina Weymouth, Jerry Harrison
26. Belinda Carlisle, Charlotte Caffey, Jane Wiedlin
27. Jerry Garcia, Pigpen McKernan, Bob Weir
28. Peter Wolf, J. Geils, Magic Dick, Danny Klein
29. Jan Berry, Dean Torrence
30. Michael McDonald, Pat Simmons, John McFree, Keith Knudsen
31. Gene Simmons, Paul Stanley, Ace Frehley, Peter Criss
32. Danny Hutton, Cory Wells, Chuck Negron

17. The Band
18. Blood, Sweat, and Tears
19. Bread
20. Cheap Trick
21. The Commodores
22. Tom Petty and the Heartbreakers
23. The Turtles
24. Steppenwolf
25. Talking Heads
26. The Go-Gos
27. The Grateful Dead
28. J. Geils Band
29. Jan and Dean
30. The Doobie Brothers
31. KISS
32. Three Dog Night

PART FOUR

Write On

☆ Lives in Print: Biographies and Autobiographies

Many people find history boring—but *people* are always interesting. Maybe that's why most people prefer to read their history in the form of someone's life story. Some of the greatest—and also some of the oddest—American books have been biographies and autobiographies.

1. *Rock, Roll, and Remember* are the memoirs of what TV personality, also known as "America's Oldest Teenager"?
2. *Leading with My Chin* is the 1996 biography of what late-night talk show host?
3. What beloved American artist's autobiography was titled *My Adventures as an Illustrator*?
4. Joe McGinniss's controversial 1993 book *The Last Brother* was a biography of what noted Massachusetts politician?
5. What country guitar legend titled his autobiography *Country Gentleman*?
6. *The King of Comedy* is the 1996 biography of what zany comedian (also known for hosting an annual telethon)?
7. The only biography Thomas Jefferson wrote was of a friend, a famous explorer. What was the book?
8. What auto executive's autobiography was the best-selling nonfiction book of 1984 and 1985?
9. What Confederate hero was the subject of Douglas Freeman's three-volume Pulitzer Prize–winning biography?
10. What great patriot's autobiography was not published until 1867, even though he died in 1790? (Hint: Go fly a kite.)
11. What belting Broadway singer titled her 1956 autobiography *Who Can Ask for Anything More*?
12. According to the title of Loretta Lynn's 1976 autobiography, whose daughter is she?

Lives in Print: Biographies and Autobiographies
(answers)

1. Dick Clark
2. Jay Leno, host of *The Tonight Show*
3. Norman Rockwell's, famous for his *Saturday Evening Post* covers
4. Edward "Ted" Kennedy
5. Chet Atkins
6. Jerry Lewis
7. *The Life of Captain [Meriwether] Lewis*, of Lewis and Clark fame
8. Lee Iacocca's of Chrysler
9. Robert E. Lee, or, as Freeman's 1935 book is titled, *R. E. Lee*
10. Benjamin Franklin's
11. Ethel Merman
12. She's a *Coal Miner's Daughter.*

13. *Kingdom of Swing* was the autobiography of what renowned clarinetist and bandleader?
14. What songwriting brothers were the subject of the 1991 biography *Fascinating Rhythm*?
15. Marquis James's Pulitzer Prize–winning biography *The Raven* is the story of what great figure in the history of Texas?
16. *His Eye Is on the Sparrow* was the autobiography of what beloved jazz and gospel singer?
17. The great poet Carl Sandburg also wrote a famous biography of what great American president? (Hint: log cabin)
18. Aviator Charles Lindbergh named his autobiography after the famous plane he flew across the Atlantic. What was it?
19. Ola Winslow won a Pulitzer Prize for her biography of what famous colonial preacher?
20. What tattooed and multicolored Chicago Bulls player titled his 1996 autobiography *Bad as I Wanna Be*?
21. *Me: Stories of My Life* was the 1991 book by what elderly movie actress? (Hint: Golden pond)
22. *A Life on the Road* is the life story of what well-traveled TV journalist?
23. *All the President's Men* and *The Final Days* are Bob Woodward and Carl Bernstein's books about what ill-fated Republican president?
24. *Profiles in Courage,* a collection of short biographies, was written by what president who was later assassinated?
25. *Where's the Rest of Me?* was the autobiography of what Republican president (and former actor)?
26. What famous TV evangelist (and founder of a university) titled his 1972 autobiography *The Call*?
27. What baseball legend's memoirs were titled *The Mick*?
28. What longtime host of a TV variety show was the subject of *Always on Sunday* and *A Thousand Sundays*?

13. Benny Goodman, known as "the King of Swing"
14. George and Ira Gershwin; one of their best-known songs was "Fascinating Rhythm."
15. Sam Houston, whose nickname "Raven" was bestowed by his Indian friends
16. Ethel Waters
17. Abraham Lincoln
18. *The Spirit of St. Louis*
19. Jonathan Edwards, a key figure in the religious movement called the Great Awakening
20. Dennis Rodman
21. Katharine Hepburn
22. Charles Kuralt; it was the best-selling nonfiction book of 1990.
23. Richard Nixon
24. John F. Kennedy
25. Ronald Reagan (He uttered the line "Where's the rest of me?" in the movie *King's Row* after discovering part of him had been amputated.)
26. Oral Roberts
27. Mickey Mantle's
28. Ed Sullivan

29. What Republican president titled his 1979 autobiography *A Time to Heal*?
30. What long-lived comedian, famous for his USO appearances, titled his memoirs *The Road to Hollywood*?
31. What actor, famous for playing Moses and Ben-Hur, wrote *In the Arena*?
32. What black education reformer's autobiography is titled *Up from Slavery*?

☆ Hot Books: American Best-Sellers

Americans have diverse tastes in reading. Best-sellers have ranged from the Bible to cookbooks to horror novels to . . . well, on and on.

1. What heavyset radio talk show host authored the nation's best-selling nonfiction books of 1992 and 1993? (Hint: dittos)
2. What high school dropout became a best-selling author of westerns and was awarded the Medal of Freedom by President Ronald Reagan?
3. What fiction book, with no human characters, was a best-seller in 1972 and 1973? (Hint: wings)
4. What novel, the best-seller of 1991, was a sequel to *Gone with the Wind*?
5. What traveling TV personality authored *A Life on the Road*, the best-selling nonfiction book of 1990?
6. The top-selling nonfiction book of 1988 was an eight-week diet for what medical condition?
7. The same author wrote the top-selling novels of 1988 (*Cardinal of the Kremlin*) and 1989 (*Clear and Present Danger*). Who?
8. The best-selling nonfiction book of 1963, *Happiness Is a Warm Puppy*, was by what world-famous cartoonist?

29. Gerald Ford
30. Bob Hope
31. Charlton Heston
32. Booker T. Washington

Hot Books: American Best-Sellers *(answers)*

1. Rush Limbaugh, author of *The Way Things Ought to Be* and *See, I Told You So*
2. Louis L'Amour
3. *Jonathan Livingston Seagull*
4. *Scarlett*, by Alexandra Ripley
5. Charles Kuralt
6. High cholesterol; the book was *The Eight-Week Cholesterol Diet*, by Robert Kowalksi.
7. Tom Clancy
8. Charles Schulz, who draws *Peanuts*

9. *Angels: God's Secret Agents* was the best-seller of 1975. What renowned evangelist wrote it?
10. What female humor columnist wrote the best-selling nonfiction books of 1978 and 1979?
11. What popular home magazine's cookbook was the best-selling nonfiction book of 1968?
12. What Bible version was the best-selling nonfiction book of 1972 and 1973?
13. What former lawyer's best-selling novels include *The Firm, The Pelican Brief,* and *The Runaway Jury*?
14. The best-selling novel of the 1800s was what antislavery tale?
15. *Fatherhood* and *Time Flies,* the best-selling nonfiction books in 1986 and 1987, were authored by what black comic?
16. *In the Kitchen with Rosie,* the best-selling nonfiction book in 1994, was written by Rosie Daley, food expert on what popular daytime talk show?
17. *It, The Tommyknockers,* and *Dolores Claiborne* were best-sellers by what king of horror novels?
18. Who published his best-selling *American Spelling Book* in 1783?
19. Rabun Gap, Georgia, gave birth to a phenomenally popular series of books on Appalachian customs. What is the name of the series?
20. What perennially popular series of reading textbooks, published from 1826 to 1920, taught Christianity as well as reading?
21. Judith Martin, Emily Post, and Amy Vanderbilt published best-sellers on what subject that concerns everyone?
22. *The Road Ahead,* by Microsoft founder Bill Gates, deals with what subject?
23. *Disclosure, Jurassic Park, The Lost World,* and other best-selling novels are by what author (who is also a movie director now and then)?

9. Billy Graham
10. Erma Bombeck, who died in 1996; the books were *If Life Is a Bowl of Cherries, What Am I Doing in the Pits?* and *Aunt Erma's Cope Book.*
11. *Better Homes and Gardens*
12. *The Living Bible,* paraphrased by Kenneth Taylor and published by Tyndale House
13. John Grisham's
14. *Uncle Tom's Cabin,* by Harriet Beecher Stowe
15. Bill Cosby
16. *The Oprah Winfrey Show*
17. Stephen King
18. Noah Webster (as in *Webster's Dictionary*)
19. Foxfire, a name given to a local plant that glows in the dark
20. The *McGuffey's Readers,* which sold an estimated 120 million copies
21. Etiquette; Judith Martin is "Miss Manners."
22. Computers, naturally
23. Michael Crichton

24. What Christian novel published in 1896 sold more than thirty million copies because it was never properly copyrighted?
25. What prolific author of inspiring rags-to-riches novels had once been run out of town for child molestation?

☆ Three "Successful" Authors

1. The phenomenal best-seller *How to Win Friends and Influence People* was by what author?
2. *Wealth Without Risk* and *Financial Self-Defense* are best-sellers by what finance whiz of the 1990s?
3. What perennially popular success author has the distinctive initials *Z.Z.*?

☆ More Lives in Print: Biographies and Autobiographies

Nothing's quite as readable as a really juicy life story (except perhaps a juicy book of trivia). Sometimes the really good ones become almost as famous as their subjects.

1. *Goddess* and *Norma Jean* are biographies of what beautiful blonde movie queen of the 1950s?
2. *Will* is the autobiography of what Watergate figure (who later became a host on talk radio)?
3. What silent film comic's story is told in the 1996 biography *Tramp*?
4. The 1979 book *Waylon and Willie* covers what two country music legends?
5. Who based her popular *Little House* books on her own childhood on the frontier?
6. *Kill Devil Hill* is the story of what two pioneers in aviation?

24. *In His Steps,* by Charles Sheldon; because publishers didn't have to pay royalties to Sheldon, they could sell the novel cheaply.
25. Horatio Alger, author of *Pluck and Luck* and other inspiring tales; Alger was serving as a minister when accused of child abuse. Interestingly, he gave most of the royalties from his best-sellers to homes for orphan boys.

Three "Successful" Authors *(answers)*

1. Dale Carnegie; the book was first published in 1936 and has been one of the best-selling books of all time.
2. Charles Givens
3. Zig Ziglar

More Lives in Print: Biographies and Autobiographies *(answers)*

1. Marilyn Monroe; Norma Jean was her real name.
2. G. Gordon Liddy, "the G man"
3. Charlie Chaplin's, whose most famous film role was the Little Tramp
4. Waylon Jennings and Willie Nelson
5. Laura Ingalls Wilder
6. Wilbur and Orville Wright; Kill Devil Hill in North Carolina was where they made their historic first flight.

7. What handsome, lean film idol of the 1950s (who died in a car crash) is the subject of the 1996 book *Rebel?*

8. What college football legend titled his autobiography *Bear?*

9. What cigar-chomping comedian titled his memoirs *100 Years, 100 Stories*—published the year he died at the age of 100?

10. *Man in Black* is the biography of what craggy-faced, deep-voiced country music legend?

11. *Brother Ray* is the biography of what blind singer, pianist, and living legend?

12. *Shooting Star* is the biography of what Western movie legend, who died in 1979?

13. *Mommie Dearest* was the spiteful biography of what movie queen (written by her own daughter)?

14. *Good Night, Mrs. Calabash* and *Schnozzola* are biographies of what big-nosed, raspy-voiced comic?

15. What female pilot, who mysteriously vanished, is the subject of *Winged Legend?*

16. *Profile of a Prodigy* is the biography of what young chess champion?

17. *The Last Billionaire* is the life story of what famous auto manufacturer?

18. What macho movie legend is the subject of *The King* and *Long Live the King?* (Hint: Frankly, Scarlett . . .)

19. What singer and actress's sad life story is told in the book *Rainbow?* (Hint: Oz)

20. What plump comic actor, who died in 1987, is the subject of *The Golden Ham?* (Hint: How sweet it is.)

21. What conservative politician who ran for president in 1964 titled his memoirs *With No Apologies?*

22. What founder of a hotel chain titled his autobiography *Be My Guest?*

7. James Dean; one of his most remembered roles was in the movie *Rebel Without a Cause*.
8. Paul "Bear" Bryant of the University of Alabama
9. George Burns, who died in 1996
10. Johnny Cash, noted for always wearing black
11. Ray Charles
12. John Wayne
13. Joan Crawford
14. Jimmy Durante
15. Amelia Earhart
16. Bobby Fischer
17. Henry Ford
18. Clark Gable, known in his day as "the King of Hollywood"
19. Judy Garland's
20. Jackie Gleason
21. Barry Goldwater
22. Conrad Hilton

23. *Death and the Magician* is a biography of what famous magician and escape artist?
24. What movie legend is the subject of *Bogie*?
25. What conservative columnist and host of the TV show *Firing Line* titled his memoirs *Overdrive* and *Cruising Speed*?
26. What astronaut is the subject of *First on the Moon*?
27. *His Way* is the biography of what ever-popular pop singer? (Hint: strangers in the night)
28. DeWitt and Lila Wallace are the subject of the book *Of Lasting Interest*. What ever-popular monthly magazine did the Wallaces publish? (Hint: condense)
29. *Last Hero* and *Coop* are biographies of what American movie legend (noted especially for his Westerns)?
30. What convicted Watergate criminal wrote about his conversion to Christianity in *Born Again*?
31. *The Marble Man* is the story of what much-beloved Confederate general?
32. *Buried Alive* is the story of what gravelly voiced rock singer who died of a heroin overdose in 1970?
33. *Stand by Your Man* is by what blonde country music queen?
34. What fast-food chain was founded by Dave Thomas, author of *Dave's Way*?

23. Harry Houdini
24. Humphrey Bogart
25. William F. Buckley
26. Neil Armstrong
27. Frank Sinatra
28. *Reader's Digest*
29. Gary Cooper
30. Charles Colson, who went on to establish the Prison Fellowship ministry after he'd served time in prison
31. Robert E. Lee
32. Janis Joplin
33. Tammy Wynette; the book's title is also the title of her best-known song.
34. Wendy's

PART FIVE

Tourists Forever

☆ Born in the U.S.A.: Famous Birthplaces

1. Memphis, Tennessee, is considered Elvis Presley's town, but what Mississippi town also has an Elvis Presley Center?
2. A log cabin near Hodgenville, Kentucky, is reputed to be the birthplace of what president of the 1860s?
3. Two southern states claim that President Andrew Jackson was born in them. Which two?
4. Ivy Green in Tuscumbia, Alabama, is the birthplace of what noted deaf and blind author?
5. What inventors, famed in the history of aviation, were both born in Dayton, Ohio?
6. What noted Confederate general's birthplace is the graceful Stratford Hall plantation in eastern Virginia?
7. What noted author's birthplace can be seen in Monroe City, Missouri? (Hint: Tom and Huck)
8. What twentieth-century president's birthplace can be visited in Denison, Texas?
9. Fairview, Kentucky, has a 350-foot monument honoring what notable Confederate statesman?
10. William Henry Harrison, the ninth president, was born at Berkeley Plantation in Virginia, but when he campaigned, he claimed to have been born in what humble type of home?
11. What twentieth-century president was born in Lamar, Missouri?
12. Niles, Ohio, has the birthplace of a popular president who was born there in 1843. Who was he?
13. What will you find in the house at George Washington's Birthplace National Monument?

Born in the U.S.A.: Famous Birthplaces *(answers)*

1. Tupelo, Mississippi, his birthplace; the Center has the house where he was born in 1935.
2. Abraham Lincoln
3. North Carolina and South Carolina; his birthplace, Waxhaw, lies near the states' boundary, which was unclear at the time of his birth. Jackson claimed he was born in South Carolina.
4. Helen Keller
5. Orville and Wilbur Wright
6. Robert E. Lee's
7. Mark Twain's; though he lived much of his life in Hannibal, he was born in Monroe City.
8. Dwight Eisenhower's; a state park named for him is also nearby.
9. Jefferson Davis, who was born there, though he made his reputation as a Mississippi senator and as president of the Confederacy
10. A log cabin, which seemed to appeal more to voters than a plantation house
11. Harry Truman; his birthplace is a state historic site.
12. William McKinley, the twenty-fifth president
13. Nothing; the house burned in 1779, but the monument maintains a museum on the site.

14. Xenia, Ohio, was the birthplace of a noted Shawnee Indian leader who tried to forge a continental Indian alliance. Who was he?

15. What famous author of Westerns was born in Zanesville, Ohio? (Hint: concentrate on the city's name)

16. Richland Center, Wisconsin, was the birthplace of what world-famous (and diminutive) architect?

17. What twentieth-century Republican president's birthplace can be visited in Whittier, California?

18. What was the significance of Virginia Dare, born August 18, 1587, on an island off North Carolina?

19. Reading, Pennsylvania, has the colonial-era birthplace of what noted frontiersman?

20. What swaggering twentieth-century president's birthplace can be visited on East Twentieth Street in Manhattan?

21. What inventor, who revolutionized American transportation, had his birthplace near Lancaster, Pennsylvania?

22. What famous author was born in New Orleans and given the name of Truman Streckfus Persons?

23. Byrdstown, Tennessee, is the site of the birthplace of a statesman known as "the Father of the United Nations." Who?

24. What twentieth-century president's birthplace is at 83 Beals Street in Brookline, Massachusetts?

☆ Big as All Outdoors: Our National Parks

Ask people about their favorite vacation destinations in the U.S., and national parks are high on the list. Something about the great outdoors (or in a few parks, the great underground) lures us. For all of people's beefing about the federal government, most people agree that the National Park Service does a fine job.

14. Tecumseh, who sided with the British in the War of 1812
15. Zane Grey
16. Frank Lloyd Wright
17. Richard Nixon's
18. She was the first white child born in America.
19. Daniel Boone, born there in 1734
20. Theodore Roosevelt's
21. Robert Fulton, inventor of the steamboat
22. Truman Capote
23. Cordell Hull, who served as the influential secretary of state under President Franklin Roosevelt
24. John F. Kennedy's

1. What Florida national park is home to the alligator, North America's largest reptile?
2. North Carolina shares what much-visited national park with Tennessee?
3. At least 120 of these hot water spouts in Yellowstone National Park have names. What are the spouts?
4. The National Park Service is part of what Cabinet department?
5. The Colorado River enters what popular national park at Marble Canyon?
6. If you are taking the three-hour Blue Tour through one of the world's largest caves, where are you?
7. If you visit Island in the Sky, Upheaval Dome, and Maze, what national park in Utah are you touring?
8. In what California park would you find the world's largest sequoia trees?
9. What mountainous Colorado park straddles the Continental Divide?
10. What popular mountain park in Virginia has the Skyline Drive running through it?
11. Texas's highest point is Guadalupe Peak in what appropriately named national park?
12. What enormous island (with a regal name) in Lake Superior is a national park?
13. What national park in southern Florida is mainly accessible by boat, not by car? (No, not the Everglades.)
14. In what California national park could you see the Devastated Area, Chaos Jumbles, and the Sulphur Works?
15. What enormous national park (with a biblical name) in Utah has the Temple of Sinawava, a large natural bowl enclosed by cliffs?
16. What California national park is noted for its waterfalls, some of the highest in the world?

Big as All Outdoors: Our National Parks *(answers)*

1. The Everglades
2. Great Smoky Mountains
3. Geysers; Old Faithful is the most famous.
4. The Interior (Funny—it's the great outdoors, but it's called the *interior.*)
5. Grand Canyon, in Arizona
6. Carlsbad Caverns National Park in New Mexico
7. Canyonlands
8. Appropriately enough, in Sequoia National Park, in California; some of the trees are over 250 feet high.
9. Rocky Mountain National Park
10. Shenandoah
11. Guadalupe Mountains
12. Isle Royale
13. Biscayne, most of which is an undeveloped tropical wilderness
14. Lassen Volcanic; the park centers around the dormant (for now) volcano, Lassen Peak.
15. Zion, one of the most visited national parks in the U.S.
16. Yosemite

17. In what national park in Montana can you see more than fifty glaciers?
18. What park in South Dakota features a cave with wind blowing in or out of it, depending on atmospheric pressure?
19. What park on the Maine coast was originally settled by French missionaries in the 1600s?
20. The smallest national park, only about five thousand acres, is in Arkansas. What is it?
21. With about eight million visitors per year, what park in the Appalachians is the most visited national park?
22. The 105-foot-high Landscape Arch is in what scenic national park in Utah?
23. What large park, straddling California and Nevada, is the lowest point in the U.S. (and one of the most desolate)?

☆ Many Mansions

Palatial homes draw us like magnets. If the owner was a celebrity, so much the better.

1. What notable Memphis mansion features a fur-covered bed, a room with carpeted walls and ceiling, and an airplane named *Lisa Marie*?
2. The awesome Biltmore estate in Asheville, North Carolina, was built by what wealthy American family? (Hint: commodore)
3. What president lived on the Virginia estate named Mount Vernon?
4. A great American auto manufacturer had a 1920s Florida home known as Mangoes. Who was he?
5. Thomas Jefferson's beautiful home near Charlottesville, Virginia, is known as what?

17. Glacier National Park, appropriately enough
18. The aptly named Wind Cave National Park in South Dakota
19. Acadia; for many years the area was part of the French colony of Acadia until taken over by the British.
20. Hot Springs
21. Great Smoky Mountains, straddling Tennessee and North Carolina
22. Arches National Park, which has more than two hundred lovely stone arches
23. Death Valley

Many Mansions (answers)

1. Graceland, home of Elvis Presley
2. The Vanderbilts; the French-style chateau has 250 rooms and a 7,500-acre estate.
3. George Washington
4. Henry Ford; the home is in Fort Myers and can be toured.
5. Monticello

6. The Nemours Mansion, a French chateau on a three-hundred-acre estate, belongs to what famous chemical makers in Delaware?

7. Mark Twain's *Tom Sawyer* and *Huckleberry Finn*, classic stories of small-town Missouri life, were published while he lived in a mansion in what New England state?

8. Though they are mansions, the summer homes of the wealthy in Newport, Rhode Island, are called by what modest name?

9. The Hermitage, outside Nashville, is the home and burial place of what president, nicknamed "Old Hickory"?

10. Springwood, a president's estate in New York, now looks as it did when he died in 1945. Who was he?

11. California's palatial Filoli House and Gardens were featured in what nighttime soap opera?

12. The lovely Joss House in Weaverville, California, was built during the gold rush by what ethnic group?

13. The stunning home Fallingwater in Pennsylvania was designed by what famous twentieth-century architect?

14. The Casements, a Florida mansion that is now a museum, was the home of what wealthy New Yorker (whose family name has come to symbolize wealth)?

15. Vizcaya, a stunning Italian Renaissance villa and gardens, is in what south Florida metropolis?

16. Arlington House, on the grounds of Arlington National Cemetery, was the home of what great Confederate general?

17. What famous home is at 1600 Pennsylvania Avenue in Washington, D.C.?

18. Federal Hill in Kentucky is the home where the state song, "My Old Kentucky Home," was written by what great songwriter?

19. House of Cash, a mansion near Nashville, now functions as a museum devoted to what country music legend?

6. The Du Pont family
7. Connecticut, his wife's home state; his house in Hartford is open for touring.
8. Cottages, strangely enough
9. Andrew Jackson
10. Franklin Roosevelt; the estate is in Hyde Park, New York.
11. *Dynasty*
12. The Chinese; the house, really a temple, has priceless tapestries and gilt scrollwork.
13. Frank Lloyd Wright; the house, graced by waterfalls, is one of his most famous designs.
14. John D. Rockefeller; you can tour the Casements at Ormond Beach, Florida.
15. Miami
16. Robert E. Lee
17. The White House
18. Stephen Foster; there is some doubt about Foster writing the song in this house, but it makes a nice story, and tourists know the house as "My Old Kentucky Home."
19. Johnny Cash, naturally

20. What Wisconsin city has the Pabst Mansion, Pabst Theatre, and Pabst Brewery?
21. What circus entrepreneur had a pretentious mansion he named Craniston?
22. The stunning Nottoway mansion in Louisiana is one of the most photographed spots in the South. It was built with money from what crop? (Hint: sweet)

☆ Unusual Museums

America has its great museums—the Smithsonian, the Museum of Radio and Television, the Art Institute of Chicago, etc. It also has its share of not-so-well-known (but still very interesting) museums, scattered across the fifty states. Let's face it: We're a museum-loving country, even if it's only a roadside display of rattlesnakes.

1. A Louisville museum honors the founder of Kentucky Fried Chicken. Who was he?
2. New Orleans has, appropriately enough, a city museum devoted to what type of music?
3. Bardstown, Kentucky, has a museum devoted to the history of what potent drink?
4. A Nashville museum is dedicated to the history of what smokable plant?
5. The Mining Museum in Platteville, Wisconsin, is devoted to what common metal? (Hint: fishing)
6. What wooden hunting items can be seen at a museum in Havre de Grace, Maryland?
7. Babe Ruth's birthplace is also a museum for what pro baseball team?
8. If you wanted to see the Navy SEAL's museum, what state would you go to?
9. The Confederate Naval Museum is, oddly, not on a coastline. Where is it?

20. Milwaukee
21. P. T. Barnum
22. Sugar cane, still a major crop in much of Louisiana. The Nottoway plantation had over seven thousand acres.

Unusual Museums *(answers)*

1. Harlan Sanders, better known as Colonel Sanders
2. Jazz, of course; New Orleans (or N'awlins) is home to Dixieland jazz.
3. Whiskey, one of Kentucky's major products
4. Tobacco; the Museum of Tobacco Art and History includes pipes, snuffboxes, and tobacco jars.
5. Lead
6. Decoys
7. The Baltimore Orioles
8. Florida; the SEAL museum is in Fort Pierce.
9. The inland city of Columbus, Georgia; it lies on the banks of the Chattahoochee River.

10. Rockford, Illinois, has a fascinating museum devoted to what type of instruments? (Hint: tick)
11. What type of folk craft has its own museum in Paducah, Kentucky? (Hint: bed)
12. What museum in Chattanooga, Tennessee, is designed for cutups?
13. What Florida city has a Lighthouse Museum, a Wreckers' Museum, and an Ernest Hemingway Museum?
14. The Pink Palace Museum in Memphis was the home of the founder of a famous supermarket chain. Which one? (Hint: oink)
15. Georgia's Crawford Long Medical Museum honors Dr. Long's most famous contribution to medicine. What was it? (Hint: knockout)
16. The International Museum of the Horse is found in what state?
17. In Cambridge, Ohio, you could visit a museum devoted to what type of pretty glass objects? (Hint: desk)
18. The Netherlands Museum is in what appropriately named Michigan city?
19. The House of Cash in Tennessee is a museum devoted to what country singer?
20. What actor's Oscar is kept in the Patton Museum, housing General George S. Patton's memorabilia?
21. In what city could you visit the B & O Railroad Museum?
22. Atlanta, Georgia's Wren's Nest museum was the home of which noted southern author?
23. The Biedenharn Foundation has a Christian museum with ancient Bibles, swords from the medieval crusades, and many other curious objects. What southern state is home to the museum?
24. What type of transportation vehicles could you see in a Wheaton, Maryland, museum?

10. Clocks and other time-keeping devices; it's called the Time Museum.
11. Quilting; it is the Museum of the American Quilter's Society.
12. The National Knife Museum, which also includes swords and razors
13. Key West; Hemingway lived in Key West for quite a while.
14. Piggly Wiggly; the founder was Clarence Saunders.
15. Ether; Long was the first person to use ether to perform (relatively) painless surgery.
16. Kentucky
17. Paperweights; the Degenhart Paperweight and Glass Museum is quite fascinating.
18. Holland, naturally
19. Johnny Cash (We hope that not many people missed this. . . .)
20. George C. Scott's; he played the general in the film *Patton.*
21. Baltimore, Maryland (It's the *B* in B & O.)
22. Joel Chandler Harris, creator of the famous Uncle Remus animal stories
23. Louisiana; it is in the city of Monroe.
24. Streetcars; Wheaton has the National Capital Trolley Museum.

25. Tombstone, Arizona's Historama museum has a narration by what noted horror movie actor?
26. What noise-making items are displayed in a museum in Evergreen, Colorado?
27. In what state could you visit Dorothy's house from *The Wizard of Oz*?
28. In what state can you walk inside a four-story museum shaped like a fish?

☆ Men and Women of Stone: Famous Statues

People love statues—maybe because there's something awesome about the human figure done in something as permanent as stone. America is filled with statues of the famous—and sometimes not-so-famous—people who have made an impact on our lives.

1. In the popular 1996 movie *Independence Day*, what famous statue is blown to smithereens by aliens?
2. What colonial founder's statue is atop City Hall in Philadelphia?
3. What U.S. president's statue is found in London's Trafalgar Square? (Hint: early)
4. Birmingham, Alabama, has an enormous iron statue of the god Vulcan, holding a torch. Though the torch is usually lighted green, what causes the torch to burn red?
5. Key Largo in Florida has a noted nine-foot underwater statue of a famous religious figure. Who?
6. If you are looking at a twenty-seven-foot statue of an Egyptian pharaoh, what Tennessee city are you in?
7. In what D.C. building could you see statues of the chief justices of the U.S.?

25. Vincent Price
26. Bells—more than five thousand from every period of history
27. Kansas; the museum is in Liberal, Kansas. (Where else would Dorothy's house be except Kansas?)
28. Wisconsin; the Freshwater Fishing Hall of Fame in Hayward is inside a giant replica of a muskellunge. An observation deck is in the fish's mouth.

Men and Women of Stone: Famous Statues
(answers)

1. The Statue of Liberty in New York
2. William Penn's, founder of the colony of Pennsylvania
3. George Washington's; this proves how broad-minded the English are, since Washington, as the leader of the American Revolution, was considered a traitor by the English.
4. Any traffic fatality in the city in the past twenty-four hours
5. Jesus; the statue, *Christ of the Deep,* can be seen from a boat or by snorkelers.
6. Memphis; the statue is on the Mud Island entertainment complex.
7. The Supreme Court building

8. A statue of George Washington on horseback stands on the grounds of what southern state capitol?

9. What state—*not* a Confederate state—has a large statue honoring Confederate general Thomas "Stonewall" Jackson?

10. What famous statue has a three-foot-wide mouth and an eight-foot-long index finger?

11. What presidential memorial in D.C. features a circular building with a huge bronze statue of the president?

12. What two fictional boys are portrayed in life-size bronze statues in Hannibal, Missouri?

13. What macho film actor is immortalized in a nine-foot bronze statue in Stephenville, Texas? (Hint: Westerns)

14. What noted British author's statue, holding an open book, is in Calistoga, California? (Hint: *Treasure Island*)

15. Sun Yat-sen, founder of the Republic of China, has a statue in what noted section of San Francisco?

16. What two figures from American folklore have huge statues in Bemidji, Minnesota?

17. What conservation character is featured in a huge statue in International Falls, Minnesota?

18. *Range Rider of the Yellowstone* is a life-size bronze statue in Billings, Montana. What western movie star posed for it? (No, not John Wayne.)

19. On Monument Avenue you can see statues of Confederate heroes like Robert E. Lee, Stonewall Jackson, and Jefferson Davis. In what southern capital is Monument Avenue?

20. What world-famous circus midget is commemorated in a statue in Bridgeport, Connecticut?

21. Skowhegan, Maine, has a twelve-ton, sixty-two-foot-high statue of an Indian chief. Of what local material is it made?

22. A famous statue at the harbor of Gloucester, Massachusetts, is of a man in what profession?

8. Richmond, Virginia
9. West Virginia, in the town of Clarksburg, Jackson's birthplace; when he was born there in 1824, the city was in Virginia, since the breakaway state of West Virginia did not form until 1861.
10. The Statue of Liberty
11. The Jefferson Memorial
12. Tom Sawyer and Huck Finn, creations of Hannibal's most famous resident, Mark Twain
13. John Wayne
14. Robert Louis Stevenson, who honeymooned in the area; he has a state park named for him.
15. Chinatown, naturally
16. Legendary lumberjack Paul Bunyan and Babe, his blue ox
17. Smokey the Bear
18. William S. Hart, a silent movie idol and probably the first real cowboy star
19. Richmond, Virginia, capital of the old Confederacy
20. Tom Thumb; P. T. Barnum, his manager, was Bridgeport's most famous resident.
21. Pine, the state tree of Maine
22. Fisherman; the town has always been a fishing center.

☆ Patriotic Places

How many family vacations and class trips center around patriotic places? Sure, we get cynical about politics (and especially about politicians), but the truth is we're fascinated by American history, particularly anything associated with the Founding Fathers of the 1700s. The phrase "George Washington slept here" still packs a punch.

1. What famous bell in Philadelphia has an inscription from Leviticus?
2. In what historic Massachusetts town could you visit the Pilgrim village and the *Mayflower II*?
3. At what historic Pennsylvania site could you sit in the Pews of the Patriots?
4. What colorful World War II general's memorial, museum, and tomb can you visit in Norfolk, Virginia?
5. Louisiana has a national historical park named for what noted French pirate?
6. Minute Man Historical Park is found in what historic Massachusetts town?
7. Federal Hall on New York's Wall Street was the site of what president's inauguration?
8. What famous Civil War speech is engraved on the walls of the Lincoln Memorial in D.C.?
9. Charlottesville, Virginia, has a memorial to the two explorers President Thomas Jefferson sent out to explore the new Louisiana Purchase. Who was this pair?
10. A cemetery in Springfield, Illinois, has the much visited tomb of what assassinated president?
11. D.C.'s Anderson House Museum is devoted to which major war? (Hint: redcoats)
12. The Museum of Our National Heritage is in what historic Massachusetts town?

Patriotic Places *(answers)*

1. The Liberty Bell; "Proclaim liberty throughout all the land unto all the inhabitants thereof" is from Leviticus 25.
2. Plymouth, of course
3. Valley Forge; the pews are in the Washington Memorial Chapel.
4. Douglas MacArthur's
5. Jean Lafitte; he was a (more or less) patriotic hero, since his gang helped Andrew Jackson defeat the British in the War of 1812.
6. Concord
7. George Washington's, in 1789
8. The Gettysburg Address
9. Meriwether Lewis and William Clark, better known as Lewis and Clark
10. Abraham Lincoln
11. The American Revolution
12. Lexington, site of the Revolutionary War's first battle

13. New Jersey has a state park commemorating Washington's famous crossing in 1776. What river did he cross?

14. At what historic Pennsylvania site could you see the Roof of the Republic, bearing state seals of all fifty states?

15. What famous rock lies under an impressive stone colonnade at a Massachusetts harbor?

16. Quincy, Massachusetts, was home to what great political family of the 1700s and 1800s?

17. The Statue of Liberty, designed by Frederic August Bartholdi, commemorates friendship between the U.S. and what nation?

18. Abraham Lincoln's Boyhood Home National Memorial is in what state? (No, not Illinois.)

19. What president's round memorial sits on the Tidal Basin in D.C.?

20. In what Maryland city could you visit the site where "The Star-Spangled Banner" was composed?

21. Virginia's lovely state capitol in Richmond was designed by what Virginia-born president?

22. Chillicothe, Missouri, has the home of what renowned World War I general?

23. Philadelphia's Philosophical Hall is home of the American Philosophical Society. What great Pennsylvania patriot started this group?

24. Houston has the San Jacinto Battleground. What war's end is commemorated here?

25. What flamboyant World War II general has a museum and memorial in Indio, California?

26. *Whites of Their Eyes* in Boston is a multimedia reenactment of what famous Revolutionary War battle?

13. The Delaware
14. Valley Forge; the roof is in the Washington Memorial Chapel.
15. Plymouth Rock, traditional site of the Pilgrims' landing in 1620
16. The Adams family, including presidents John and John Quincy
17. France; it was the French people who gave the statue.
18. Indiana, just south of Lincoln City
19. Thomas Jefferson's
20. Baltimore; the bombing of its Fort McHenry during the War of 1812 inspired Francis Scott Key to write the anthem.
21. Thomas Jefferson
22. John J. "Black Jack" Pershing; the town also has the one-room school where Pershing taught before entering West Point.
23. Benjamin Franklin
24. Texas's war of independence from Mexico, which ended in 1836
25. George S. Patton; the site was once a training ground for survival in North Africa.
26. Bunker Hill; it's in the specially designed Bunker Hill Pavilion.

☆ World-Class Parks: World Heritage Sites

A special few places in America have made an impression on the United Nations. In fact, the UN has given the named World Heritage Sites to certain locations that have a unique historical or natural significance. The good ole U.S.A. has its share of these—sixteen, to be exact. Some of these are ones you've probably visited, and some may surprise you.

1. What national park is noted for a distinctive blue haze that hangs over the hilltops?
2. What million-acre national park in Florida is almost half water?
3. If you see Bright Angel Point, Grandview Point, and Desert View, what Arizona national park are you visiting?
4. What Colorado national park's name means "green table"?
5. If you are visiting Bridalveil Falls, El Capitan, and Clouds Rest, what stunning California national park are you in? (Hint: a foe of Bugs Bunny)
6. *Liberty Enlightening the World* in New York is better known by what name?
7. Crescent City, California, is the site of what national park named for a large tree? (Hint: patio furniture)
8. What building in Pennsylvania was the site of the adoption of the Declaration of Independence?
9. Cave City, Kentucky, is near what much visited national park?
10. The University of Virginia campus and a home named Monticello were both designed by an early U.S. president. Who?
11. The awesome geyser named Old Faithful is in what much visited national park in Wyoming?

World-Class Parks: World Heritage Sites *(answers)*

1. Great Smoky Mountains, naturally; it's shared with Tennessee and North Carolina.
2. The Everglades, of course
3. Grand Canyon
4. Mesa Verde, in southwestern Colorado; the "table" is a great plateau, towering above the surrounding valleys.
5. Yosemite (Remember the character "Yosemite Sam"?)
6. The Statue of Liberty
7. Redwood National Park
8. Independence Hall, in Philadelphia
9. Mammoth Cave
10. Thomas Jefferson; the university is in Charlottesville, Virginia, and Monticello is nearby.
11. Yellowstone; actually, Wyoming shares it with Idaho and Montana.

12. The beautiful Olympic National Park lies near the Pacific Ocean in what western state?
13. The Chaco Culture National Historic Park features pueblos built by prehistoric Indians. In what southwestern state would you find it?
14. The Wrangell-Elias National Park, with over 8 million acres, is in what huge state?
15. In what tropical park can you see lush vegetation growing around volcanoes?
16. The only prehistoric city in the U.S. is buried under Cahokia Mound site in what midwestern state?

☆ Gray and Blue: Civil War Sites

The war—what they used to call "the Late Unpleasantness"—ended in 1865 . . . or did it? It certainly hasn't ended in Americans' memories, because people love to read about it, talk about it, and visit historic sites connected with it. Throughout the South, and even in a few northern locations, are battlefields, museums, and other attractions reminding us that from 1861 to 1865 the Blue vs. Gray game was the great topic.

1. What much visited battlefield in Pennsylvania has a 307-foot observation tower?
2. What name is given to the giant granite mountain in Georgia, carved with figures of Confederate heroes?
3. And what three men's figures are carved on it?
4. You can tour the White House of the Confederacy in which two southern states?
5. Appomattox Court House in Virginia commemorates a fateful meeting between what two generals?
6. The Museum of the Confederacy is in what capital city?
7. The Andersonville National Historic Site in Georgia is a memorial to what sort of institution?

12. Washington; the park features a rain forest, glaciers, and rare elk.
13. New Mexico
14. Alaska
15. The Hawaii Volcanoes National Park
16. Illinois

Gray and Blue: Civil War Sites *(answers)*

1. Gettysburg
2. Stone Mountain
3. Confederate President Jefferson Davis, General Robert E. Lee, and General Thomas "Stonewall" Jackson
4. Montgomery, Alabama, the first capital, and Richmond, Virginia, the second; both capitals have the homes that President Jefferson Davis lived in.
5. Robert E. Lee and U. S. Grant, who met to bring an end to the Civil War in Virginia
6. Richmond, Virginia, also the Confederacy's capital
7. A notorious Confederate prison, famed for its horrid living conditions; it is now also a memorial for all American prisoners of war.

8. What much-visited island fort near Charleston, South Carolina, is considered the first battle site of the Civil War?

9. Fairview, Kentucky, has a 350-foot monument honoring what notable American statesman?

10. The Confederama is a Civil War museum in what long-suffering Tennessee city?

11. Gettysburg, Pennsylvania, has a museum that was the house used as headquarters by what Confederate general?

12. What state shares the Chickamauga and Chattanooga National Military Park with Tennessee?

13. What was the fate of Evelynton, a lovely Virginia plantation belonging to Southern secession agitator Edmund Ruffin?

14. On what Virginia battleground would you find the Crater, an enormous depression caused by gunpowder exploding underground?

15. Chancellorsville, Virginia, was the site of the fatal wounding of a famous Confederate general—by his own men. Who was he?

16. What prestigious college in Lexington, Virginia, has the grave of Robert E. Lee *and* the grave of Lee's horse, Traveller?

17. Fredericksburg and Spotsylvania National Military Park contains the tiny house where a renowned Confederate general died. Who was he?

18. What famous 1865 event is reenacted every year in Durham, North Carolina's Bennett Place?

19. The Poison Spring Battleground commemorates a Civil War battle in what state?

20. The annual Chambersfest in Chambersburg, Pennsylvania, commemorates an unpleasant Civil War incident. What?

8. Fort Sumter, a federal post that was fired on by Confederates in April 1861
9. Jefferson Davis, who was born there, though he made his reputation as a Mississippi senator and as president of the Confederacy
10. Chattanooga, which saw more than its share of fighting during the war
11. Robert E. Lee
12. Georgia; it is the largest of the Civil War battle sites.
13. Yankee soldiers burned it during the Civil War; however, the restored plantation is open for touring.
14. Petersburg, Virginia; the explosion was set off by Yankee miners who had tunneled under the Confederate defenses.
15. Thomas "Stonewall" Jackson, who had just won the battle shortly before being shot by friendly fire; his amputated arm was given a separate burial, and the site can be visited.
16. Washington and Lee University (which had the "and Lee" added to its name after Lee served it as president)
17. Thomas "Stonewall" Jackson; the small house is kept as it was the day Jackson died there in 1863.
18. The surrender of Confederate General Joseph Johnston to Union General William Sherman
19. Arkansas
20. The town was burned by the troops of Confederate General Jubal Early.

21. The Eternal Light Peace Memorial is at what Civil War battlefield site?
22. The Bloody Pond is a gruesome sight at the Shiloh National Military Park, a famous Civil War battlefield. In what state is it?
23. What southern capital has the Cyclorama, with a forty-two-foot-high, 360-degree painting of the Union-ravaged city?
24. What southern capital has Monument Avenue, called "the most beautiful street in America" and dedicated to the Confederacy?
25. Whose monuments are found on Monument Avenue? (There are five altogether.)

☆ Three Sea Parks

1. You can visit Sea World theme parks in Florida, California, Ohio, and what other state?
2. What state's John Pennekamp Coral Reef State Park was the first undersea park in the U.S.?
3. The National Aquarium is not in Washington but in what nearby metropolis?

☆ Unusual Sights

Sure, it's fun to visit Civil War battlefields, graves of famous people, and historic mansions. But Americans have always enjoyed visiting the unusual and the offbeat, too. In a country this big, we have a lot to choose from—volcanoes, pygmy trees, houses made of bottles, . . . well, you get the idea.

1. In what Pennsylvania town are the streetlights shaped like chocolate kisses?

21. Gettysburg, Pennsylvania
22. Tennessee
23. Atlanta, Georgia
24. Richmond, Virginia
25. President Jefferson Davis, Gen. Robert E. Lee, Gen. "Stonewall" Jackson, Gen. J. E. B. Stuart, and oceanographer Matthew Fontaine Maury. (If you're familiar with Maury, you're a *real* Civil War buff.)

Three Sea Parks *(answers)*

1. Texas; it's near San Antonio.
2. Florida's; it's in Key Largo, and it has an interesting nine-foot *Christ of the Deep* statue.
3. Baltimore

Unusual Sights *(answers)*

1. Hershey, naturally; the town is the headquarters for the famous candy company.

2. Virginia Beach's Mount Trashmore is a city park built over what useful piece of land?

3. What bulky animals were first exhibited in the U.S. in 1796?

4. What state capital has a working oil well on its grounds?

5. Blizzard Beach, a water-slide park made to look like a snow-covered ski resort, is part of what Florida entertainment complex?

6. The Mirage Hotel has a volcano that erupts every fifteen minutes. In what glitzy Nevada city is it?

7. In what charming, historic southern port could you see "earthquake bolts" on the walls of houses?

8. Nashville's Downtown Presbyterian Church has what unusual (and ancient) style of architecture inside?

9. Odessa, Texas, has an enormous crater produced by what celestial phenomenon?

10. What fictional Indian hero is depicted by a fifty-two-foot fiberglass statue in Ironwood, Michigan?

11. If you are walking through a desert under a glass dome at Mitchell Park, in what midwestern city are you?

12. What is distinctive about the "Stalacpipe" formation in Virginia's Luray Caverns?

13. The Artist's Palette, Dante's View, and Devil's Golf Course are stunning sites in which low-lying California park?

14. Fossilized sea reptiles fifty feet long can be seen at the Berlin-Ichthyosaur State Park in what western state?

15. Fairplay, Colorado, has a monument to Prunes. What sort of creature was Prunes?

16. What type of mountain can be toured at New Mexico's Capulin National Monument? (Hint: hot)

17. What substance used for making plaster of paris composes the White Sands National Monument in New Mexico?

2. A landfill; in a city with no hills, the city put its trash to good use.
3. Elephants
4. Oklahoma City; the city sits on an enormous oil field.
5. Disney World
6. Las Vegas, where else?
7. Charleston, South Carolina; the bolts are designed to stabilize the buildings in the event of an earthquake.
8. Egyptian; the church was built in 1849, a time when the discovery of King Tut's tomb in Egypt had made Egyptian the trendy style of the day.
9. A meteor striking the earth thousands of years ago
10. Hiawatha
11. Milwaukee, Wisconsin; the glass dome is part of the park's horticultural conservatory.
12. It is a musical organ, using specially tuned stalactites to produce the sounds.
13. Death Valley National Monument
14. Nevada; the park also contains Berlin, a ghost town.
15. A burro who carried supplies to the mines around Fairplay for more than sixty years (Not many donkey monuments in America . . .)
16. A volcano, over a mile in circumference and 415 feet deep
17. Gypsum; almost all normal beach sand is silica.

18. What huge South Dakota building, done in Byzantine architecture, is decorated with colored corn?
19. Atlantic City, New Jersey, has a six-story animal visitors can walk through. What is it?
20. What enormous southwestern plant is called "organ pipe" because its thirty or more arms resemble pipes of a church organ?
21. The city of Enterprise, Alabama, has a monument to the boll weevil, an insect known for destroying cotton plants. Why was the monument built?
22. Of what unusual material is the fourteen-ton Cross in the Woods in Indian River, Michigan? (Hint: picnic tables)
23. What is unusual about the two-hundred-year-old trees in Van Damme, California?

☆ More Patriotic Places

1. Construction began in 1732 on what Philadelphia building where the Continental Congress met?
2. What D.C. museum is devoted to the faces of famous Americans?
3. What historic raid originated in Boston's Old South Meeting House?
4. The National Colonial Farm in Maryland is a reconstruction of what type of farm?
5. The 221-foot granite monument in Boston commemorates what famous Revolutionary War battle?
6. What beautiful D.C. building is entitled to one copy of every book printed in the nation?
7. The original manuscript of what great patriotic song can be seen at the Maryland Historical Society?
8. Berkeley Plantation in Virginia was the site where the world's most famous (and saddest) bugle call was written. What was it?

18. The Corn Palace, one of America's more unusual buildings
19. An elephant named Lucy
20. A cactus; the Organ Pipe Cactus National Monument is in Arizona.
21. Because of the weevil's destruction of cotton crops, area farmers had to learn to diversify with other crops.
22. Redwood—which does not grow in Michigan; the tree was over two thousand years old. The fifty-five-foot cross holds a seven-ton bronze Jesus.
23. They are tiny, due to poor soil conditions. The Pygmy Forest is a favorite tourist stop.

More Patriotic Places *(answers)*

1. Independence Hall
2. The National Portrait Gallery
3. The Boston Tea Party in 1773, in which the colonists protested the heavy tax on tea
4. A tobacco plantation
5. Bunker Hill, fought near Boston in June 1775
6. The Library of Congress
7. "The Star-Spangled Banner," composed near Baltimore
8. "Taps," composed by Union soldier Daniel Butterfield as his troops occupied the plantation

9. D.C.'s huge slab of black granite is a memorial to veterans of what war?

10. Charlottesville, Virginia, has a memorial to the two men Thomas Jefferson sent out to explore the new Louisiana Purchase. Who were they?

11. The historic town of Chester, Pennsylvania, has a stone marking the 1682 arrival of what noted Englishman?

12. What colonial Virginia city, a favorite tourist destination, was originally called Middle Plantation?

13. What Revolutionary War patriot's home can be visited in Burlington, Vermont? (Hint: a brand of furniture)

14. Fredericksburg, Virginia, has a museum devoted to what Virginia-born president, with a famous "doctrine" named for him?

15. What noted World War II general and Nobel Peace Prize winner has a museum in Lexington, Virginia?

16. Philadelphia has a memorial to Thaddeus Koscuiszko, a European soldier who aided in the Revolutionary War. What nationality was he?

17. If you visited the Old Barracks Museum in Trenton, New Jersey, you could see how soldiers lived during what great war?

18. The Virginia homes Red Hill and Scotchtown are now museums. Both belonged to what Revolutionary War patriot, known for his "Give me liberty or give me death" speech?

19. The U.S.'s first bank, founded by Alexander Hamilton, is in what historic city?

20. Mt. Kisco, New York, has the home of the Supreme Court's first chief justice and an author of The Federalist Papers. Who was he?

21. East Haddam, Connecticut, has a schoolhouse where a noted patriot, executed by the British, once taught. Who was he?

9. Vietnam
10. Meriwether Lewis and William Clark, better known as Lewis and Clark
11. William Penn; the town had been settled by Swedes several years before Penn arrived to take charge.
12. Williamsburg
13. Ethan Allen, leader of the Green Mountain Boys
14. James Monroe, the fifth president; the museum is in his former law office.
15. George C. Marshall; it is on the VMI campus.
16. Polish
17. The American Revolution
18. Patrick Henry
19. Philadelphia
20. John Jay
21. Nathan Hale ("I only regret that I have but one life to give for my country"—remember?)

22. What famous colonial author's home can be visited in New Rochelle, New York? (Hint: *Common Sense*)
23. The Chalmette National Historical Park near New Orleans commemorates the last land battle between the U.S. and what European country?
24. Fentress County, Tennessee, is noted as the home of what much-decorated World War I hero?
25. In what D.C. building could you see the Rotunda and Statuary Hall?
26. What twentieth-century president's summer home was on the Canadian island of Campobello?
27. The phrase "Equal Justice Under Law" is carved on the front of what Washington, D.C., building?

☆ A Day at the Beach

For most of human history, beaches were . . . well, just useless stretches of sand. Then, sometime in the 1800s, people actually began to like the feel of sand between their toes and salt water on their skin (not to mention jellyfish, bugs, sharks, melanoma, etc.). No wonder some of the country's hottest vacation spots are its fine beaches.

1. What Florida town, famous for its wide beach that cars can drive on, is a favorite for students on spring break?
2. What southern state has an incredibly long coastline but no beaches?
3. What popular tourist town in Florida was built upon sand dredged out of Biscayne Bay?
4. What Great Lakes state has freshwater beaches at Saugatuck and at Warren Dunes?
5. Within Everglades National Park in Florida, the beaches are not composed of sand but of what substance?

22. Thomas Paine, author of *Common Sense* and other essays
23. Britain; the battle was the last engagement of the War of 1812.
24. Alvin York, subject of the Gary Cooper movie *Sergeant York;* York was famed for capturing 132 German soldiers.
25. The Capitol
26. Franklin Roosevelt's; the estate is now in the Roosevelt Campobello International Park.
27. The Supreme Court

A Day at the Beach *(answers)*

1. Daytona Beach, which shares the "Spring Break Capital" title with Fort Lauderdale, further south
2. Louisiana; its coastline is mostly comprised of marshes and bayous, not sand beaches.
3. Miami Beach
4. Michigan
5. Shells

6. What Virginia resort area is connected with the Eastern Shore by the seventeen-mile-long Chesapeake Bay Bridge-Tunnel?

7. What appropriately named California resort town is noted for its five-mile-long, five-hundred-foot-wide beach?

8. In what New Jersey resort area would you find Caesar's, Grand Hotel, Harrah's, Merv Griffin's, and the Trump Regency?

9. What posh Florida city was named for the dense stands of coconut trees there?

10. New England's most famous peninsula is a tourist playground about seventy miles long, with old fishing villages and sandy beaches. What is it?

11. Redondo Beach has the international festival of what typically Californian sport?

12. Jones Beach is a favorite summer getaway for what northeastern metropolis?

13. The Canaveral National Seashore is in what state?

14. What does the resort town of Ocean City, New Jersey, lack that nearby Atlantic City has?

15. Rehoboth Beach, a favorite weekend haunt for D.C. people, is in what tiny state?

16. You can lounge on Lake Michigan beaches at Foster Avenue, Thirty-First Street, and Calumet Park in what metropolis?

17. What state has gulf beaches at Padre Island, Galveston, and Bryan Beach?

18. Some of the volcanic sands on "the Big Island" of Hawaii are what distinctive color?

19. What state's beautiful Sanibel Island beaches are considered America's hot spot for shell collectors?

6. Virginia Beach
7. Long Beach
8. Atlantic City, a gambling mecca as well as a beach town
9. Palm Beach, naturally
10. Cape Cod
11. Surfing
12. New York City
13. Florida, just south of the Kennedy Space Center
14. Alcohol; the founders decreed that the family resort would never sell alcohol, and it never has.
15. Delaware
16. Chicago; you'll probably do more lounging than swimming, since Lake Michigan is too chilly for most people.
17. Texas
18. Black
19. Florida's; Sanibel is near Fort Myers.

☆ More Unusual Sights

1. What large state has more than forty active volcanoes?
2. By what better name do we know the Los Angeles La Brea asphalt deposits?
3. What bird (associated with oceans) is depicted in a monument in landlocked Salt Lake City?
4. In what northwestern state could you go swimming in the Lava Hot Springs? (Hint: potato)
5. America's largest formation of sand dunes is not near an ocean but in what plains state?
6. What state's capitol, dating from 1969, has legislative chambers shaped like volcano cinder cones?
7. What huge federal building near D.C. has seventeen miles of hallways?
8. The ghost town of Rhyolite in Death Valley, California, has a unique house made of what glass containers?
9. What flat wasteland covered with salt stretches across Utah almost all the way to Nevada? (Hint: a Pontiac model)
10. If you are driving California's Avenue of the Giants, what giants do you see?
11. Athens, Georgia, has a notorious double-barreled weapon, the only one of its kind. What sort of weapon is it?
12. Bell Labs headquarters in New Jersey has a sixty-foot likeness of what electrical component?
13. What type of ancient homes can you see in Utah's Hovenweep National Monument?
14. At what world-famous Florida attraction could you visit the Island in the Sky?
15. What is distinctive about Chattanooga's Lookout Mountain train ride?
16. What southwestern state's capitol has a round kiva-like design that resembles the Indian sun sign?

More Unusual Sights *(answers)*

1. Alaska
2. The La Brea tar pits
3. The seagull; a flock of them saved the Mormon settlers in 1848 by devouring a destructive plague of grasshoppers.
4. Idaho
5. Nebraska
6. Hawaii
7. The Pentagon
8. Beer and liquor bottles—over twelve thousand of them in the "Bottle House."
9. The Bonneville Salt Flats
10. Redwood trees, some over three hundred feet tall; they're in Humboldt Redwoods State Park in California.
11. A double-barreled cannon, used only once during the Civil War
12. A transistor
13. Cliff dwellings, known as pueblos
14. Cypress Gardens; the tropical island 150 feet above the water offers a superb view of the beautiful gardens.
15. It is on an incline, one of the steepest railways in the world, offering wonderful views of the area.
16. New Mexico's, in Santa Fe

17. Of what unusual wood is the fourteen-ton Cross in the Woods made in Indian River, Michigan?

18. Santa Barbara, California, has an enormous old tree whose branches are wide enough to shade ten thousand people. What sort of fruit tree is it? (Hint: Newton)

19. What Arizona national monument centers around a large cone-shaped mountain of volcanic cinders?

20. San Jose, California's Mystery House is a curious item built by the widow of a noted gun manufacturer. Who?

21. Kissimmee, Florida, has a futuristic house made of what common plastic?

22. The Hilton Hawaiian Village in Honolulu has a pond featuring what cold-water birds?

23. In what Virginia college's museum could you see General "Stonewall" Jackson's stuffed horse on display?

17. Redwood—unusual because it does not grow in Michigan. The tree was over two thousand years old. The fifty-five-foot cross holds a seven-ton bronze Jesus.
18. A fig tree, believed to be the largest in the U.S.
19. Sunset Crater Volcano National Monument
20. Winchester, known for the famous Winchester rifles; the widow believed she would never die so long as she kept building, so the house is a hodgepodge of blank walls, secret passageways, and stairways going nowhere. (She did die, by the way.)
21. Polyurethane; the home, Xanadu, is open to the public.
22. Penguins—rather out of place in the tropics
23. VMI, the Virginia Military Institute; Jackson's horse Little Sorrel looks surprisingly lifelike.

PART SIX
Be a Sport

☆ Great American Athletes: Common Bonds

If you saw the names of three famous American athletes, would you recognize the sport they had all played? Find out. Just for fun, we'll throw in coaches as well as players. Keep in mind that the names here are from both present and past.

1. Lee Trevino, Larry Nelson, Dave Stockton
2. Harmon Killebrew, Arky Vaughn, Cal Ripken
3. Steve Lewis, David Wottle, Ray Barbuti
4. Shug Jordan, Woody Hayes, Knute Rockne
5. May Sutton, Chris Evert-Lloyd, Evelyn Sears
6. Jim Brown, Willie Wood, Tom Landry
7. Bill Walton, Bob Cousy, Oscar Robertson
8. Albert White, Phil Boggs, Bob Webster
9. Cliff Battles, Johnny Unitas, Doak Walker
10. Phil Esposito, Gordie Howe, Wayne Gretzky
11. Janet Evans, Tiffany Cohen, Theresa Andrews
12. Hugh Duffy, William Dickey, Willie Mays
13. Frank Shorter, Roger Kingdom, Hayes Jones
14. Scott Hamilton, David Jenkins, Richard Button
15. Matt Biondi, Jim Montgomery, John Weismuller
16. Thad Vann, Pop Warner, John Heisman
17. Ray Bourque, Luc Robitaille, Bobby Orr
18. Nate Archibald, Norm Nixon, Guy Rodgers
19. Andre Phillips, Edwin Moses, Glenn Hardin
20. Joe Guyon, Sonny Jurgenson, Terry Bradshaw
21. Lisa Wagner, Dana Stewart, Carol Norman
22. Phil Mahre, Joe Levins, A. J. Kitt
23. Luke Appling, Charles Comiskey, Ty Cobb
24. William Hoyt, Charles Dvorak, Don Bragg
25. Rick Carey, Brian Goodell, Mark Spitz
26. Tony Zale, Dick Tiger, Terry Downes

Great American Athletes: Common Bonds
(answers)

1. Golf
2. Baseball
3. Track and field
4. College football coaches
5. Tennis
6. Football
7. Basketball
8. Diving
9. Football
10. Hockey
11. Swimming
12. Baseball
13. Track and field
14. Figure skating
15. Swimming
16. College football coaches
17. Hockey
18. Basketball
19. Track and field
20. Football
21. Bowling
22. Skiing
23. Baseball
24. Track and field (pole vault, to be specific)
25. Swimming
26. Boxing, middleweight

27. Ty Murray, Lewis Field, Paul Tierney
28. Alex English, Paul Arizin, Moses Malone

☆ Sports Nicknames

1. He was born George Herman Ruth, but the world knows him by what one-word name?
2. What heavyweight boxing champion of the 1940s was "the Brown Bomber"?
3. Nicknamed "Stan the Man," he won seven National League batting titles between 1943 and 1957. Who was he?
4. What pro football notable of the 1970s was "Broadway Joe"?
5. What baseball legend, known as "the Georgia Peach," was the first inductee in the Baseball Hall of Fame?
6. What Boston Celtics pro, known as "Mr. Basketball," died at age ninety-eight in 1995?
7. What baseball legend was known as "the Iron Horse"?
8. What boxing legend was known as "the Manassa Mauler"?
9. What player for the Harlem Globetrotters was known as "the Clown Prince of Basketball"?
10. Baseball great Jerome Herman Dean was better known by what name?
11. What bare-knuckles boxing champion was known as "the Boston Strong Boy"?
12. "Joltin' Joe" and "the Yankee Clipper" were the same baseball star, married to Marilyn Monroe. Who?
13. What football legend was "the Galloping Ghost"?
14. What Boston Celtics legend was "Mr. Basketball," even though he was only six-foot-one?
15. What heavyweight boxing champ modestly called himself "the greatest"?
16. Who is golf's "Golden Bear"?

27. Rodeo
28. Basketball

Sports Nicknames (answers)

1. "Babe"
2. Joe Louis
3. Stan Musial
4. Joe Namath
5. Ty Cobb
6. Nat Holman
7. Lou Gehrig
8. Jack Dempsey, born in Manassa, Colorado
9. Meadowlark Lemon
10. Dizzy
11. John L. Sullivan, also known as "the Great John L."
12. Joe DiMaggio (also known as "the Mr. Coffee man")
13. Red Grange
14. Bob Cousy
15. Cassius Clay, or Muhammad Ali; not everyone agreed with his nickname, including those who called him "the Louisville Lip."
16. Jack Nicklaus

17. What quick-tempered baseball legend was both "the Kid" and "the Splendid Splinter"?
18. What women's tennis grand slam winner was "Little Mo"?
19. What golfer, known as "the world's greatest woman athlete," is honored with a museum in Beaumont, Texas?
20. What National League batting champ was "Charlie Hustle"?
21. What boxing notable of the old days was called "Gentleman Jim"?
22. What baseball legend from Alabama was "the Say Hey Kid"?

☆ Six Olympic Questions

1. What Southern capital hosted the Summer Olympics in 1996?
2. The U.S. boycotted the 1980 Moscow Olympics because the Soviet Union had invaded what Asian country?
3. What great Native American athlete had to return his 1912 Olympic medals because he had played semipro baseball?
4. What two Olympic swimming medalists later went on to play Tarzan in the movies?
5. The U.S. Olympic Complex, which trains more than fifteen thousand athletes each year, is in what Colorado city?
6. What swimmer, who later endorsed swimming pools and milk, won seven gold medals in the 1972 Olympics?

17. Ted Williams
18. Maureen Connolly
19. Babe Zaharias
20. Pete Rose
21. Jim Corbett
22. Willie Mays

Six Olympic Questions *(answers)*

1. Atlanta, Georgia; if you missed this, don't admit it to anyone.
2. Afghanistan; a total of sixty-six nations did not participate.
3. Jim Thorpe; in 1983 the Olympic Committee officially returned the medals to the children of the late Thorpe.
4. Johnny Weismuller and Buster Crabbe
5. Colorado Springs
6. Mark Spitz

☆ More Great American Athletes: Common Bonds

Given the names of three famous athletes, you could, no doubt, immediately remember the popular sport they all played. Could you do it even if we threw in a few less familiar sports? And coaches? Maybe even animals?

1. Horton Smith, Sam Snead, Sandy Lyle
2. Jim Clark, Rodger Ward, Bill Vukovich
3. John Bike, Fred Lewis, Paul Haber
4. Chris Waller, Scott Keswick, Lance Ringnald
5. George Foreman, Archie Moore, Larry Holmes
6. Craig Perret, Gary Stevens, Michael Kinane
7. Carl Lewis, Steve Scott, Mark Nenow
8. Monica Selles, Steffi Graf, Tracy Austin
9. James Foxx, Edwin Matthew, Mickey Mantle
10. James Lightbody, Bob Schul, Lee Evans
11. George DiCarlo, Matt Vogel, Rod Strachan
12. Walter Camp, John McKay, "Bear" Bryant
13. Dick Butkus, Bob Lilly, Fran Tarkenton
14. Wes Unseld, Dave Cowens, Larry Bird
15. Pete Weber, Dell Ballard, Gary Dickinson
16. Pat Setlsam, Michael Ralston, Eric Klein
17. Rick Barry, Mike Newlin, Larry Nance
18. Rick Kehoe, Brett Hull, Ken Wharram
19. Terry Taylor, Barry Asher, Rich Mersek
20. Joe Walcott, Max Baer, Evander Holyfield
21. Alice Marble, Margaret Court, Pauline Betz
22. Jim Lindquist, Mike Miller, Brian Voss
23. Lisa Dennehy, Elise Brinich, Sheila Young
24. Don Budge, Ken Rosewall, John McEnroe
25. Larry Noggle, Del Miller, Glen Garnsey
26. John Llewellyn, Mark Reiland, Tom Brands
27. Charles Coody, Doug Ford, Arnold Palmer

More Great American Athletes: Common Bonds
(answers)

1. Golf
2. Auto racing
3. Handball
4. Gymnastics
5. Boxing, heavyweight
6. Horse racing; they were jockeys, not horses.
7. Track and field
8. Tennis
9. Baseball
10. Track and field
11. Swimming
12. College football coaches
13. Football
14. Basketball
15. Bowling
16. Speed skating
17. Basketball
18. Hockey
19. Bowling
20. Boxing, heavyweight
21. Tennis
22. Bowling
23. Speed skating
24. Tennis
25. Harness racing drivers
26. College wrestling
27. Golf

28. Greg Oly, Tom Grannes, Matt Trimble
29. Ezzard Charles, Floyd Patterson, Jack Sharkey
30. Frank Parker, Bill Tilden, Rod Laver
31. Bob Goalby, Bernhard Langer, Jack Nicklaus
32. Tom Sneva, Wilbur Shaw, Michael Andretti
33. Kerri Strug, Shannon Miller, Kim Kelley
34. Xandra, Thermel, However
35. Glen Rice, Bobby Hurley, Bill Walton
36. Kay Cockerill, Lou Dill, Anne Quast
37. Richard Schultz, Bret Brian, Jeffrey Macy
38. A. J. Foyt, Rick Mears, Al Unser

☆ Sports Firsts

1. What annual sports mega-event was first held January 15, 1967, at Memorial Coliseum in Los Angeles?
2. What midwestern city became, in 1904, the first U.S. host of the Olympics?
3. What major sporting event was held for the first time in Louisville, Kentucky, in 1875?
4. What sport was first played officially between the college teams of Rutgers and Princeton in November 1869?
5. What items were used for the first time in the 1892 heavyweight boxing championship?
6. What game was played for the first time in the U.S. at the Staten Island Cricket and Baseball Club in 1874? (Hint: neither cricket nor baseball)
7. What sort of pitch did Candy Cummings throw for the first time in 1867?
8. What pro sport attempted its first *spring* season in 1983?
9. What very useful piece of protective equipment was first worn by a baseball player in 1875?
10. The Buffalo Germans were the first championship pro team in what great American sport?

28. Speed skating
29. Boxing, heavyweight
30. Tennis
31. Golf
32. Auto racing
33. Gymnastics
34. Greyhound racing (names of dogs, in case you were puzzled)
35. Basketball
36. Golf
37. Weight lifting
38. Auto racing

Sports Firsts *(answers)*

1. Super Bowl I, Green Bay vs. Kansas City (Green Bay won 35–10.)
2. St. Louis
3. The Kentucky Derby
4. Football (Rutgers won, by the way.)
5. Gloves
6. Tennis, which a young woman had brought with her from Bermuda
7. A curve
8. Football
9. A catcher's mask
10. Basketball

11. Boxing's first official heavyweight champ (1882–92) was what Boston bare-knuckles legend?
12. The first inductees to the Baseball Hall of Fame were Christy Mathewsón, Walter Johnson, Honus Wagner, and what two legends?
13. The first case of a pro football team leaving California was announced in 1995. What midwestern city were the Rams departing for?

☆ All-Around Athletes: A Sports Grab Bag

You may consider yourself a football whiz, or a baseball buff, or an auto racing expert. But now see how well you do with a grab bag of questions from all sorts of sports.

1. An 1880 football conference decided that how many players from each team could be on the field at one time?
2. What pro sport was shortened by eighteen games in 1995 due to a prolonged strike?
3. The Masters, the U.S. Open, the British Open, and the PGA are the four major tournaments in what sport?
4. The Vezina Trophy goes to the best goalkeeper in what pro sport?
5. What violent sport is "the sweet science"?
6. What European immigrant group is credited with bringing bowling to America?
7. Hambletonian winners are champions in what sport? (Hint: neigh)
8. What pro baseball player set a new record in 1995 by playing in 2,131 consecutive games?
9. What great American sport did James Naismith invent after his indoor versions of lacrosse, rugby, and soccer proved too rough?

11. John L. Sullivan, "the Boston Strong Boy"
12. Babe Ruth and Ty Cobb
13. St. Louis

All-Around Athletes: A Sports Grab Bag *(answers)*

1. Eleven, of course; prior to 1880 there were sometimes twenty-five men per team.
2. Baseball
3. Golf
4. Hockey
5. Boxing, oddly enough
6. The Dutch (Remember the story of Rip Van Winkle?)
7. Harness racing
8. Cal Ripken Jr., who beat Lou Gehrig's longstanding record
9. Basketball (which is still more popular than indoor lacrosse)

10. What caused bowling to change from nine pins to ten pins?

11. What sport entered American culture after some U.S. college students saw it played in Canada in the winter of 1894?

12. What sports-governing organization resulted from President Theodore Roosevelt's concern about deaths and injuries in football games?

13. What boxing legend made history by winning the heavyweight championship twice, more than twenty years apart?

14. The Breeders' Cup is given in what professional sport?

15. What popular winter sport was played with "mixed teams" of pros and amateurs until 1910?

16. In what sport were "mufflers" used in the old days?

17. What future movie actor and accused murderer won football's Heisman Trophy in 1968?

18. The Magic is the NBA team of what fast-growing Florida metropolis?

19. The Lady Byng Trophy is awarded annually for "gentlemanly conduct" in what ungentle pro sport?

20. When James Naismith invented basketball in 1891, how many players were on each team? (Hint: *not* five)

21. What is the most common pitch in pro baseball?

22. In 1996 the Cleveland Browns moved to Baltimore and became what team?

10. The law; in the early days, there was so much gambling and corruption that the game of ninepins was outlawed in some areas. The way around the law was simple: add another pin.
11. Hockey, which is, by birth, a Canadian sport
12. The NCAA, National College Athletic Association
13. George Foreman, 1973 and 1995
14. Horse racing, of course
15. Hockey
16. Boxing; this was the old name for the gloves. They were used only for *training* bouts, not actual matches, which were all bare knuckles.
17. O. J. Simpson, who played for USC at the time
18. Orlando
19. Hockey
20. Nine (It must have been crowded out there. . . .)
21. The fastball
22. The Baltimore Ravens

☆ Still More Great American Athletes: Common Bonds

Given the names of three well-known athletes, you could, of course, think of the sport they all played. Could you do it even if we threw in a few less familiar sports? And coaches? And even animals?

1. Cap Anson, Chick Hafey, Brooks Robinson
2. Mary Meagher, Sharon Strouder, Tracy Caulkins
3. Carol Heiss, Peggy Fleming, Dorothy Hamill
4. Biff Jones, Clarence Munn, George A. Munger
5. Tommy Freeman, Marty Servo, Johnny Saxton
6. Dean Oliver, Phil Lyne, Dave Appleton
7. Jerry Bailey, Pat Day, Willy Shoemaker
8. Lorraine Hanlon, Janet Lynn, Rosalynn Sumners
9. Pablo Morales, Melvin Stewart, David Wharton
10. Dutch Clark, George Musso, Roger Staubach
11. Bernard King, Michael Jordan, Bob Pettit
12. Carl Lewis, Robert Hayes, Joe DeLoach
13. Harry Lowell, Larry Robinson, Eric Vail
14. Vince Lucci, Luke Karen, Bob Hochrein
15. Ken Shelley, Todd Eldredge, Christopher Bowman
16. Mike Weaver, Leon Spinks, Buster Douglas
17. Pep Youngs, Joseph Tinker, Lou Gehrig
18. Mal Anderson, Stan Smith, Hugh Doherty
19. John Campbell, Carl Allen, Bill Fahy
20. Kenny Monday, Chris Campbell, Bruce Baumgartner
21. David Robinson, Keith Smart, Pervis Ellison
22. Barry Sanders, Doug Flutie, John Latimer
23. Glenna Collett, Beth Daniel, Beverly Hanson
24. Danny Sullivan, Gaston Chevrolet, Johnny Rutherford
25. Lionel Simmons, Ralph Sampson, Walter Berry
26. Andy Bathgate, Max Bentley, Bobby Hull
27. Ed Deins, Mike Putzer, Tom Howery

Still More Great American Athletes: Common Bonds *(answers)*

1. Baseball
2. Swimming
3. Figure skating
4. College football coaches
5. Boxing, welterweight
6. Rodeo
7. Horse racing jockeys
8. Figure skating
9. Swimming
10. Football
11. Basketball
12. Track and field
13. Hockey
14. Bowling
15. Figure skating
16. Boxing, heavyweight
17. Baseball
18. Tennis
19. Harness racing drivers
20. Wrestling
21. Basketball
22. Football
23. Golf
24. Auto racing
25. Basketball
26. Hockey
27. Bowling

PART SEVEN

The Bad &
the Ugly

☆ Criminals Great and Small

1. Kansas City, Missouri, has made a museum of a bank robbed by what famous outlaw brothers?
2. What South Carolina mother went to prison in 1995 for drowning her two sons in a lake?
3. What two notorious California brothers went to prison in 1996 for murdering their parents?
4. What football legend was acquitted in 1995 of murdering his ex-wife and her friend?
5. What Mexican desperado was pursued by General John Pershing in 1916?
6. The man accused of murdering a wrestler who lived on his palatial estate in 1995 was a member of what wealthy family? (Hint: chemical company)
7. For what horrible crime was General Ulysses S. Grant arrested in Kane, Pennsylvania?
8. What famous criminal ended his days as a shoe salesman and was never brought to trial?
9. Toguri D'Aquino, convicted of doing propaganda broadcasts for the Japanese in World War II, is better known by what name?
10. What famous aviator paid fifty thousand dollars to get back his kidnapped infant?
11. What wild-eyed killer of the 1960s had set up a commune for his "family" at the Spahn ranch near Los Angeles?
12. What convicted Watergate criminal (and future talk radio host) wrote the book *Will*?
13. What famous criminal gang has a museum in Coffeyville, Kansas?
14. The Dry Tortuga islands off the south end of Florida received four famous criminals as prisoners in 1865. Who were they? (Hint: assassination)

Criminals Great and Small *(answers)*

1. Jesse and Frank James and their gang; it was the first bank Jesse James robbed in broad daylight.
2. Susan Smith
3. The Menendez brothers, Lyle and Erik
4. O. J. Simpson
5. Pancho Villa, who was notorious for raiding border areas
6. The Du Ponts
7. Fishing without a license
8. Frank James, brother of the more famous Jesse James
9. "Tokyo Rose," the name she used in the broadcasts
10. Charles Lindbergh; though the ransom was paid, the baby was found dead.
11. Charles Manson, whose "family" was responsible for the murder in 1969 of actress Sharon Tate and four others
12. G. Gordon Liddy
13. The Dalton gang
14. The conspirators involved in the plot to assassinate Abraham Lincoln

15. What heiress, kidnapped by the radical Symbionese Liberation Army, was convicted of armed robbery in 1976?

16. What marine colonel gained national fame for his role in the Iran-Contra scandal of the 1980s?

☆ Bars and Stripes Forever: Jails and Prisons

1. What convicted Watergate criminal later established a Christian ministry for prisoners?

2. "Old Sparky" in the Texas Prison Museum is what sort of apparatus?

3. What item was used in Wickenburg, Arizona, to hold prisoners until the town jail was built?

4. What type of criminals were taken to California's Prisoner Rock?

5. The Spanish word *calabozo* gave what slang term to the American vocabulary?

6. What famous Civil War figure was imprisoned in Fort Lee after the war?

7. Georgia has a national historic site dedicated to all American prisoners of war. What is the site?

8. What great American circus entrepreneur had been jailed for libel while he was a newspaper editor?

9. During the Revolutionary War, what type of people were imprisoned in the Old New Gate Prison in Connecticut?

10. What notable religious leader was killed by a mob while he was in the old jail in Carthage, Illinois? (Hint: polygamy)

11. The famous Leavenworth federal penitentiary is in what state?

12. What famous California island prison closed in 1963 and is now a museum?

15. Patty Hearst
16. Lt. Col. Oliver North, whose convictions were overturned; he later became an author and noted radio talk show host.

Bars and Stripes Forever: Jails and Prisons
(answers)

1. Charles Colson, who founded Prison Fellowship
2. An electric chair
3. A large tree, now known as the Jail Tree; rowdy prisoners were fastened to it with chains.
4. Public drunks; they were told to either dry up on the island or swim the (sobering) distance to the shore.
5. "Calaboose," still used as a slang term for jail; the Spanish word means "dungeon" or "jail."
6. Confederate president Jefferson Davis; his cell can still be visited there.
7. Andersonville, site of a Confederate prison for Yankee soldiers
8. P. T. Barnum
9. Tories, supporters of the British; it was originally a copper mine.
10. Joseph Smith, founder of the Mormons
11. Kansas
12. Alcatraz, which held many notorious prisoners, including Al Capone

13. In 1890 murderer William Kemmler became the first man to be executed by what method?
14. What Revolutionary War agitator was freed from a French prison by James Monroe in 1794?
15. What state prison in Ossining was built with convict labor in 1825?
16. Which of the original colonies was planned as a settlement for people from England's debtors' prisons?
17. What country music legend recorded his hit "A Boy Named Sue" at San Quentin Prison?
18. Alvin "Creepy" Karpis spent the record amount of time, twenty-eight years, in what notorious island prison?
19. The nation's most famous prison riot occurred in 1971 at Attica prison in what state?
20. What young actor, once married to singer-actress Madonna, served prison time in the 1990s?

☆ Assassinations and Some Attempts

1. What alleged presidential assassin was killed by Jack Ruby on November 24, 1963?
2. What federal agency took on the job of guarding the president after William McKinley's assassination in 1901?
3. What southern governor and presidential candidate was shot while campaigning at a mall in 1972?
4. What assassination was the Warren Commission appointed to investigate in 1964?
5. Chicago mayor Anton Cermak was killed by assassin Guiseppe Zangara in 1933. What newly elected president was Zangara actually aiming for?
6. The year 1881 was the "year of three presidents" in American history. Who were they?

13. Electrocution; this occurred in New York's Auburn Prison.
14. Thomas Paine, author of *Common Sense* and other propaganda pieces
15. Sing Sing
16. Georgia; as today, prisons were overcrowded. The English thought the far-off wilderness of America would be a good place to send them.
17. Johnny Cash
18. Alcatraz
19. New York; the riot killed forty-three inmates and guards.
20. Sean Penn, who resumed his acting career upon release

Assassinations and Some Attempts *(answers)*

1. Lee Harvey Oswald, arrested for shooting John F. Kennedy
2. The Secret Service
3. George Wallace, shot by Arthur Bremer at a Maryland shopping mall
4. The assassination of John F. Kennedy, which occurred in November 1963
5. Franklin D. Roosevelt
6. Rutherford Hayes (whose term had ended), James Garfield (newly elected, then assassinated), and Chester Arthur (president after Garfield's assassination)

7. What popular president of the 1800s was the first to survive an assassination attempt? (Hint: Old Hickory)
8. What Democratic presidential candidate was fatally shot in 1968 by Sirhan Sirhan, a Jordanian?
9. What important site is the burial place of Louisiana's assassinated governor, Huey Long, the "Kingfish"?
10. The Dr. Samuel Mudd House can be toured in Waldorf, Maryland. What is Mudd's claim to fame?
11. Washington, D.C.'s performing arts center is named for which assassinated president?
12. Buffalo, New York, has a statue of a twentieth-century president assassinated there. Who?
13. What president, assassinated in 1881, had said of the presidency, "What is there in this place that a man should ever want to get in it?"
14. Ford's Theatre in D.C. was the scene of what famous assassination?
15. "The Sixth Floor" is a Dallas, Texas, museum devoted to what famous assassination?
16. What Republican president's shooting in 1981 caused the Oscars broadcast to be delayed?
17. What Republican president did Squeaky Fromme try to assassinate in 1975?
18. What president was, in 1950, almost fatally shot by Puerto Rican nationalists?
19. The Surratt House in Clinton, Maryland, focuses on the escape of what presidential assassin?
20. When Abraham Lincoln was shot, which of his Cabinet members was also critically wounded?
21. What former president was shot at while campaigning for president in Milwaukee in 1912? (Hint: bear)

7. Andrew Jackson; the spunky Jackson turned on the assailant and beat him senseless with a cane.
8. Robert F. Kennedy
9. The grounds of the state capitol in Baton Rouge
10. Dr. Mudd treated the broken leg of runaway assassin John Wilkes Booth, quite unaware that Booth had just shot Abraham Lincoln. Mudd was imprisoned but later pardoned.
11. John F. Kennedy
12. William McKinley, killed in 1901
13. James Garfield
14. Abraham Lincoln's, in 1865; the theatre has been restored to its appearance at the time Lincoln was shot.
15. John F. Kennedy's; the fatal shot came from the sixth floor of the Texas School Book Depository, now a museum.
16. Ronald Reagan's; he was shot (but not killed) by John Hinckley Jr. It was appropriate that the Oscars telecast was postponed, since Reagan had been a movie actor.
17. Gerald Ford
18. Harry Truman
19. John Wilkes Booth, who shot Lincoln; the Surratt family aided Booth in his attempted escape.
20. William Seward, Lincoln's secretary of state, famous for having purchased Alaska for the U.S.; unlike Lincoln, Seward survived.
21. Teddy Roosevelt, who escaped unhurt

☆ Three Executions

1. By what method was antislavery radical John Brown executed in 1859?
2. What leader of a slave revolt was hanged after murdering his master's family and fifty other people in 1831?
3. What bloodthirsty pirate was finally captured and hanged in 1701?

☆ Massacres and Other Violent Deaths

1. What type of execution did Pocahontas save John Smith from?
2. What notorious outlaw was killed by members of his own gang for ten thousand dollars in reward money?
3. What notorious duel between two well-known politicians took place in July 1804?
4. What religious cult leader led a thousand followers to commit mass suicide in Guyana in 1978?
5. What president condemned the Soviet Union for shooting down a Korean jet, killing 269 people?
6. Albert DeSalvo, sentenced to life in prison for strangling several women, is better known by what name?
7. When Mary Jo Kopechne drowned in a car in 1969, what politician had been driving the car?
8. What Chicago gangster chief ordered the famous St. Valentine's Day Massacre?
9. Lima, Ohio, was the site of a famous killing by a gangster's henchmen. Who was he?
10. Las Cruces, New Mexico, takes its name from the crosses *(las cruces)* over the graves of white settlers massacred by what Indian tribe?
11. When a TWA jet and a United jet collided in midair in 1956, in what Arizona scenic landmark did they crash?

Three Executions *(answers)*

1. Hanging, the usual method in the 1800s
2. Nat Turner
3. William Kidd, better known as Captain Kidd

Massacres and Other Violent Deaths *(answers)*

1. Being clubbed to death—*not*, as is commonly thought, from being beheaded
2. Jesse James
3. The duel of Aaron Burr and Alexander Hamilton; Hamilton died.
4. Jim Jones, head of Jonestown
5. Ronald Reagan; this occurred in 1984.
6. The Boston Strangler; he was sentenced in 1967.
7. Senator Edward Kennedy of Massachusetts
8. Al Capone
9. John Dillinger; his gang's murder of Lima's sheriff led to a successful nationwide manhunt for Dillinger.
10. The Apaches
11. The Grand Canyon; the crash killed 128 people.

12. What notorious Confederate raider sacked the town of Lawrence, Kansas?

13. Antislavery newspaper editor Elijah Lovejoy died at the hands of a pro-slavery mob. What was he trying to protect when he died?

14. What pacifist Christian group saw thirty of its members butchered by bayonets at New Jersey's Hancock House?

15. Massacre Rocks State Park commemorates an ambush of immigrants in 1862. In what northwestern state did this take place?

16. The Wyoming Massacre took place in what state? (Hint: *not* Wyoming)

17. What famous flood occurred in 1889 when the South Fork Dam broke?

18. What notorious gunman died, and is buried, in Glenwood Springs, Colorado?

19. How many people were actually killed in the famous Boston Massacre of 1770?

20. What western legend was holding a "dead man's hand" (two aces and two eights) when he was gunned down?

21. St. Joseph, Missouri, has the home of what famous outlaw, shot there in 1882?

22. During what 1786–87 rebellion by debt-ridden Massachusetts farmers were about forty men killed?

23. What black preacher led an 1831 revolt in Virginia in which over fifty people were killed?

24. Davy Crockett, Jim Bowie, and William Travis all died defending what famous site in San Antonio, Texas?

25. William Bonney, who died at age twenty-one and claimed to have killed one man for every year of his life, was better known by what name?

26. What notorious pirate, along with his crew, was killed at Ocracoke Island, North Carolina, in 1718?

12. William "Bloody Bill" Quantrill; his gang burned the town and killed 150 people.
13. His printing press
14. The Quakers; the massacre occurred in 1778, when three hundred British soldiers attacked.
15. Idaho
16. Pennsylvania; the Wyoming River lent its name to the later state of Wyoming.
17. The Johnstown flood in Pennsylvania; more than two thousand people died.
18. Doc Holliday, who died in 1887; his tombstone says, ironically, "He died in bed."
19. Six, shot down by British troops; although it was a key event leading to the American Revolution, it was not a major event in terms of body count.
20. Wild Bill Hickok
21. Jesse James, who was living under the alias "Mr. Howard"
22. Shay's Rebellion
23. Nat Turner, who was captured and executed
24. The Alamo
25. Billy the Kid
26. Edward Teach, better known as "Blackbeard"

27. The old jail in Carthage, Illinois, was the site of the killing of a noted American religious leader. Who?
28. What religious cult's compound in Texas was stormed by federal agents in a long siege in 1993?
29. What New York City skyscraper was bombed by terrorists in 1993, killing seven people and injuring a thousand?
30. Pan Am flight 103, blown apart by a terrorist bomb in 1988, exploded over what country?
31. What had John Lennon done for Mark David Chapman just before Chapman shot him in New York in 1980?
32. In what Middle Eastern country were 240 U.S. Marines killed by suicide bombers in 1983?
33. Nearly a hundred people were killed in a New York City riot in July 1863. What federal practice were the rioters protesting?
34. What object, moving at 180 mph, killed eleven people in Covington, Georgia, in 1969?

☆ More Criminals Great and Small

1. In the infamous St. Valentine's Day Massacre of 1929, what gang leader's men rubbed out rivals from Bugs Moran's gang?
2. Anne Bonny and Mary Read dressed as men and engaged in what form of nautical crime in the 1700s?
3. CIA agent Aldrich Ames went to prison in 1994 for selling state secrets to what nation?
4. What famous woman was acquitted for the 1892 ax murders of her father and stepmother?
5. What two Italian radicals were executed for a 1920 double murder at a Massachusetts shoe factory?
6. In 1953 Julius and Ethel Rosenberg were executed for treason for selling atomic-bomb secrets to what nation?

27. Joseph Smith, founder of the Mormons
28. The Branch Davidians, under leader David Koresh; eighty-seven people died, including seventeen children.
29. The World Trade Center
30. Scotland; the explosion killed all the passengers, most of whom were Americans, and eleven people on the ground.
31. Autographed his latest album, *Double Fantasy*
32. Lebanon
33. The draft for the Civil War; until March 1863, the Union army had been all volunteer. New York was not supportive of the war or of President Lincoln.
34. A drag racing car, which smashed into spectators, killing eleven and injuring dozens of others

More Criminals Great and Small *(answers)*

1. Al Capone's
2. Piracy; both were notoriously cruel, and Anne had left her respectable Charleston husband to become the mistress of the infamous pirate Calico Jack.
3. The Soviet Union; Aldrich had been a double agent, passing on information to the KGB.
4. Lizzie Borden; her case still excites a lot of interest.
5. Sacco and Vanzetti, whose case is still being debated today
6. The Soviet Union; they were convicted of treason, and President Eisenhower refused to grant them a pardon.

7. Denmark Vesey and thirty-six supporters were executed in 1822 for organizing a revolt of what sort of people?

8. In what comfortable place was gangster chieftain Umberto Anastasia murdered in 1957?

9. In 1958 fourteen-year-old Cheryl Crane stabbed and killed Johnny Stompanato for threatening her mother. What beautiful blonde movie queen was her mother?

10. What secretary of the treasury and right-hand man of George Washington was blackmailed for an adulterous affair?

11. What did Alferd Packer do to his five snowbound companions after robbing and murdering them in Colorado in 1874?

12. What sheriff collected a five-hundred-dollar reward for gunning down (in the dark) gunslinger Billy the Kid?

13. What western bandit with a colorful name would rob stagecoaches with an unloaded gun and leave behind a poem?

14. Belle Starr, the notorious "Bandit Queen" of the old West, was murdered in what cowardly fashion?

15. What was the profession of Tom Horn, who was executed in 1903 for killing a fourteen-year-old boy?

16. What beloved American song crooner spent thirty days in jail for drinking during the Prohibition era?

17. The bloodthirsty, lecherous José Gasparilla set up his pirate lair and harem in what gulf coast city?

7. Slaves; the slave revolt was in Charleston, South Carolina.
8. A barber's chair; the man known as "Lord High Executioner" was killed by two gunmen.
9. Lana Turner; Crane was acquitted, with the jury calling it justifiable homicide.
10. Alexander Hamilton; the blackmail was a plot on the part of the woman and her husband.
11. Ate them; he was eventually sentenced to forty years in prison for cannibalism.
12. Pat Garrett
13. Black Bart, whose real name was Charles E. Boles; he called himself a poet and signed his poems "Black Bart, Po-8."
14. She was shot in the back; there is still a mystery about who her murderer was.
15. He was a hired gun, probably the most famous in the West, paid by powerful cattle ranchers to kill off small-time settlers.
16. Bing Crosby; he went to jail in 1930, after being stopped by a policeman who smelled liquor on his breath.
17. Tampa, Florida; the city still celebrates a Gasparilla Carnival every year (overlooking the character of the real Gasparilla, a thoroughly despicable character).

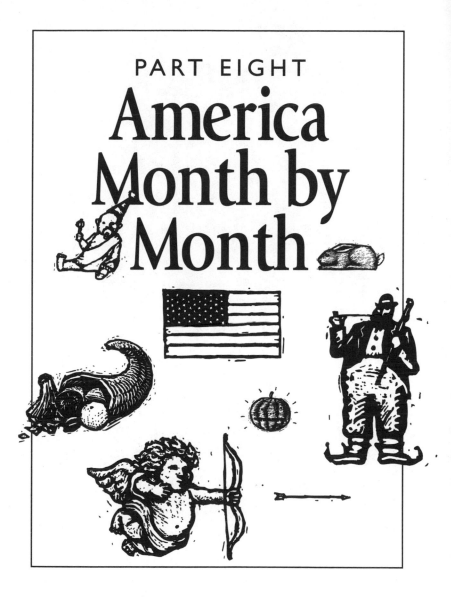

PART EIGHT

America
Month by
Month

☆ January

1. What parade, held on January 1, 1954, became the first nationwide TV broadcast in color?
2. What riotous party season kicks off on January 6 in New Orleans every year?
3. In January 1957 President Eisenhower proclaimed his Eisenhower Doctrine, pledging aid to any Middle Eastern nation battling what political force?
4. The forty-ninth star was added to the U.S. flag in January 1959 because of what new state?
5. What web-footed green celebrity was Grand Marshal of the Tournament of Roses Parade in January 1996?
6. What large state's Spindletop Gusher set off an oil boom on January 10, 1901?
7. On January 3, 1863, artist Thomas Nast gave the world the now standard picture of what Christmas personage?
8. Russian-born Vladimir Zworykin landed in the U.S. on January 1, 1919. What world-changing appliance did Zworykin invent?
9. The first dime with this president's portrait on it was issued January 30 (his birthday) in 1946. Who? (Hint: check your pockets)
10. What flippable toy did the Wham-O company introduce in January 1957?
11. What little-seen continent did American explorer John Davis sight in January 1840 and claim for America?
12. James Marshall found a gold nugget on January 24, 1848, setting off a gold rush in what western state?
13. What unsuccessful Republican presidential candidate was awarded the Presidential Medal of Freedom in January 1997?
14. What president claimed he had spotted a UFO in Georgia in January 1969?
15. What Confederate general's birthday, January 19, used to be celebrated as a holiday in many southern states?

January *(answers)*

1. The Tournament of Roses Parade in California
2. Mardi Gras season, or carnival, which lasts until Ash Wednesday
3. Communism
4. Alaska
5. Kermit the Frog
6. Texas's
7. Santa Claus; Nast didn't invent him, but his image of Santa became the standard one.
8. Television
9. Franklin Roosevelt's
10. The Frisbee
11. Antarctica (At the time, no one much cared to dispute America's claim.)
12. California
13. Bob Dole, who had lost in the 1996 presidential race; Dole had been Senate majority leader.
14. Jimmy Carter
15. Robert E. Lee's

☆ February

1. What famous children's hospital, founded by entertainer Danny Thomas, opened in February 1962?
2. What famous chain of hamburger stands did Ray Kroc purchase from its original owners in February 1960?
3. For what invention did Alexander Graham Bell apply for a patent in February 1876?
4. In February 1733 the last of England's thirteen colonies was established on the Atlantic coast. What was it?
5. The famous Liberty Bell tolled its last time on February 23, 1846, in honor of which president's birthday?
6. What circus entrepreneur saw his star midgets, Tom Thumb and Lavinia Warren, married in February 1863?
7. What item (for personal protection) did Samuel Colt patent in February 1836?
8. What famous gangland massacre occurred February 14, 1929?
9. What astronaut (and future U.S. senator) became, in February 1962, the first American to orbit the earth?
10. What dry and sunny southwestern state became the forty-eighth state on Valentine's Day 1912?
11. What general (and future president) defeated Mexican general Santa Anna at Buena Vista on February 23, 1847?
12. What was the destination of the eighty-six blacks who left New York on a ship in February 1820?
13. What phenomenally popular English novelist was the toast of New York in February 1842? (Hint: Tiny Tim)
14. What honored general was named general-in-chief of the Confederate armies in February 1865?
15. What popular family magazine, noted for its Norman Rockwell covers, published its last issue February 8, 1969?

February *(answers)*

1. St. Jude's, in Memphis, Tennessee
2. McDonald's
3. The telephone, naturally
4. Georgia, beginning with the settlement of Savannah
5. George Washington's (which is actually February 22)
6. P. T. Barnum
7. The famous Colt revolver
8. The St. Valentine's Day Massacre in Chicago
9. John Glenn
10. Arizona
11. Zachary Taylor, "Old Rough and Ready"
12. Africa; it was the first organized effort of American blacks to resettle there.
13. Charles Dickens; Dickens's popularity in the U.S. waned considerably after he made cutting remarks about the Americans.
14. Robert E. Lee
15. *The Saturday Evening Post,* which was resurrected in the 1980s and is still being published

☆ March

1. What new nation adopted its constitution on March 11, 1861, one week after Abraham Lincoln was inaugurated president?
2. What fateful event took place in San Antonio, Texas, on March 6, 1836?
3. What president (whose name reminds you of a vacuum cleaner) signed a law on March 3, 1931, making "The Star-Spangled Banner" the national anthem?
4. What two famous ironclad ships battled near Norfolk, Virginia, on March 9, 1862?
5. What president was shot in March 1981, causing the temporary cancellation of the Academy Awards telecast?
6. What event in the life of a U.S. president used to take place in March but is now held in January?
7. What novel item did Elisha Otis install in a New York public building in March 1857?
8. What enormous chunk of land did America buy from Russia in March 1867 (for two cents per acre)?
9. In the first Congress, which met in March 1789, how many states sent representatives?
10. What boxing champ, imprisoned for three years on a morals charge, was released March 25, 1995?
11. What president was born March 15, 1767, in a log cabin on the North Carolina–South Carolina frontier? (Hint: Old Hickory)
12. What color is the Chicago River dyed each year on March 17?
13. What poet and horror story author was booted out of West Point in March 1831 for skipping classes and chapel?
14. Texas celebrates Texas Independence Day on what day?
15. Who sent the fateful telephone message "Mr. Watson, come here, I want you!" on March 10, 1876?

March *(answers)*

1. The Confederate States of America
2. The fall of the Alamo to the Mexicans
3. Herbert Hoover
4. The *Monitor* (a Union ship) and the *Merrimack* (Confederate); the battle was a draw.
5. Ronald Reagan
6. His inauguration
7. An elevator
8. Alaska
9. Only eleven; Rhode Island and North Carolina sent no one.
10. Mike Tyson, who went on to fight again
11. Andrew Jackson
12. Green, for St. Patrick's Day
13. Edgar Allan Poe
14. March 3
15. Alexander Graham Bell, who accidentally sent the first telephone message after he spilled some acid on himself

☆ April

1. What Mexican food chain announced on April 1, 1996, that it had purchased the Liberty Bell?
2. What California disaster on April 18, 1906, destroyed 25,000 buildings and left 225,000 homeless?
3. What great leader took his oath of office on April 30, 1789?
4. What beautiful Hollywood actress married Prince Rainier III in April 1956 and retired from acting?
5. For what new position were seven military test pilots chosen by NASA in April 1959?
6. What huge sports arena opened April 9, 1965, with President Johnson in attendance?
7. What distant (and cold) destination did Admiral Robert Peary reach in April 1909?
8. Which three great American wars all began in the month of April?
9. What flighty festival is held on the Washington Monument grounds every April?
10. The Cape Henry Memorial in Virginia Beach, Virginia, marks what fateful event of April 1607?
11. Samuel Adams and John Hancock were awakened by an alarm on the night of April 18, 1775. Who gave the alarm?
12. Which state celebrates San Jacinto Day on April 21?
13. What federal fort near Charleston, South Carolina, was fired upon on April 12, 1861?
14. What famous German-born scientist died April 18, 1955, with his brain being preserved for study?
15. What Indian woman did Englishman John Rolfe marry on April 14, 1614?

April *(answers)*

1. Taco Bell; it was their April Fool's joke.
2. The San Francisco earthquake
3. George Washington
4. Grace Kelly
5. Astronauts—the very first group
6. The Houston Astrodome
7. The North Pole
8. The Revolutionary War, the Civil War, and the Spanish-American War
9. The kite-flying festival
10. The first landing spot of the English in America
11. Paul Revere; the Battle of Lexington took place the next day.
12. Texas
13. Fort Sumter; the incident kicked off the Civil War.
14. Albert Einstein
15. Pocahontas

☆ May

1. What notable Georgia city did Union general William T. Sherman torch in May 1864?
2. In May 1963 James Whittaker became the first American to reach what peak in the Himalayas?
3. The longest sports game in modern history, May 31, 1964, was 7 hours and 23 minutes long. What sport?
4. Missouri celebrates each May 8 as a tribute to what Missouri-born president?
5. What world-famous event is held the first Saturday in May in Louisville, Kentucky?
6. What beloved Confederate general died May 10, 1863, after being wounded by friendly fire?
7. What famous New York skyscraper opened in May 1931?
8. What high office did George Washington turn down on May 22, 1782?
9. What impeached president was finally acquitted on May 16, 1868?
10. What nationwide celebration began on May 10, 1876?
11. When Coca-Cola first went on sale on May 8, 1886, what now illegal drug did it contain?
12. What watery Florida region was the site of the notorious ValuJet crash in May 1996?
13. What establishment did twenty-four New York financiers open in May 1792?
14. What amazing telecommunications device did inventor Samuel Morse demonstrate for Congress in May 1843?
15. What runaway political leader was captured by federal agents in Georgia on May 10, 1865?

May *(answers)*

1. Atlanta
2. Mount Everest
3. Baseball; it was the Giants vs. the Mets.
4. Harry Truman; May 8 is Truman Day.
5. The Kentucky Derby, held at Churchill Downs
6. Thomas "Stonewall" Jackson, who had just won a ringing victory at the Battle of Chancellorsville
7. The Empire State Building
8. King; Washington wisely saw that it would be inconsistent to break away from England and its king and then set up a kingdom in America.
9. Andrew Johnson, who became president after the assassination of Lincoln
10. The centennial, honoring America's hundredth birthday
11. Cocaine, in a small amount
12. The Everglades; the crash of the twenty-year-old jet killed all 110 people aboard and raised public concern about air travel safety.
13. The New York Stock Exchange
14. The telegraph
15. Jefferson Davis, president of the defeated Confederacy

☆ June

1. What "super" movie actor was paralyzed after falling from a horse in June 1995?
2. Who became the world's most famous kite flyer in June 1752?
3. What makeup mogul, whose name is a household word, died in June 1996 at the age of 91?
4. What collectibles convention is held each June in Ocean City, New Jersey? (Hint: bubble gum)
5. A 221-foot granite monument in Boston commemorates what famous Revolutionary War battle, fought in June 1775?
6. What group of counties that had broken away from a Confederate state became a new U.S. state in June 1863?
7. What fifty-four-year-old president sneaked into New York in June 1844 to marry a twenty-four-year-old?
8. In June 1957 the *Mayflower II* landed in Plymouth, Massachusetts, after duplicating the 1620 voyage of what group?
9. What huge statue arrived in New York in packing cases in June 1885?
10. What European nation landed spies on the east coast of the U.S. in June 1942?
11. What state celebrates each June 11 as King Kamehameha I Day?
12. What president died at age eighty-five on June 28, 1836, and was buried at his Virginia estate, Montpelier?
13. What frightfully expensive movie epic with Elizabeth Taylor and Richard Burton premiered June 12, 1963? (Hint: pyramids)
14. What egotistical boxing champ was fined for draft evasion on June 20, 1967?
15. On June 7, 1968, Sirhan Sirhan was arrested for the assassination of what Democratic presidential candidate?

June *(answers)*

1. Christopher Reeve, best known for playing Superman in several movies
2. Benjamin Franklin, who flew his kite in a thunderstorm, proving that lightning is electricity
3. Max Factor
4. Baseball cards
5. Bunker Hill
6. West Virginia, which had broken from (surprise!) Virginia
7. John Tyler, first president to wed while holding that office; his wife Julia bore him seven children.
8. The Pilgrims, who had sailed on the original *Mayflower*
9. The Statue of Liberty
10. Germany; they were captured and executed.
11. Hawaii
12. James Madison
13. *Cleopatra*
14. Muhammad Ali, or Cassius Clay, if you like
15. Robert F. Kennedy

☆ July

1. What fateful Civil War battle in Pennsylvania took place July 1–3, 1863?
2. What was distinctive about the new U.S. flag flown July 4, 1960?
3. What state capital has a Lincoln Fest every July?
4. What great American author lived at Walden Pond beginning in July 1845?
5. What historic city hosts the Freedom Festival every July?
6. What notorious (and very young) killer was gunned down by Pat Garrett on July 14, 1881?
7. What two early presidents both died on July 4, 1826?
8. What famous statesman was killed in a duel with Aaron Burr on July 11, 1804?
9. What assassinated president's son was present when President James Garfield was assassinated July 2, 1881?
10. In July 1996, what two California brothers were given life sentences for murdering their wealthy parents?
11. In July 1995 the Walt Disney Company acquired what TV network for nineteen billion dollars?
12. What female aviator mysteriously disappeared over the Pacific Ocean on July 2, 1937?
13. What detested federal tax was instituted in July 1862?
14. Who walked near the Sea of Tranquility on July 20, 1969?
15. In July 1995 what South Carolina mother was found guilty of drowning her two sons in a lake?

July *(answers)*

1. Gettysburg
2. It was the first to have fifty stars.
3. Springfield, Illinois, where Lincoln had served in the state legislature
4. Henry David Thoreau, who wrote *Walden*
5. Philadelphia
6. Billy the Kid
7. John Adams, the second president, and Thomas Jefferson, the third
8. Alexander Hamilton
9. Abraham Lincoln's son Robert; he must have wondered if he was a jinx.
10. Lyle and Erik Menendez
11. ABC
12. Amelia Earhart
13. The income tax
14. The first men on the moon, Neil Armstrong and Buzz Aldrin
15. Susan Smith

☆ August

1. What lethal item did Paul Tibbets deliver to Hiroshima, Japan, on August 6, 1945?
2. What was the significance of Virginia Dare, born August 18, 1587, on an island off North Carolina?
3. What huge mountainside sculpture was begun in August 1927?
4. A national wood-carving championship is held each August in Grand Rapids, Minnesota. What less-than-delicate instruments are used in the carving?
5. What nonpro baseball league has its world series each August in Williamsport, Pennsylvania?
6. New Haven's Connecticut Tennis Stadium is host to what international tournament each August?
7. When the British sacked Washington, D.C., in August 1814, First Lady Dolley Madison saved which presidential portrait?
8. A telephone installed in Milwaukee's city hall in August 1896 had what new (and circular) feature?
9. What federal count, done every ten years, began in August 1790?
10. What amazing (and profitable) fluid did Edwin Drake discover in Pennsylvania in August 1859?
11. What military medal, awarded to men wounded in battle, was first bestowed in August 1782?
12. What long-lived, frizzy-haired comic strip girl made her debut in August 1924? (Hint: Arf!)
13. What head of a detective agency arrested notorious Confederate spy Rose Greenhow in July 1861?
14. On August 18, 1988, presidential candidate George Bush said, "Read my lips," followed by what three words?
15. What Deep South state celebrates August 30 as Huey Long Day? (Hint: crawfish)

August *(answers)*

1. The atomic bomb
2. She was the first white child born in America.
3. Mount Rushmore in South Dakota, the Four Presidents, sculpted by Gutzon Borglum
4. Chain saws
5. Little League; Williamsport is the headquarters of Little League.
6. The Volvo International
7. George Washington's
8. A dial
9. The Federal Census
10. Petroleum; it was America's first oil strike.
11. The Purple Heart
12. "Little Orphan Annie," drawn by Harold Gray, one of the most popular comic strips of all time
13. Allan Pinkerton; Greenhow was a Washington socialite who was a master at prying information out of federal bigwigs.
14. "No new taxes." While president, he broke that promise, which probably played a part in his defeat in 1992.
15. Louisiana, which Long served as both governor and senator

☆ September

1. Margaret Gorman was the first winner of what famous beauty pageant, first held in September 1921?
2. In September 1777 what metal object was removed from Philadelphia and hidden in a church in Allentown, Pennsylvania?
3. At what Virginia site were the ruins of an English fort from the 1600s discovered in September 1996?
4. What kidnapped heiress was captured by FBI agents in September 1975?
5. What notable military surrender occurred on September 2, 1945?
6. What famous pledge appeared in the *Youth Companion* on September 8, 1892?
7. What poem (later an anthem) was written by Francis Scott Key on September 14, 1814?
8. What renowned traitor of the Revolutionary War was burned in two-faced effigy on September 30, 1780?
9. What famous frontiersman (who did *not* wear a coonskin cap) died in September 1820 after gorging on sweet potatoes?
10. What Republican senator resigned in September 1995 after his scandalous diary became public knowledge?
11. What assassinated president's son was present when President William McKinley was assassinated on September 6, 1901?
12. The submarine *Nautilus*, commissioned in September 1954, was the first to be powered by what source?
13. What gigantic auto company was founded by William C. Durant in September 1908?
14. What Confederate leader's birthday is celebrated on the first Sunday in September?
15. What state with a large Indian population celebrates Cherokee Strip Day on September 16?

September *(answers)*

1. Miss America; the pageant is still held every September in Atlantic City.
2. The Liberty Bell
3. Jamestown, site of the 1607 settlement; never before had anyone seen actual pieces of the original fort.
4. Patty Hearst, who had been kidnapped by the Symbionese Liberation Army in 1974
5. Japan surrendered to the U.S.; this was V-J Day.
6. The Pledge of Allegiance to the Flag
7. "The Star-Spangled Banner," which Key wrote after watching the British bombard a fort in Baltimore
8. Benedict Arnold
9. Daniel Boone
10. Bob Packwood
11. Abraham Lincoln's son Robert, who must have believed he was a jinx
12. Nuclear power
13. General Motors
14. Confederate president Jefferson Davis, who was born in Kentucky
15. Oklahoma

☆ October

1. Fearing nuclear attack, what did President Kennedy tell the country in October 1961 that a "prudent family" should build for itself?
2. On October 19, 1968, what former First Lady married Greek tycoon Aristotle Onassis on his private island Skorpios?
3. What powerful federal body begins its session on the first Monday in October?
4. In what gulf coast state could you attend Shrimporee every October?
5. What prickly metal item, much used by farmers, was patented by Joseph Glidden in October 1783?
6. What imposing New York statue was officially dedicated on October 28, 1886?
7. What great city fire of October 8, 1871, was supposed to have been started by a lantern kicked over by Mrs. O'Leary's cow?
8. The town of Independence, Kansas, has a Neewollah festival in October. What holiday is being celebrated?
9. What major sports event was going on when an earthquake struck San Francisco in October 1989?
10. What troubled period of history began on "Black Tuesday" in October 1929?
11. What midwestern state with a large Scandinavian population celebrates Leif Eriksson Day on October 10?
12. What nation's forces raided the small town of St. Albans, Vermont, on October 19, 1864, moving in from Canada? (Hint: gray uniforms)
13. What former California governor entered the Democratic presidential race in October 1992, claiming he would accept no contribution larger than one hundred dollars?
14. The cornerstone for what famous Washington home was laid on October 13, 1792?
15. The clothing item known as a "slide fastener" went on sale in October 1914. By what name do we know this common item?

October *(answers)*

1. A fallout shelter
2. Jackie Kennedy
3. The Supreme Court
4. Texas, at Aransas Pass on the coast
5. Barbed wire
6. The Statue of Liberty
7. The Great Chicago Fire (which definitely happened, even if the cow story isn't true)
8. Halloween—which, spelled backwards, is Neewollah (Americans are a clever people, yes?)
9. The World Series
10. The Great Depression; "Black Tuesday" was October 29, 1929.
11. Minnesota; Eriksson was a Viking, and the Vikings were Scandinavian, so . . .
12. The Confederacy; they managed to rob a bank in the process.
13. Edmund "Jerry" Brown, who did not get the Democratic nomination
14. The White House
15. The zipper

☆ November

1. What Democratic president was assassinated in Dallas, Texas, in November 1963?
2. What state celebrates Will Rogers Day on November 4?
3. What famous American document was signed in the Provincetown, Massachusetts, harbor on November 11, 1620?
4. What famous (and very short) speech did President Lincoln deliver on November 19, 1863?
5. In November 1883 what divided the country into four sections?
6. What militant atheist was the guest on the first *Donahue* show on November 6, 1967?
7. The November 21, 1980, episode of what nighttime soap was one of the top-rated TV shows of all time? (Hint: Who shot . . . ?)
8. In November 1994, what former president revealed he had Alzheimer's disease?
9. What is the significance of the first Tuesday after the first Monday in November?
10. In what Muslim nation were sixty-three Americans taken hostage in November 1979?
11. All Saints' Day is celebrated November 1 in what Deep South state?
12. What jumped from twenty-nine cents to thirty-two cents in November 1994?
13. What Wisconsin serial killer was killed by a fellow prisoner in November 1994?
14. What day in November is generally the busiest shopping day of the year?
15. In November 1994, what forty-five-year-old became the oldest man to win a boxing title?

November *(answers)*

1. John F. Kennedy
2. Oklahoma, Rogers' home state
3. The Mayflower Compact, drawn up by the Pilgrims; it was America's first written agreement on self-government.
4. The Gettysburg Address
5. The creation of four time zones; they were necessary because trains were now running coast to coast, and clocks needed to be synchronized.
6. Madalyn Murray O'Hair
7. *Dallas;* this was the episode when America learned who shot J. R. Ewing.
8. Ronald Reagan
9. It's Election Day.
10. Iran; this began one of the longest hostage crises in U.S. history.
11. Louisiana
12. The price of a stamp
13. Jeffrey Dahmer, who was serving fifteen life sentences
14. The Friday following Thanksgiving
15. George Foreman; he knocked out heavyweight champion Michael Moorer in the tenth round.

☆ December

1. What lofty D.C. memorial was finally completed on December 6, 1884, after 105 years of construction?
2. The Treaty of Ghent, signed in December 1814, ended what war between the U.S. and Britain?
3. What red "Tickle Me" doll was *the* Christmas toy in 1996?
4. Walter Williams died in December 1959 at the age of 117. He was the last surviving veteran of what war?
5. What offbeat singer and ukulele player married Miss Vicki on *The Tonight Show* in December 1969?
6. The classic Army-Navy Football Game is held in what historic city?
7. What general lived at Valley Forge, Pennsylvania, beginning in December 1777?
8. What southern state laid the groundwork for the Confederacy by passing the Ordinance of Secession in December 1860?
9. What president, dying on December 14, 1799, was the only president to die in the 1700s?
10. What inventor cut the world's first record by singing "Mary Had a Little Lamb" into his new machine?
11. What very "dry" period of American history ended officially on December 5, 1933?
12. What notorious attack occurred at 7:55 A.M. on December 7, 1941?
13. What type of commercial aired for the last time on December 31, 1970? (Hint: puff)
14. What was given to Barney Clark during an eight-hour operation in December 1982?
15. In December 1928 Admiral Richard Byrd established "Little America" in what remote (and chilly) location?

December *(answers)*

1. The Washington Monument
2. The War of 1812, which lasted longer than just 1812
3. Elmo
4. The Civil War
5. Tiny Tim, whose single hit song was his falsetto "Tiptoe Thru' the Tulips with Me"; he died in December 1996.
6. Philadelphia, the first Saturday in December
7. George Washington, along with his poorly supplied troops
8. South Carolina
9. George Washington
10. Thomas Edison; he did this on December 6, 1877.
11. Prohibition; there was (needless to say) a great deal of toasting on that day.
12. The Japanese attack on Pearl Harbor in Hawaii
13. Cigarette ads
14. An artificial heart
15. Antarctica

PART NINE

A Sense of Place

you are here

☆ The Name Game: Sources of States' Names

Do you know how *your* state got its name? Some people do, some don't. It's a fascinating subject because the states' names reflect the diversity of the American experience—the Indians, English settlers, French settlers, Polynesians. One state is even named for a president.

1. Which state on the Pacific coast is named for a U.S. president?
2. What state, which originally called itself Kanawha, was a breakaway from a state that had joined the Confederacy?
3. What western state, the site of Yellowstone Park, was named for a river valley in Pennsylvania?
4. What two states were named for the English king Charles I?
5. What popular vacation state's name is from the Spanish word for "flowery"?
6. Which state (one that shares its name with a river) has a name meaning "big river"?
7. What state with a large Indian population takes its name from an Indian word meaning "red man"?
8. What tiny state was named for a small Greek island?
9. What huge state (whose state motto is "Friendship") is named for the Indian word for friend?
10. What state with a lot of French place names was named for the French king Louis XIV?
11. What large western state was named for a mythical land in an old Spanish novel?
12. What large state takes its name from the Eskimo word meaning "great lands"?
13. What southwestern state is named for the country it borders?

The Name Game: Sources of States' Names
(answers)

1. Washington, naturally; the area was originally named Columbia, by the way.
2. West Virginia, which until 1862 was part of Virginia
3. Wyoming, named for the Wyoming Valley in Pennsylvania
4. North Carolina and South Carolina, which were originally one colony; the Latin form of the name *Charles* is *Carolus.*
5. Florida; the Spanish explorer Ponce de Leon named it *Pascua Florida* in 1513. The name means "flowery Easter," which was the day he named it.
6. Mississippi
7. Oklahoma; the word is Choctaw.
8. Rhode Island, named for the island of Rhodes
9. Texas, which in old days was also spelled Texias, Tejas, and Teysas
10. Louisiana, of course
11. California, a name that first appeared in 1510
12. Alaska, from the Eskimo (or Aleut) word *alakshak*
13. New Mexico

14. What mountainous New England state is named for the French words meaning "green mountain"?
15. What midwestern state with thousands of lakes has a name meaning "land of sky blue waters"?
16. What state's name means "land of Indians"?
17. What southern state, settled by the English in 1732, was named for the king of England at that time?
18. What state on the Atlantic was named for the unmarried queen of England?
19. What state, famous for its dairy farms, takes its name from the Indian word for "grassy place"?
20. What mountainous state, which shares its name with a river, has the Spanish name meaning "red"?
21. What large western state's name is the Spanish word for "mountainous"?
22. The Indian word for "flat river" is the name of what very flat state?
23. What tiny state on the east coast was named for a governor of Virginia?
24. The District of Columbia was named for what famous explorer?

☆ State Symbols

All fifty states have an official state flower and state bird. Most have gone way beyond that and have state reptiles, state beverages, etc. We can't possibly cover all of them here, but you'll find some of the more amusing state symbols in this section.

1. What New England state has the sperm whale as its state animal?
2. Alabama's state bird is the yellowhammer. What sort of bird is it?
3. Virginia's state beverage is what all-natural product?

14. Vermont, from the French *vert* (green) and *mont* (mountain)
15. Minnesota; the name is from the Sioux Indians.
16. Indiana, naturally
17. Georgia, named for King George II
18. Virginia, named for Queen Elizabeth I, who was widely known as the Virgin Queen
19. Wisconsin
20. Colorado
21. Montana
22. Nebraska
23. Delaware, named for Lord De La Warr, an early governor of Virginia
24. Christopher Columbus, of course (Did anyone miss this?)

State Symbols *(answers)*

1. Connecticut (A case where the state animal is almost as big as the state itself.)
2. It's a species of woodpecker known (by bird experts) as the yellow-shafted flicker; oddly, it's the one species of woodpecker that spends more time on the ground than in trees.
3. Milk

4. Wisconsin's state insect is able to produce food. What is it?
5. Mississippi's state water mammal is what intelligent creature?
6. Holly is not only a familiar Christmas symbol but also the state tree of what tiny eastern state?
7. The desert tortoise is the official reptile of what large western state?
8. New York's state flower, chosen by its schoolchildren, is what familiar garden flower?
9. The Appaloosa is the official horse of what mountainous western state? (Hint: potato)
10. What New England state's official rock is the Roxbury pudding stone?
11. What gulf coast state has (appropriately) the pelican as the state bird and the crawfish as the state crustacean?
12. What common red bird of the backyard is the favorite choice for state bird?
13. The willow ptarmigan, a bird of snowy regions, is the state bird of what large state?
14. What southwestern state has the frijole and the chili as its state vegetables?
15. The humuhumunukunukuapuaa is the state fish of what island state?
16. The American buffalo is the state animal of what two plains states (which formerly had thousands of buffalo)?
17. The Baltimore oriole is the appropriate state bird for what eastern state?
18. What drink (colored red) is the state beverage of Ohio?
19. What southern state's animal is the raccoon and its insects the ladybug and firefly? (Hint: music)
20. What southwestern state has the cactus wren as its bird and the saguaro cactus as its flower?
21. The Rocky Mountain bighorn sheep is the animal for what state?

4. The honeybee
5. The porpoise
6. Delaware
7. California
8. The rose
9. Idaho
10. Massachusetts (If you knew this, consider yourself an M.T., Master of Trivia. Or maybe you live in Massachusetts. . . .)
11. Louisiana
12. The cardinal; seven states have it as the state bird.
13. Alaska, where else?
14. New Mexico
15. Hawaii, naturally (If you can't pronounce the name of this fish, you are not alone.)
16. Both Kansas and Oklahoma
17. Maryland
18. Tomato juice
19. Tennessee's (The people who chose the raccoon clearly had never had one get into their garbage cans.)
20. Arizona
21. Colorado

22. Orange juice is the state beverage for what state? (Hint: *not* California)
23. The state flower of Kentucky is pretty but makes many people sneeze. What is it?
24. The moose is the official animal for what woodsy New England state?
25. Massachusetts's state drink is what type of juice? (Hint: Thanksgiving)
26. Minnesota's state bird is what wild-voiced water creature?
27. Although it doesn't go "Beep! Beep!" it is New Mexico's state bird. What?
28. The Scotch bonnet, a symbol for North Carolina, is what type of item? (No, *not* a hat.)
29. The mountain boomer, a symbol for Oklahoma, is what type of creature?
30. What busy water creature is Oregon's state animal?
31. Rhode Island's state bird is what appropriately named breed of chicken?
32. The shag is the official dance of what southern state? (Hint: It could have been the Charleston.)
33. South Dakota has what howling creature as its state animal?
34. What spicy item is, appropriately, the state dish of Texas?
35. Utah has no coastline, but its state bird is what saltwater bird?

☆ Three "Golden" Places

1. The Pittsburgh site where the Monongahela and Allegheny Rivers flow together to form the Ohio River is called what?
2. The world's tallest suspension bridge, connecting San Francisco with Marin County, is what?
3. When Spain claimed possession of the Golden Isles of Guale in the 1500s, which future state were they looking at?

22. Florida
23. Goldenrod
24. Maine
25. Cranberry
26. The loon
27. The roadrunner, which bears a *slight* resemblance to the one in the cartoons
28. A seashell
29. A lizard, also known as the collared lizard; it's the state reptile.
30. The beaver
31. The Rhode Island red
32. South Carolina
33. The coyote
34. Chili
35. The seagull—which lives on lakes and rivers as well as on seas

Three "Golden" Places *(answers)*

1. The Golden Triangle
2. The Golden Gate Bridge
3. Georgia; several of the state's islands are still called the Golden Isles.

☆ Great and Grand and Big Places

Maybe size impresses us easily. We see a river, lake, valley, whatever, and give it a name beginning with "Grand" or "Big" or "Great." In some cases, the people who come later understand how the place got its name. And in other cases, they scratch their heads and wonder, "What's *grand* about this place?"

1. The bodies of water known as Huron, Ontario, Michigan, Erie, and Superior are collectively known as what?
2. What mountainous national park in Tennessee and North Carolina is the most visited park in the U.S.?
3. The greatest source of water power in the U.S. is what "grand" dam in the Northwest?
4. If you see Bright Angel Point, Grandview Point, and Desert View, what Arizona national park are you visiting?
5. The Grand Canyon of the South is in what mountainous state? (Hint: horses)
6. Grand Caverns in Virginia once served as barracks for what Confederate general's troops?
7. What enormous swamp, straddling the border of North Carolina and Virginia, was explored by George Washington in the 1760s? (Hint: has a gloomy name)
8. What great river of the West (which shares its name with a state) was formerly called the Grand River?
9. What Texas metropolis is often referred to as "Big D"?
10. What shallow lake in Utah is twice as salty as the ocean?
11. Where was the Republic of the Rio Grande?
12. What much-loved singer and actress was born Frances Gumm in Grand Rapids, Minnesota? (Hint: Oz)
13. What appropriately named national park is at a major bend in the Rio Grande river in Texas?
14. What national park in western Wyoming has a name meaning "large bosom"?
15. The Continental Divide also goes by what name?

Great and Grand and Big Places *(answers)*

1. The Great Lakes, of course
2. Great Smoky Mountains
3. Grand Coulee
4. The Grand Canyon
5. Kentucky
6. Thomas "Stonewall" Jackson's, during the Civil War
7. The Great Dismal Swamp
8. The Colorado
9. Dallas
10. The Great Salt Lake, naturally
11. Around Laredo, Texas; a large area along the river was for several years a disputed "no man's land."
12. Judy Garland
13. Big Bend
14. Grand Teton
15. The Great Divide

16. What enormous ten-thousand-foot mountain in Colorado has a fifty-square-mile area at its summit?
17. What appropriately named Michigan city sits on the Grand River?
18. In northern Wyoming, a river and mountain range are both named for a type of wild sheep. What?
19. Big Diomede (along with Little Diomede) is a chilly island between the U.S. and what nation?
20. What prickly name is given to the wilderness area northeast of Houston, Texas?
21. Big Round Top was a key battle site in what famous Civil War battle fought in Pennsylvania?
22. What river, named for an Indian tribe, forms the boundary between Iowa and South Dakota?
23. The familiar trail that colonial settlers followed from Pennsylvania south to Virginia and North Carolina was called what?
24. Before Lewis and Clark began exploring America's West, what general name did Americans give to all land west of the Mississippi River?

☆ Counting the Counties

Every state has its oddly named places, and this is nowhere more true than in the names of counties. Given a few counties, see if you can name the state.

1. Otter Tail, Blue Earth, Big Stone, Crow Wing, Yellow Medicine (a Great Lakes state)
2. Tuscaloosa, Tallapoosa, Coosa, Montgomery, Limestone (a southern state)
3. Calaveras, Contra Costa, El Dorado, Mendocino, San Bernardino (a western state)
4. St. Bernard, St. Landry, St. John the Baptist, St. Helena, St. Tammany (a Deep South state)

16. Grand Mesa
17. Grand Rapids
18. Bighorn
19. Russia; both the Diomedes are in the Bering Strait between Russia and Alaska.
20. Big Thicket
21. Gettysburg
22. The Big Sioux
23. The Great Wagon Road; it was the main path that German and Scotch-Irish settlers followed as they settled the South.
24. The Great American Desert

Counting the Counties *(answers)*

1. Minnesota
2. Alabama
3. California
4. Louisiana (Technically, Louisiana has *no* counties—the divisions are called *parishes.*)

5. Cattaraugus, Saratoga, Schenectady, Wyoming, Onondaga (a northeastern state)
6. Box Elder, Sanpete, Wasatch, Carbon, Salt Lake (a western state)
7. Eau Claire, Fond du Lac, Green Lake, Door, Iron (a Great Lakes state)
8. Hernando, De Soto, Indian River, Manatee, Okeechobee (a southern state)
9. Rio Arriba, Guadalupe, Los Alamos, Dona Ana, Santa Fe (a southwestern state)
10. Kankakee, Rock Island, Winnebago, Jo Daviess, Bureau (a Great Lakes state)
11. Berks, Bucks, Beaver, Lackawanna, Susquehanna (a mid-Atlantic state)
12. Apache, Cochise, Mohave, Navajo, Yavapai (a southwestern state)
13. Androscoggin, Kennebec, Penobscot, Sagadahoc, Piscataquis (a New England state)
14. Licking, Defiance, Muskingum, Pickaway, Ashtabula (a Great Lakes state)
15. Jeff Davis, Jim Hogg, Jim Wells, Live Oak, Palo Pinto (a western state)
16. Charles City, James City, Appomattox, Isle of Wight, Spotsylvania (a southern state)
17. Lewis and Clark, Beaverhead, Powder River, Musselshell, Sweet Grass (a far western state)
    . . . and in case you were wondering:
    - California has the biggest county (San Bernardino, twenty thousand square miles)
    - Texas is the state with the most counties (254)
    - Alaska has no counties
    - Delaware has the next fewest (3)
    - The most common name for a county is (surprise!) Washington (found in thirty-one states).

5. New York
6. Utah
7. Wisconsin
8. Florida
9. New Mexico
10. Illinois
11. Pennsylvania
12. Arizona
13. Maine
14. Ohio
15. Texas
16. Virginia (Yes, there really is a Charles City County.)
17. Montana

☆ The Name Game: Sources of States' Names (Part 2)

1. What is the only state with a Polynesian name?
2. What southern state takes its name from the word for Cherokee Indian villages? (Hint: music)
3. What watery state's name is Chippewa for "big water"?
4. What very short state name is an Indian word meaning "fine river"?
5. What state, originally named New Amsterdam, was named for a county in England?
6. What midwestern state's name is the Indian word meaning "warriors"?
7. What state on the Pacific has a name that no one knows the origin of?
8. What southwestern state's Pima Indian name means "little spring place"?
9. What northeastern state was named for its founder, a leader of the Quakers in England?
10. What two states' common name is the Sioux word meaning "friend" or "ally"?
11. What New England state with a one-syllable name was named for a province in France?
12. What state, noted for its gambling, has a Spanish name meaning "snowclad"?
13. What state on the Chesapeake Bay was named for the wife of a king of England?
14. What northeastern state is named after a small island off the coast of England (and famous for its dairy cows)?
15. What prairie state's short name is Indian for "beautiful land"?
16. What New England state (which shares its name with a river) has a Mohican name meaning "long river place"?
17. What state with a large Mormon population takes its name from a Navajo word?

The Name Game: Sources of States' Names (Part 2) *(answers)*

1. Hawaii; the name may mean "homeland."
2. Tennessee, from the Cherokee word *tanasi*
3. Michigan, from the Indian words *michi gama.*
4. Ohio, which is also the name of a major river
5. New York, named for old York in northeastern England
6. Illinois, from the Algonquin Indian word *illini*
7. Oregon; the name may be from an Indian word, but no one is sure.
8. Arizona
9. Pennsylvania, named for founder William Penn; Pennsylvania means "Penn's woodlands."
10. North and South Dakota
11. Maine
12. Nevada
13. Maryland, named for King Charles I's wife, Henrietta Maria
14. New Jersey, named for the island of Jersey
15. Iowa
16. Connecticut
17. Utah, probably from the Navajo word *ute*

18. The Sioux word for "south wind people" is the name for what flat, windy state?
19. What state's name is the Algonquin word for "river of big canoes"? (Hint: Mark Twain)
20. The Indian word for "gem of the mountains" is the name for what northwestern state?
21. What is the only New England state named for a place in old England?
22. What southern state is named for a branch of the Creek Indian tribe? (Hint: "Bear" Bryant)
23. The Indian word for "meadowland" is the name for what state famous for tobacco and horses?
24. What southern state's name is Indian for "downstream people"? (Hint: Ozarks)
25. The Indian word meaning "large hill place" is the name of what New England state? (Hint: Pilgrims)

18. Kansas
19. Missouri
20. Idaho, sometimes known as the Gem State
21. New Hampshire, named for the English county of Hampshire
22. Alabama, from the Indian word *alibamons*
23. Kentucky
24. Arkansas
25. Massachusetts

PART TEN

Breezing through History

☆ Purchases, Duels, Dictionaries: 1800 to 1809

1. What famous purchase, doubling the size of the U.S., took place April 30, 1803?
2. In March 1807, what leader signed a bill making the importation of slaves illegal?
3. Who were the two famous leaders of the Corps of Discovery that started up the Missouri River in 1804?
4. In a famous duel July 11, 1804, who shot and killed Alexander Hamilton?
5. When Congress moved to its permanent home in D.C. in 1800, what Pennsylvania city did they move from?
6. What abolitionist fanatic, executed in 1859, was born in Torrington, Connecticut, in 1800?
7. The U.S. Military Academy was established in 1802 at what site in New York state?
8. What famous D.C. institution, which has a copy of every book printed in the U.S., was founded in 1800?
9. Who published his first dictionary in 1806?
10. The federal post at Fort Dearborn on Lake Michigan, founded in 1803, later became what metropolis?

☆ Wars, National Anthems, Ships: The 1810s

1. It was called the War of 1812, but what year did it end?
2. What future U.S. president (nicknamed "Old Hickory") was an important leader in the First Seminole War in 1817?
3. What future state, a vacation paradise, did the U.S. obtain from Spain in 1819?
4. For helping in the 1814 Battle of New Orleans, what famous Louisiana pirate was pardoned by President James Madison?

Purchases, Duels, Dictionaries: 1800 to 1809
(answers)

1. The Louisiana Purchase
2. Thomas Jefferson
3. Lewis and Clark
4. Aaron Burr
5. Philadelphia
6. John Brown, famed for his ill-fated raid on the Harpers Ferry arsenal
7. West Point
8. The Library of Congress
9. Noah Webster
10. Chicago

Wars, National Anthems, Ships: The 1810s
(answers)

1. 1814
2. Andrew Jackson
3. Florida
4. Jean Lafitte

5. The "star-spangled banner" that inspired Francis Scott Key to write his poem in 1814 had how many stars?
6. What frontiersman, who died at the Alamo, had fought with Andrew Jackson in the Creek War of 1814?
7. What war was dubbed "Mr. Madison's War"?
8. What crop began to be cultivated in Dennis, Massachusetts, in 1816? (Hint: Thanksgiving)
9. What key American financial institution opened in 1817? (Hint: Wall Street)
10. The ship *Savannah* was the first vessel to cross the Atlantic using what energy source?

☆ Elections, Textbooks, New Religions: The 1820s

1. What president made a famous 1823 proclamation, telling European nations not to meddle in American affairs?
2. Andrew Jackson won the popular vote in the 1824 election, but what New Englander (and son of a president) became president?
3. The 1827 book *Tamerlane and Other Poems* was the first book by what poet and horror story master?
4. What New England state didn't achieve statehood until 1820, even though it was settled in the 1600s?
5. What religious sect, usually associated with Utah, began in 1820 in Palmyra, New York?
6. What huge territory (later a state) did President Andrew Jackson try to buy from Mexico in 1829?
7. What sort of Americans began immigrating to the British colony of Sierra Leone in 1820?
8. What ever-popular series of reading textbooks began publication in 1826?

5. Fifteen, for there were fifteen states at that time; it had fifteen stripes also.
6. Davy Crockett
7. The War of 1812, when James Madison was president
8. Cranberries; more specifically, they began to be cultivated *commercially* at that time.
9. The New York Stock Exchange
10. Steam

Elections, Textbooks, New Religions: The 1820s
(answers)

1. James Monroe; the proclamation is known as the Monroe Doctrine.
2. John Quincy Adams, who won over the vote in the Congress
3. Edgar Allan Poe
4. Maine
5. The Mormons, founded by Joseph Smith
6. Texas; Mexico refused at that time.
7. Blacks; they were free blacks, part of the first organized immigration of black Americans to Africa.
8. *McGuffey's Readers*

9. What was congressional leader Henry Clay's reward for helping John Quincy Adams win the 1824 presidential election?
10. Los Angeles's oldest house, built in 1820, was damaged by what natural phenomenon?

☆ Rebellions, Inventions, Resignations: The 1830s

1. What large area (and future state) declared its freedom from Mexico in 1835?
2. Davy Crockett was at what infamous battle site on March 6, 1836?
3. In 1832 John C. Calhoun became the first politician in what post to resign?
4. In 1835 what famous leader was made commander of the Texan army?
5. What new (and nonedible) item did New York's Delmonico Restaurant offer its customers, beginning in 1836?
6. What state was settled by five Indian tribes that were forced out of the eastern U.S. beginning in 1830?
7. Nat Turner led a rebellion of what type of people in 1831?
8. What amazing communications invention did Samuel Morse spring on the world in 1835?
9. What religious group settled at Nauvoo, Illinois, in 1839, before later moving on to Utah?
10. Abner Doubleday of New York codified the rules for what great American sport?

9. Adams made him secretary of state. Historians refer to this as the "Corrupt Bargain."
10. An earthquake, what else?

Rebellions, Inventions, Resignations: The 1830s
(answers)

1. Texas
2. The Alamo (Remember?)
3. Vice president
4. Sam Houston
5. Printed menus
6. Oklahoma, originally known as the Indian Territory
7. Slaves; his band killed 57 whites in Virginia.
8. The telegraph
9. The Mormons
10. Baseball

☆ Tippecanoe, Gold Rushes, Walden Pond: The 1840s

1. What tragic 1840s event in Ireland sent many Irish off to America?
2. What large nation voted to become a state of the U.S. in 1845?
3. What future U.S. state established itself in 1849 as the State of Deseret? (Hint: Mormons)
4. What "silicon" city was California's first capital, beginning in 1849?
5. What war began under President James K. Polk and General Zachary Taylor in 1846?
6. What name was given to the three-hundred-mile-long strip of California land that precipitated gold fever in the 1840s?
7. What large Protestant denomination split into Southern and Northern sections over the issue of slavery in 1844?
8. What great author lived at Walden Pond from July 1845 to September 1847?
9. What president suffered such an executive burnout that he died three months after leaving office in 1849?
10. What president, known as "Tippecanoe," died in 1841 after only one month in office?

☆ Oil, Debates, Literary Classics: The 1850s

1. What Asian nation was opened to U.S. trade by Commodore Perry in 1853? (Hint: JVC)
2. What famous political debates took place in Illinois in 1858?
3. What famous armored car company was founded in 1852 to carry gold and other valuables?

Tippecanoe, Gold Rushes, Walden Pond: The 1840s *(answers)*

1. The potato famine, causing widespread starvation
2. The Republic of Texas
3. Utah
4. San Jose
5. The Mexican War
6. The Mother Lode
7. The Baptists
8. Henry David Thoreau, author of *Walden, or, Life in the Woods*
9. James K. Polk
10. William Henry Harrison, who was succeeded by Vice President John Tyler. ("Tippecanoe and Tyler, Too")

Oil, Debates, Literary Classics: The 1850s *(answers)*

1. Japan
2. The debates between Abraham Lincoln and Stephen Douglas
3. Wells Fargo

4. What best-selling antislavery novel was published in 1852?

5. What world-changing industry began at Titusville, Pennsylvania, in 1859?

6. The purpose of San Jacinto Clubs, formed in the 1850s, were to promote what Texas hero as a presidential candidate?

7. What classic novel about a whale was published in 1851?

8. The Comstock Lode, containing both gold and silver, was discovered in 1859 in what state?

9. What organization, now noted for teaching swimming, was founded in 1851?

10. John Frémont became the first presidential candidate of what major political party in 1856?

☆ Secession, Impeachment, Generals: The 1860s

1. What fateful battle was fought in July 1863 in Pennsylvania?

2. What president never appeared at his 1865 impeachment trial?

3. What inventor's lock, introduced around 1860, was noted for its small and flat key?

4. What southern state laid the groundwork for the Confederacy by passing the Ordinance of Secession in December 1860?

5. What momentous step did twenty-six counties of western Virginia take in 1861?

6. What type of flavoring did the first chewing gum, introduced in 1869, have?

7. What major candidate in the 1860 presidential election was not even on the ballot in ten southern states?

8. What large territory (later a state) was purchased from Russia in 1867?

4. Harriet Beecher Stowe's *Uncle Tom's Cabin*
5. Petroleum; Edwin Drake drilled the first oil well in that year.
6. Sam Houston
7. Herman Melville's *Moby Dick*
8. Nevada
9. The Young Men's Christian Association, the YMCA
10. The Republicans

Secession, Impeachment, Generals: The 1860s
(answers)

1. Gettysburg, a key Union victory in the Civil War
2. President Andrew Johnson
3. Linus Yale's, who also introduced the combination lock
4. South Carolina
5. They voted to break away to form the new state of West Virginia.
6. None
7. Abraham Lincoln, who won
8. Alaska

9. Jefferson Davis took office as president of what new nation in 1861?
10. What Georgia city (later the state capital) was destroyed by Union general Sherman in his 1864 "March to the Sea"?

☆ Dime Stores, Massacres, Mark Twain: The 1870s

1. What general met his match at Little Bighorn in Montana on June 25, 1876?
2. What cleaning device did Melvin Reuben Bissell introduce in 1876?
3. What Chicago shoe salesman became a world-famous evangelist in the 1870s?
4. What great city burned in 1871 at the rate of about sixty-five acres per hour?
5. What novel type of orange (now one of the most popular varieties) was introduced into California in 1873?
6. What deaf inventor patented the phonograph in 1878?
7. What famous five-and-dime store opened in 1879 in Utica, New York?
8. What religious group, now known for its door-to-door evangelism, was started by Charles Taze Russell in 1872?
9. What nationwide celebration was staged in 1876?
10. What great American children's book was published by Mark Twain in 1876? (Hint: whitewashing a fence)

☆ Statues, Monuments, Tar Baby: The 1880s

1. What *very* large woman has been holding a torch in New York since 1886?
2. What major change in 1883 caused the U.S. to be divided into four sections? (Hint: clock)

9. The Confederate States of America
10. Atlanta—not a major city at that time, in spite of what you might guess by watching *Gone with the Wind*

Dime Stores, Massacres, Mark Twain: The 1870s (*answers*)

1. George Custer
2. The carpet sweeper
3. D. L. Moody, who founded Chicago's Moody Bible Institute
4. Chicago
5. The navel orange, which sprang from a genetic mutation in groves in Brazil
6. Thomas Edison
7. Woolworth's
8. The Jehovah's Witnesses
9. The nation's hundredth birthday, the centennial
10. *Tom Sawyer*

Statues, Monuments, Tar Baby: The 1880s (*answers*)

1. The Statue of Liberty
2. The creation of time zones

3. What future state, populated only by Indians, was opened for white settlement in 1889?
4. What was the actual purpose of the first air conditioner, built in 1880? (Hint: *not* cooling)
5. The Yankee from Hartford is the main character in what popular 1889 novel by Mark Twain?
6. What world-changing invention did Thomas Edison develop in 1889, using flexible film invented by George Eastman?
7. What famous New York City bridge opened in 1883?
8. What tall D.C. landmark, modeled on an Egyptian obelisk, was completed in 1885?
9. What plantation storyteller did Joel Chandler Harris introduce in his 1881 book? (Hint: Brer Rabbit)
10. What Christian group, famous for working with the urban poor, began work in the U.S. in 1880?

☆ Battleships, Poetry, Dime Novels: The 1890s

1. What war began after the U.S. battleship *Maine* was blown up in Havana, Cuba?
2. Who was the last president to be born in the nineteenth century? (Hint: general)
3. What very shy woman poet published a few collections of her poems in the 1890s?
4. What Asian country was the focus of the U.S. Open Door Policy of 1899?
5. What did H. S. Thompson's Chicago eating establishment, which opened in 1891, *not* have?
6. What cheap type of detective and adventure novels were popular in the 1890s?

3. Oklahoma, called the Indian Territory at the time
4. Dehumidifying air and inhibiting growth of bacteria; the unit was in a brewery in Alexandria, Virginia.
5. *A Connecticut Yankee in King Arthur's Court*
6. The motion picture
7. The Brooklyn Bridge
8. The Washington Monument, which took thirty-six years to build
9. Uncle Remus
10. The Salvation Army, which had already been active in England

Battleships, Poetry, Dime Novels: The 1890s
(answers)

1. The Spanish-American War, which began in 1898
2. Dwight Eisenhower, born in 1890
3. Emily Dickinson
4. China; the U.S. wanted to open it as an international market.
5. Waiters; Thompson decided he could offer lower prices by having self-service—the nation's first cafeteria.
6. Dime novels

7. What new ride, introduced at the Chicago World's Fair in 1893, was 280 feet high with 36 cars holding 40 people each?

8. What popular indoor team sport was invented in 1895 by William Morgan at a Massachusetts YMCA?

9. What five-borough metropolis came into existence in 1898?

10. What valuable substance was discovered in Alaska in 1896?

7. The Ferris wheel
8. Volleyball
9. New York City, with the merger of Manhattan, Brooklyn, the Bronx, Queens, and Staten Island
10. Gold, leading to the Klondike Gold Rush

PART ELEVEN

The Mighty Dollar

☆ Pitching Power: Advertising in America

1. What dough company claims that "Nothin' says lovin' like somethin' from the oven"?
2. What fast-food chain told people "You deserve a break today"?
3. What athletic shoes should you buy "Because life is not a spectator sport"?
4. What handsome actor pitched Chaz cologne and Close-Up toothpaste before becoming a Hawaii private eye?
5. What federal agency, known as the FTC, checks on claims made by advertisers?
6. What vegetable company logo could you see—fifty-five feet tall—in Blue Earth, Minnesota? (Hint: Ho ho ho)
7. What breakfast cereal calls itself "The Breakfast of Champions"?
8. Leo the Lion is the symbol of what major Hollywood movie studio?
9. What oil company uses a flying red horse as its symbol?
10. What company, known for soaps and other household items, tops the U.S. in money spent on advertising?
11. What "pocketed" animal is the logo for Pocket Books?
12. What hair product used the slogan "A little dab'll do ya"?
13. The American Advertising Museum is not in New York or California but in what northwestern state?
14. What coffee is supposed to be "Good to the last drop"?
15. According to the late John Cameron Swayze, what brand of watch "Takes a licking but keeps on ticking"?
16. What brand of breath mints claimed it was "Two, two, two mints in one"?
17. Josephine the plumber was the pitchwoman for what familiar home powder?

Pitching Power: Advertising in America *(answers)*

1. Pillsbury
2. McDonald's
3. Reebok
4. Tom Selleck, *Magnum, P.I.*
5. The Federal Trade Commission
6. The Jolly Green Giant, standing in Green Giant Park
7. Wheaties
8. Metro-Goldwyn-Mayer, MGM
9. Mobil
10. Procter and Gamble
11. A kangaroo
12. Brylcreem
13. Oregon, in the city of Portland
14. Maxwell House
15. Timex
16. Certs
17. Comet cleanser

18. What type of daytime TV series got its name from all the ads for household products?
19. What snow-white laundry detergent called itself "99 and $^{44}/_{100}$% Pure"?
20. According to TV ads, what federal horror produced Excedrin Headache No. 1040?
21. Among company logos, Mr. Peanut and Johnny Walker carry what object in their hands?
22. What Chattanooga tourist attraction has been advertised on billboards, birdhouses, and barn sides around the world?
23. In the 1970s "I can't believe I ate the whole thing" was the pitch line for what fizzy product?
24. What auto rental company says, "We try harder"?
25. What is the connection between Utah's Mount Ben Lomond and the Paramount movie company?

☆ Three Millionaires

1. What restored colonial city in Virginia was built mainly with the help of millionaire John D. Rockefeller?
2. James Stockdale and Pat Choate were vice presidential running mates for what millionaire candidate of the 1990s?
3. What reclusive millionaire, who died in 1976, piloted a flying boat known as the *Spruce Goose*?

18. Soap operas
19. Ivory Snow
20. A tax audit
21. A cane
22. Rock City
23. Alka-Seltzer
24. Avis
25. The mountain was the model for the mountain in Paramount's logo.

Three Millionaires *(answers)*

1. Williamsburg
2. Ross Perot, who ran for president in 1992 and 1996
3. Howard Hughes

☆ Business, American Style

President Calvin Coolidge claimed that "the business of America is business." Well, there *must* be something more to us than just business. But business and industry are fascinating subjects since they affect us every day, like it or not.

1. What has been America's top aircraft maker for thirty years?
2. What department store chain first marketed tires under the Allstate brand?
3. What insurance company's trademark came from a signature on the Declaration of Independence?
4. What chain of discount stores outranks all others in the Fortune 500 list?
5. What seafood restaurant chain has 29 percent of the market in the U.S.?
6. In 1982, what very old communications firm was acquired by MCI?
7. What TV network did the Disney company acquire in 1996?
8. Brewery giant Anheuser-Busch also owns what salty snack company?
9. What New England city, home to more than fifty insurance companies, is Insurance Town, U.S.A.?
10. What millionaire and presidential candidate founded Electronic Data Systems in 1962 after having worked for IBM?
11. Illinois's Morton Arboretum, a stunning collection of trees, is named for what common kitchen substance?
12. The elegant home Hillwood in D.C. is connected with what major breakfast food company?
13. What tire company did Charles Goodyear establish?
14. The Pittsburgh Symphony Orchestra performs in a hall named for what food company? (Hint: ketchup)

Business, American Style *(answers)*

1. Boeing ("If it's not Boeing, I'm not going.") As of December 1996, Boeing is even bigger, since it merged with McDonnel-Douglas.
2. Sears, which today owns Allstate Insurance (which followed in 1931)
3. John Hancock
4. Wal-Mart
5. Red Lobster
6. Western Union
7. ABC
8. Eagle Snacks (The two were a logical combination.)
9. Hartford, Connecticut
10. Ross Perot
11. Salt; to be specific, the money for the arboretum was given by the Morton Salt Company.
12. Post; the home was furnished with money from founder C. W. Post.
13. He didn't; the Goodyear Tire Company is named in his honor, since he invented durable rubber.
14. Heinz

15. What noted maker of collectible plates and coins is in Media, Pennsylvania?
16. Wealthy businessman Henry Flagler made one southern state a popular tourist destination by building hotels and railroads. Which state?
17. What associations, known as BBBs, protect consumers from unethical business practices?
18. You can tour the E-One factory in Florida. What sort of important vehicles are made there? (Hint: dalmatians)
19. After Dairy Queen, what is America's most profitable chain of ice cream stores? (Hint: hyphen)
20. Jani-King and ServiceMaster are America's biggest providers of what essential service?
21. What oil company, once known as Esso, then Enco, is the biggest in the U.S.?

☆ Money Matters

1. The $100 bill had Benjamin Franklin's picture on it. Whose picture is on the new $100 bill, issued in 1996?
2. What U.S. coin has a torch on its reverse side?
3. U.S. paper money is made of 25 percent linen and 75 percent of what other fiber?
4. All U.S. dollar coins since 1794 (except one) had what animal on them?
5. What words first appeared on U.S. coins in 1864?
6. What assassinated president's portrait appeared on a half-dollar coin in the 1960s?
7. What western city's U.S. mint turns out over 5 billion coins each year?
8. What historic coin-making operation can be toured in Philadelphia?
9. Which Cabinet department oversees the production of currency in the U.S.?
10. What distinction does Citibank of New York hold?

15. The Franklin Mint
16. Florida
17. Better Business Bureaus
18. Fire trucks
19. Baskin-Robbins
20. Commercial cleaning
21. Exxon (If you remember Esso, you're showing your age. . . .)

Money Matters *(answers)*

1. Benjamin Franklin's; you have to look closely to see the details in how the bill is redesigned.
2. The dime
3. Cotton
4. An eagle
5. In God We Trust
6. John F. Kennedy's
7. Denver's
8. The U.S. Mint
9. The Treasury, naturally
10. The largest bank (in assets) in the U.S.

11. What New England state coined its own money while it was an independent republic for fourteen years?
12. The Roman numeral for what year appears on the back of a one-dollar bill?
13. What item on a one-dollar bill has thirteen stars, thirteen stripes, thirteen arrows, thirteen olives, thirteen rows of stones, and a thirteen-letter motto?
14. What agency, known as the Fed, oversees the nation's banking system?
15. In 1786, what future president wisely proposed a decimal money system, with a dollar unit divided into ten silver pieces or a hundred copper pieces?
16. The first American mint was established in 1652 in what major colonial city?
17. What was radically different about the money used to pay Massachusetts soldiers in 1690? (Hint: billfold)
18. In 1834 Congress declared an official ratio of sixteen to one for what two metals?
19. What crop could be used in place of cash in the Virginia colony?
20. In 1900 the U.S. formally placed its money on what standard?
21. The "security thread" in the new $100 bill issued in 1996 will glow under what type of light?

☆ Lavish Spending

1. What federal agency can now be sued for up to $1 million for "reckless collection"?
2. What $92 million music museum opened in Cleveland, Ohio, in 1995?
3. What sporty car did Ford introduce in April 1964 for a price of $2,368?
4. What renowned western mine yielded more than $1 billion in gold and silver?

11. Vermont, which also ran its own postal service
12. 1776
13. The Great Seal of the U.S.
14. The Federal Reserve
15. Thomas Jefferson, who thought the old British system of pounds, shillings, etc. was too confusing
16. Boston
17. It was *paper* money, the first paper money in America, and quite radical at the time.
18. Gold (sixteen) to silver (one)—that is, one ounce of gold was worth sixteen times one ounce of silver. In a day of (relatively worthless) paper money, we forget how important these matters were in times past.
19. Tobacco; ministers in the colony were paid in tobacco instead of in gold.
20. Gold
21. Ultraviolet; the new hundred is the first of a new set of bills that are (supposedly) harder to counterfeit.

Lavish Spending *(answers)*

1. The Internal Revenue Service, as dictated by a law passed in 1996
2. The Rock and Roll Hall of Fame and Museum
3. The Mustang (How times—and prices—do change.)
4. The Comstock Lode in Nevada

5. What writer, famous for *The Call of the Wild,* was the first American author to earn $1 million?

6. What publishing tycoon backed out of the 1996 presidential race after spending $30 million of his own money?

7. What large chunk of land was purchased from Russia for the amount of $7.2 million?

8. What world-changing item (with wheels) went on sale in 1908 for $850?

9. What child star was making $300,000 per film during the Great Depression?

10. The city of Frederick, Maryland, was occupied by Gen. Jubal Early, who charged the residents a $200,000 ransom. In what war did this take place?

11. In 1898 the *New York Journal* offered a $50,000 reward for the capture of those thought to have sunk what ship?

12. The Castle, built from the bounty of silver mines, was known as "the house of silver doorknobs." Where is it?

13. What D.C. museum was established with a half-million dollars from an Englishman who had never set foot in the U.S.?

14. What New York City building has about one-third of the world's supply of gold bullion?

15. What famous British relics were housed for a while at the U.S. gold depository at Fort Knox?

16. What gorgeous building in Salt Lake City is decorated with more than twelve thousand square feet of twenty-four-karat gold leaf?

17. What item, weighing more than 1,800 pounds, was found in Colorado's Smuggler Mine?

18. What golfer became, in 1963, the first to earn over $100,000 in one year?

5. Jack London; a million was an extravagant sum in those days.
6. Steve Forbes
7. Alaska
8. The Model T, marketed by Henry Ford
9. Shirley Temple
10. The Civil War; Early was a general for the Confederacy. The $200,000 ransom was to prevent his troops from destroying the town.
11. The *Maine;* the sinking was the key event leading to the Spanish-American War.
12. Virginia City, Nevada, site of the famous Comstock Lode mine
13. The Smithsonian Institution; James Smithson, a scientist, left his entire fortune to the U.S. Interestingly, he is buried in D.C.
14. The Federal Reserve Bank
15. The Crown Jewels, which are normally kept in the Tower of London; they were kept in the U.S. while World War II was raging in Europe.
16. Symphony Hall, home of the Utah Symphony
17. A silver nugget
18. Arnold Palmer

19. What former Union general was president when Congress passed "the Grab Act," doubling the president's salary and hiking its own by 50 percent?
20. What president submitted the first *trillion-dollar* budget to Congress?
21. What actor, in 1969, bought his glamorous actress wife a million-dollar, sixty-nine-carat diamond?
22. What Elizabeth Taylor movie, made in 1963, cost $37 million and was, at the time, the most expensive movie ever made? (Hint: pyramid)
23. What popular singer paid a $240,000 ransom in 1963 to recover his kidnapped son (who happened to have the same name)?
24. For what historical American document did Ira Corn of Dallas pay $404,000 in 1969? (Hint: 1776)

☆ More Business, American Style

1. What chain of discount stores also owns Waldenbooks and Borders Books? (Hint: blue light specials)
2. If you toured the Philip Morris Cabarrus Center in North Carolina, what crop would you be learning about?
3. High Point, North Carolina, is the center for what major industry? (Hint: wood)
4. Kannapolis, North Carolina, is a noted textile town. What famous manufacturer has its headquarters there?
5. What manufacturing innovation, now a standard practice, did Eli Whitney introduce to his musket factory?
6. Q-R-S Music in Buffalo, New York, manufactures music rolls used in what type of instrument?
7. What U.S. industrial giant has its headquarters in Winston-Salem, North Carolina? (The town name should give you a hint.)
8. The CavOilCade Festival in Port Arthur, Texas, honors what industry?

19. U. S. Grant; the "Grab Act" was passed in 1873.
20. Ronald Reagan, in 1987
21. Richard Burton, who gave the present to Elizabeth Taylor
22. *Cleopatra*
23. Frank Sinatra; Frank Jr. was released unhurt and most of the money was recovered. Many people suspected the family had planned the whole thing as a publicity stunt.
24. The Declaration of Independence

More Business, American Style *(answers)*

1. Kmart
2. Tobacco; the Cabarrus Center is one of Philip Morris's key tobacco manufacturing facilities.
3. Furniture manufacture, one of the state's key industries
4. Cannon, famous for towels and linens; in fact, the town was named for the Cannon company.
5. Interchangeable parts
6. Player piano; their factory can be toured.
7. R. J. Reynolds Tobacco
8. Petroleum, the backbone of the city's economy

9. Riverside, California, is the center of what noted California industry? (Hint: juice)
10. Which automaker is usually number one in the Fortune 500 list of companies?
11. In terms of number of locations, what is the biggest fast-food chain in the U.S.?
12. What giant computer company was founded by Steve Jobs and Steve Wozniak?
13. What computer giant was founded by a nineteen-year-old named Bill Gates?
14. What motel chain was founded by realtor Cecil Day?
15. What company's 1894 catalog billed it as "the Cheapest Supply House on Earth"?
16. In 1907, what Philadelphia-based paper company introduced the paper towel?
17. What convenience store chain, with over ten thousand outlets, outranks all others in the U.S.?
18. Leon Leonwood Bean founded what mail-order clothing company?
19. Ben Franklin Stores don't sell kites or lightning rods, but they do sell what?
20. If you "crack up," you might call the Novus mobile repair shops, which repair what?
21. America's largest pizza chain has what semi-Italian name?
22. ERA, Coldwell Banker, and Century 21 are the biggest moneymakers in selling what?
23. Marcus Samuel ran a shop that sold boxes decorated with shells. His son, Marcus Jr., founded what much bigger company?
24. David McConnell, a book salesman, started what door-to-door company after finding that potential book-buyers liked to get free samples of cologne?

9. Orange growing
10. General Motors
11. McDonald's, followed closely by Subway
12. Apple
13. Microsoft
14. Days Inns
15. Sears
16. Scott
17. 7-Eleven
18. L. L. Bean, of course
19. Craft items
20. Windshields
21. Little Caesar's (Yes, it really is bigger than Pizza Hut.)
22. Real estate; they're the three biggest chains of real estate franchises.
23. Shell Oil, which the younger Marcus named after his dad's business
24. Avon; he found the fragrance market much more profitable than the book market.

PART TWELVE

Faith Matters

☆ That Gospel Sound

A trip to any record store in the U.S. will convince you that Christian music is no longer "fringe" music. It's gone mainstream and is being discovered by new listeners. But many people are aware that it's been part of American music since the very beginning.

1. The annual awards for gospel music are known by what name? (Hint: bird)
2. The Gospel Music Hall of Fame is in what city, famous for its music connections?
3. What pretty female vocalist became a major crossover artist in the 1990s, making a splash with *Heart in Motion* and *House of Love*?
4. Mother Maybelle Carter, one of the queens of gospel music, was the mother-in-law of what country music legend ("the Man in Black")?
5. What country singer, famous for "Wichita Lineman," started recording Christian albums in the 1980s?
6. What baritone singer has been a featured performer in the Billy Graham crusades?
7. "Oh Happy Day," an old gospel song, was a worldwide hit in 1969 for what black choral group?
8. What denomination, noted for its work among the poor, is also famous for its brass bands?
9. At the funeral of gospel music queen Mahalia Jackson, what "queen of soul" sang "Precious Lord"?
10. The pop-gospel group the Jordanaires sang backup for what rock-and-roll legend?
11. What pop music legend, born Richard Wayne Penniman, has recorded gospel albums but is better known for "Tutti Frutti" and "Good Golly, Miss Molly"?
12. What clean-cut pop singer, famous for his "white buck" shoes, shifted to gospel recording in the 1970s?

That Gospel Sound *(answers)*

1. The Dove Awards, first awarded in 1969
2. Nashville, Tennessee; Nashville has longtime connections with gospel as well as with country.
3. Amy Grant
4. Johnny Cash, whose wife is June Carter Cash
5. Glen Campbell
6. George Beverly Shea
7. The Edwin Hawkins Singers
8. The Salvation Army
9. Aretha Franklin, who has recorded at least one gospel album
10. Elvis Presley
11. Little Richard
12. Pat Boone

13. What black pop singer toured with the Billy Graham Crusades in her later years?

14. *Angel Band*, an album of old-time hymns, was recorded by what long-haired, sweet-voiced country music legend?

15. Leonard Slye, "king of the cowboys" in the movies, recorded both western and gospel. By what name do we know him?

16. What famous country quartet recorded a two-disk set *The Holy Bible—The New and Old Testaments*?

☆ The Bible on the American Map

The fight over separation of church and state goes on and on, but one thing's for sure: The Bible has made a definite impact on the naming of places in America.

1. What Minnesota metropolis, named for an apostle, was originally named Pig's Eye?

2. Where is Hell in the U.S.?

3. Which gulf state has counties named St. James, St. John the Baptist, and St. Mary?

4. Jacob's Pillow Dance Festival takes its name from the story of Jacob sleeping on a stone pillow. In what state is the festival held?

5. What state has a capital whose name refers to the Lord's Supper and baptism?

6. What California city is named for angels?

7. There are several Bethlehems in the U.S. Which state has the largest?

8. What is the largest U.S. city with a biblical name?

9. What is the only U.S. capital named after a city in the Old Testament?

10. What east coast state has a city named after an angel?

11. In what state would you find Mount Sinai?

12. Which state has both Bethlehem and New Bethlehem?

13. Ethel Waters
14. Emmylou Harris
15. Roy Rogers
16. The Statler Brothers

The Bible on the American Map *(answers)*

1. St. Paul
2. There isn't one, but there is a Hell's Canyon on the border between Idaho and Oregon.
3. Louisiana; actually, they aren't counties, but *parishes*—Louisiana's equivalent of counties.
4. Massachusetts
5. California; Sacramento is the Spanish word for sacrament.
6. Los Angeles, of course
7. Pennsylvania; Bethlehem has a population of about 70,000.
8. Philadelphia, Pennsylvania
9. Salem, Oregon; Salem is mentioned in Genesis 14. The name means "peace," and it has been a popular name on the U.S. map.
10. Maryland; the city is St. Michaels, named for the archangel Michael.
11. New York
12. Pennsylvania

13. Which southwestern state has a city named Trinity?
14. In what state would you find the biblically named Bethany, Bethel, and Bethlehem?
15. What beach with a biblical name is Delaware's most popular tourist attraction?
16. Where can you see the parting of the Red Sea?
17. In what New England city would you find the exhibit *Light Unto My Path: Exploring the Bible in Sight and Sound?*
18. Where can you see the Ten Commandments carved in stone in letters five feet high (probably the grand example of a large-print Bible)?
19. The enormous Cathedral of St. John the Divine has a notable Bible Garden. What metropolis is it in?
20. In what state is Bible Hill?

☆ Faith Groups, American Style

America is a melting pot in many ways, including religion. Not only have Christians, Jews, and other major religions managed to coexist, but America has also made its own unique contributions to the list of world religions.

1. In the 1600s they were called Separatists in England, but what name do we know them by? (Hint: Thanksgiving)
2. What Christian group, famous for its work in the slums of London, came to the U.S. in the late 1800s?
3. Silver Spring, Maryland, is the world headquarters for what religious group? (Hint: Saturday)
4. If you visit an area settled by Moravian Christians, what will you find in God's Acre?
5. The Christians formerly called "holy rollers" in jest are today called by what name?
6. When the U.S. separated from Great Britain, what did America's Church of England churches become?

13. Texas
14. Connecticut
15. Rehoboth Beach, a favorite spot for visitors from D.C. and Baltimore
16. At Universal Studios in Hollywood, California; it recreates the special effects used in the film *The Ten Commandments*.
17. Boston
18. On a mountainside at Field of the Wood, North Carolina; a border around the Commandments measures the length of a football field.
19. New York City
20. Tennessee

Faith Groups, American Style *(answers)*

1. Pilgrims
2. The Salvation Army, which quickly gained a reputation for its charitable work
3. The Seventh-day Adventists
4. Tombstones; the Moravians gave this name to cemeteries.
5. Pentecostals, or charismatics, or both
6. Episcopalian

7. What Christian denomination was noted for its frontier "circuit riders," preachers who traveled from settlement to settlement?

8. The Society of Friends, a Christian denomination, is better known by what name?

9. The denomination known as the Lutheran Church—Missouri Synod has its headquarters in what state?

10. Pleasant Hill, Kentucky, has a restored village of what unique religious group?

11. What Christian denomination—the largest in Texas—has a state historical center that includes the site of Sam Houston's baptism?

12. The German Christian immigrants who insisted on baptism by total immersion were known by what appropriate name?

13. In the religious camp meetings of the 1800s, what item could not be sold within two miles of the gatherings?

14. In the colonial period a "gathered" church consisted of what type of people?

15. The Church of Jesus Christ of Latter-day Saints, headquartered in Utah, is better known by what name?

16. What better name are "the plain people" Christians known by? (Hint: Pennsylvania)

17. What religious sect, founded by Charles Taze Russell, is noted for its door-to-door evangelism?

18. What group founded by Mary Baker Eddy has its "mother church" and headquarters in Boston? (Hint: noted for its reading rooms)

19. After Roman Catholicism, what is the nation's largest Christian denomination? (Hint: water)

20. What key social issue in the 1800s caused many of America's denominations to split into southern and northern branches?

7. The Methodists
8. The Quakers
9. Missouri—St. Louis, to be specific (Did anyone miss this?)
10. The Shakers, known for their simple lifestyle and their well-made furniture; Shaker Village is a popular tourist stop.
11. The Baptists
12. The Dunkers, today known as Church of the Brethren
13. Alcohol; local authorities feared disorder if liquor were available at the meetings.
14. Those who could claim to have had a definite conversion experience
15. The Mormons
16. The Amish, a branch of the Mennonites that chooses to remain aloof from the surrounding culture
17. The Jehovah's Witnesses
18. Christian Science, which publishes the famous newspaper *The Christian Science Monitor*
19. The Southern Baptist Convention (which, since it exists in all fifty states, is hardly *southern* anymore)
20. Slavery; many of the churches reunited after the Civil War, but some existed separately for many years.

☆ Settling for Belief

Americans are proud—rightly so—of having the freedom of
religion. It has been, from the very beginning, one of the
main attractions of the country. In fact, the country would
not be what it is today without settlers who came here
looking for freedom of worship. Remember the Pilgrims?
They were just the beginning. . . .

1. Which of the thirteen colonies attracted the widest range
   of Christian denominations?
2. What Mormon leader persuaded thousands to emigrate
   to Nauvoo, Illinois?
3. The town of Valdese was settled by a persecuted Christian
   group called the Waldensians. What southern state is
   Valdese in?
4. What North Carolina city with a hyphenated name was
   settled by Christian Moravians fleeing persecution in
   Europe?
5. The Turkey red wheat that made Kansas a wheat haven
   was introduced by what religious group?
6. What American colonizer had been kicked out of
   England's Oxford University for his nonconformist
   religious views?
7. Newark, New Jersey's largest city, began as a small
   settlement by what Christian group?
8. What simple-living Christian group requires its married
   men to wear beards (but not mustaches), black coats, and
   low-crowned black hats?
9. What historic city's first settlers, the Quakers, lived in
   caves until the city itself was built?
10. By what more common name do we know the Germans
    from the Rhineland and Palatinate who settled in
    Pennsylvania in the 1700s?

Settling for Belief *(answers)*

1. Pennsylvania, which William Penn planned as a "holy experiment" in religious toleration
2. Brigham Young, who later led the Mormon trek to Utah
3. North Carolina
4. Winston-Salem, which is also famous (as you might guess from the name) as a tobacco town
5. Mennonites, who had immigrated from Russia
6. William Penn, later a leader of the Quakers and founder of Pennsylvania
7. The Puritans (How things do change. . . .)
8. The Amish, found in Pennsylvania and elsewhere
9. Philadelphia's
10. The Pennsylvania Dutch

11. Bethlehem, Pennsylvania, originated in 1741 with a devout group of German-speaking Christians. Who were they?

12. What religious colonizer left Massachusetts and bought land from the Narragansett Indians in 1636?

13. What Christian denomination in the U.S. grew because of the many German and Scandinavian immigrants?

14. Puritan pastors Thomas Hooker, Theophilus Eaton, and John Davenport founded settlements that became what colony in New England?

15. What colony, founded by George and Cecil Calvert, was planned as a refuge for English Catholics?

16. What colony was founded in the 1600s because Sweden's King Gustavus Adolphus wanted to convert the Indians to Christianity?

11. The Moravians, who were not only devout but highly industrious
12. Roger Williams, founder of the Rhode Island colony
13. The Lutherans; this was the official state church in Scandinavia and much of Germany.
14. Connecticut
15. Maryland; the colony, however, guaranteed religious freedom to Protestants.
16. Delaware, which later came under English control

PART THIRTEEN
Political Potpourri

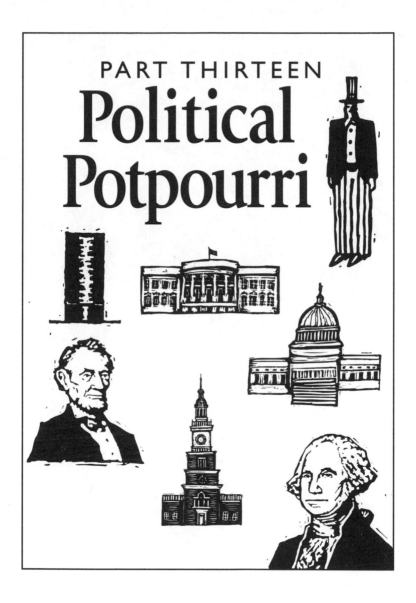

☆ Waiting in the Wings: U.S. Vice Presidents

Is the vice president just a "standby," the official whose only purpose is to fill in if the president dies? Well, that has happened on enough occasions to make it important. But in fact, this job, only "one heartbeat away from the presidency," has some other duties, as you can read in the Constitution. Besides that, a few of the vice presidents have been rather amusing characters.

1. What early vice president called the office "the most insignificant office that ever the invention of man contrived"?
2. When the vice president presides over the Senate, what is his title?
3. What vice president under President William McKinley claimed that McKinley "had no more backbone than a chocolate éclair"? (Hint: bull moose)
4. Who, in 1973, became the first man *appointed* to the office of vice president?
5. Vice President Thomas Marshall, serving under Woodrow Wilson, stated that "What this country needs is a good five-cent" what?
6. What one-syllable word did Vice President Alben Barkley coin as shorthand for his position?
7. If the U.S. president and vice president were both unable to serve, what official would be president?
8. What vice president was famed for killing Cabinet member Alexander Hamilton in a duel?
9. Huron, South Dakota, has a drugstore owned by a famous Democratic senator and vice president until his death. Who?

Waiting in the Wings: U.S. Vice Presidents
(answers)

1. John Adams, who was George Washington's vice president and, afterwards, president himself
2. President of the Senate
3. Theodore Roosevelt, who became president upon McKinley's death
4. Gerald Ford, who was appointed by Richard Nixon to replace the scandal-plagued Spiro Agnew
5. Cigar; the statement is Marshall's only claim to fame.
6. Veep; Barkley was veep 1949–53.
7. The Speaker of the House
8. Aaron Burr
9. Hubert Humphrey, vice president under Lyndon Johnson; the store is still in his family.

10. What group of people was Spiro Agnew referring to in 1969 when he called them an "unelected elite" that dictated what people thought was "news"?
11. John C. Calhoun became, in 1832, the first man to resign as vice president. Who was the president he had continually locked horns with?
12. The first veep to become president on the death of the president was John Tyler, who succeeded what man who served only a month?
13. John Breckinridge, veep under James Buchanan, later served which other nation as a Cabinet member and general?
14. What president, who served a *long* time, had the greatest number of veeps?
15. What vice president ran for president against John F. Kennedy in 1960 and lost?
16. Gerald Ford's veep was, like Ford himself, appointed instead of elected. Who was this man, a member of one of New York's richest families?
17. What tight-lipped veep under Warren Harding quipped "Gotta eat somewhere" when people commented that his position required him to attend a lot of official dinners?
18. How many vice presidents have become president when the president died?

☆ Three Ambassadors

1. What former child actress was appointed ambassador to Ghana in 1974 by Gerald Ford?
2. What millionaire and father of a president served as ambassador to Great Britain from 1938 to 1940?
3. What president had served as ambassador to France from 1785 to 1789?

10. TV newscasters—specifically, the top newscasters at the major networks
11. Andrew Jackson; theirs was the absolute worst case of relations between president and vice president.
12. William Henry Harrison, who caught pneumonia at his inauguration and never recovered; Tyler was sometimes referred to as "the Accidental President."
13. The Confederacy
14. Franklin Roosevelt, who served 1933–45, had three—John Garner, Henry Wallace, and Harry Truman.
15. Richard Nixon, who had been vice president under Eisenhower; he ran again in 1968 and 1972 and won.
16. Nelson Rockefeller
17. Calvin Coolidge, who became president upon Harding's death
18. Eight—John Tyler (after W. H. Harrison), Millard Fillmore (after Taylor), Andrew Johnson (after Lincoln), Chester Arthur (after Garfield), Theodore Roosevelt (after McKinley), Calvin Coolidge (after Harding), Harry Truman (after F. D. Roosevelt), and Lyndon Johnson (after Kennedy). If you named all these, give yourself the M.Triv. degree and treat yourself to a day at the beach.

Three Ambassadors *(answers)*

1. Shirley Temple Black
2. Joseph P. Kennedy, father of John F., Robert, and Ted
3. Thomas Jefferson

☆ Party of Three: America's Political Third Parties

No, there weren't always just two major political parties (and still aren't, actually). Sometimes the third party serves a useful purpose, bringing key issues to the public's attention. And sometimes the third parties are . . . well, just plain weird.

1. Who ran for president in 1992 and 1996 as the Reform candidate?
2. What former Alabama governor and third-party candidate was shot at a Maryland mall in 1972?
3. What well-known author of a book on baby and child care ran as the People's candidate in 1972?
4. William Z. Foster ran in 1932 as the first candidate of what party associated with eastern Europe?
5. What major national party split in the 1860 election, running a southern candidate and a northern candidate?
6. Former Republican president Theodore Roosevelt ran in 1912 on his newly formed Progressive party. By what animal name is the party better known?
7. Corruption in U. S. Grant's Republican administration led to a "new and improved" Republican party candidate in 1872. What name did candidate Horace Greeley give to his party?
8. Peter Cooper of New York ran in 1876 as the candidate for a party with a name we apply to dollar bills. What?
9. What issue motivated the formation of the Prohibition party in 1884?
10. Eugene Debs ran for president five times as the candidate for what pro-government, pro-welfare party (which controls most countries in Europe)?
11. What former Republican from Illinois ran as a liberal Independent against Ronald Reagan and Jimmy Carter in 1980?

Party of Three: America's Political Third Parties
(answers)

1. Ross Perot
2. George Wallace; he was confined to a wheelchair afterward but went home and was elected Alabama governor again.
3. Benjamin Spock, whose famous child care books have sold millions of copies
4. The Communists; he did not get even one percent of the vote.
5. The Democrats, who ran John Breckinridge (South) and Stephen Douglas (North); the split gave the election to a Republican named Abraham Lincoln.
6. The Bull Moose party; Roosevelt claimed he was eager to run and felt as "fit as a bull moose." He lost.
7. Liberal Republicans, who also garnered some Democratic votes; Greeley lost, and Grant was reelected.
8. The Greenback party; Cooper got barely one percent of the vote.
9. Opposition to alcohol; it ran candidates in the next seven elections.
10. The Socialist party
11. John Anderson, who lost to Reagan and got no electoral votes

12. A former western explorer ran in 1856 on the new (and at that time *third*) Republican party. Who was he?
13. What former president, who had been elected as a Democrat in 1836, ran as the Free Soil candidate in 1848?
14. What long-lived South Carolina senator (still serving in the 1990s) ran for president in 1948 on the States' Rights ticket?
15. The American Independent candidate in 1968 was what flamboyant Alabama governor?
16. The first major third party in America ran in 1832 on a platform of opposition to secret fraternal groups. What appropriate name did the party have?
17. James Birney ran for president in 1844 as an avowed antislavery man. What was the name of his party?
18. Roger McBride ran in 1976 as the first candidate of what party emphasizing individualism and minimal government?
19. Silas Swallow's last name made him an inappropriate candidate in 1904 for what party?
20. James Stockdale and Pat Choate were the vice presidential running mates of what candidate of the 1990s?
21. What Christian denomination was the Know-Nothing political party of the 1800s opposed to?

☆ Foreign Relations

America was settled in an age when European nations made a sport of fighting each other. The world hasn't changed much, has it? Nations still fight, or sometimes just "rattle their sabers" at each other.

But foreign relations aren't all nasty. Often as not, we've had some pleasant, happy relations with other countries. The questions here concern the happy times . . . and the other times.

12. John C. Frémont, who lost to Democrat James Buchanan
13. Martin Van Buren; the Free Soil folks were basically an antislavery party. Van Buren lost.
14. Strom Thurmond, whose longevity still amazes people
15. George Wallace, who got 14 percent of the vote and forty-six electoral votes
16. The Anti-Masonic party; its 1832 presidential candidate, William Wirt, got 8 percent of the vote.
17. Liberty; he got only 2.3 percent of the vote and no electoral votes.
18. The Libertarians
19. Prohibition
20. Ross Perot
21. Catholics, as well as all foreigners

1. In what appropriate country did the 1951 Walt Disney film *Alice in Wonderland* premiere?
2. The Treaty of Ghent ended which nineteenth-century war with Britain?
3. The *New York Herald* financed an expedition to locate what famous African explorer?
4. What Caribbean island nation won its freedom in the Spanish-American War of 1898?
5. What future state was liberated from Mexico by the U.S. in 1836?
6. The French people gave the Statue of Liberty to the U.S. What country was to provide the pedestal?
7. The U.S. ambassador to the Court of St. James is, in fact, ambassador to what nation?
8. Besides being an author and an inventor, Benjamin Franklin was also American ambassador to what European country?
9. "My Country, 'Tis of Thee" is sung to the tune of what country's national anthem?
10. Fulton, Missouri, has a museum devoted to what great British statesman of the twentieth century?
11. What valuable gas did the U.S. refuse to sell to the Hitler government in Germany?
12. What future president became governor of the Philippines in 1901? (Hint: a real heavyweight)
13. What French-born soldier of the Revolutionary War was made an honorary U.S. citizen?
14. The English drinking song "To Anacreon in Heaven" lent its tune to what familiar patriotic song?
15. In 1959, vice president Richard Nixon visited the Soviet Union, and what Soviet leader visited the U.S.?
16. What country had tried to build a canal in Panama before the U.S. stepped in?

Foreign Relations *(answers)*

1. England; its author, Lewis Carroll, was English, and it is a *very* English book, though Americans have always loved it.
2. The War of 1812
3. David Livingstone; they found him. ("Dr. Livingstone, I presume?")
4. Cuba; technically, Cuba was under U.S. protection until 1902, when it became fully independent.
5. Texas, which then became an independent republic—for nine years
6. The U.S. itself
7. Great Britain
8. France
9. Britain's; the tune is the same as "God Save the King."
10. Winston Churchill, who delivered his famous "Iron Curtain" speech in Fulton in 1946
11. Helium, used in dirigibles; since the U.S. was the world's only producer, the Germans had to use the dangerously flammable hydrogen.
12. William Howard Taft
13. The Marquis de Lafayette
14. "The Star-Spangled Banner"
15. Nikita Khrushchev
16. France

17. What Revolutionary War agitator helped write France's constitution in the 1790s?
18. What was unusual about the 1918 play *Lincoln*, by John Drinkwater?
19. What Native American tribe's name is used by the French to refer to hoodlums?
20. What noted author and lecturer was a friend of English authors William Wordsworth, Thomas Carlyle, and Samuel Taylor Coleridge?
21. The Azilum community in Pennsylvania was built by refugees from what revolution of the 1790s?
22. What large item from England was sent to Fulton, Missouri?
23. What German soldier, a hero in the Revolutionary War, was known as "the Drillmaster"?
24. Invasion plans for the Bay of Pigs in Cuba were first drawn up under what president?
25. Painter Emanuel Leutze used Germany's Rhine River as his backdrop for his painting of George Washington crossing what river?

17. Thomas Paine, author of *Common Sense* and other propaganda pieces
18. It premiered in England and was written by an Englishman.
19. The Apaches'
20. Ralph Waldo Emerson
21. The French Revolution; many nobles, fearing for their lives, fled France and settled here. *Azilum* means "asylum" or "refuge."
22. A seventeenth-century church, which had been badly bombed by the Germans in World War II; it was dismantled and then completely reassembled in Fulton.
23. Baron von Steuben
24. Dwight Eisenhower; the actual invasion took place under his successor, Kennedy.
25. The Delaware; the actual scene isn't nearly as dramatic as Leutze's famous painting.

PART FOURTEEN

A Many-Cultured
Culture

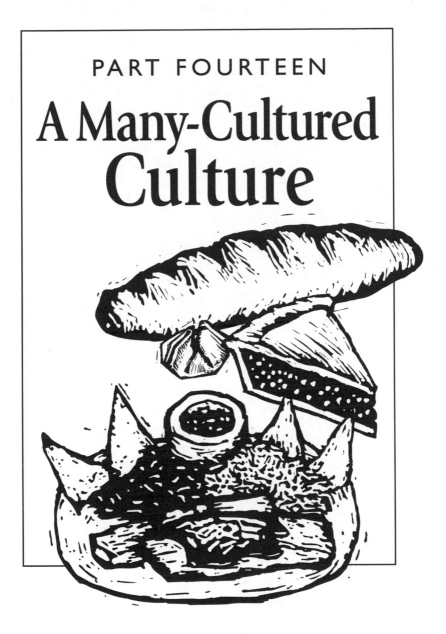

☆ Melting Pot: A Nation of Immigrants

English, Irish, French, Spanish, German, Chinese, etc., etc. Each of us (Native Americans excepted) have roots in some other nation. This mixture has only helped make America a rich and fascinating place.

1. What Florida metropolis has a Little Havana section?
2. What historic city on the Mississippi River was founded by Frenchman Jean-Baptiste Le Moyne in 1718?
3. The seaport of Belfast was named by its Scotch-Irish settlers for their hometown. What New England state is it in?
4. Hanamatsuri is a festival held by the Japanese community in Los Angeles. What religious figure's birthday does it honor?
5. What Norwegian explorer—an early visitor to America—is honored in a park in Duluth, Minnesota?
6. What country took over the colony of Louisiana when the French wanted to be rid of it?
7. What noted Spanish explorer arrived in Florida on Easter morning in 1513?
8. What notorious French pirate helped Andrew Jackson defeat the British in the Battle of New Orleans?
9. In Chicago, what ethnic group holds a celebration of Revolutionary War soldier Baron von Steuben?
10. New Glarus, Wisconsin, has a reconstruction of a village from what European nation?
11. Columbus, Ohio, has an annual *Haus und Garten* tour in what ethnic neighborhood?
12. If you wanted to see Danish, Finnish, German, and Norwegian farm buildings all in one place, what Wisconsin attraction would you visit?

Melting Pot: A Nation of Immigrants *(answers)*

1. Miami, known for its many Cuban immigrants
2. New Orleans (or, if you prefer, N'awlins)
3. Maine
4. Buddha
5. Leif Eriksson, who sailed to America around the year 1000
6. Spain; this changing of hands explains the interesting mix of cultures in Louisiana.
7. Ponce de Leon, noted for his search for the fountain of youth
8. Jean Lafitte, one of the more colorful figures in Louisiana's history
9. The Germans (The baron was German, of course.)
10. Switzerland; settled by the Swiss, New Glarus is often referred to as "Little Switzerland." The *old* Glarus is in Switzerland.
11. German; *Haus und Garten* means "house and garden."
12. Old World Wisconsin, with more than fifty preserved nineteenth-century farm buildings. It's in the town of Eagle.

13. Salado, Texas's annual Gathering of the Clans celebrates what heritage?
14. What Wisconsin metropolis grew due to the influence of the Forty-Eighters?
15. What popular and historic California resort town takes its name from the Spanish friars who settled there in the 1600s?
16. What name is given to the people of French and Spanish heritage living in New Orleans?
17. What German-settled California metropolis was originally planned as a winemaking center? (Hint: Disneyland)
18. Czech Village, a popular tourist attraction, is in Cedar Rapids in what midwestern state?
19. What Great Lakes city has a German Fest, Irish Fest, Festa Italiana, and Festa Mexicana all within the same month? (Hint: brew)
20. Gallipolis, Ohio, was founded by aristocrats fleeing from what troubled nation in the 1790s?
21. Besides New York, which colony was established by Dutchman Peter Minuit?
22. Lindsborg, Kansas, has a St. Lucia Festival, indicating the town's ethnic group. What group settled the town? (Hint: meatballs)
23. The first Russian cathedral in America was in what far western state?

☆ Going Native: The American Indians

What term is correct now—*Indians* or *Native Americans*? People disagree about that, but there's no disagreement over the key role Indians—or Native Americans—have played in the American saga. If you doubt the Indian impact, look at

13. Scotch, naturally
14. Milwaukee; the Forty-Eighters were an influential group of German refugees who settled in 1848.
15. Carmel, named for the order of Carmelite Friars who came with the Spanish settlers
16. Creoles, noted for their delicious cooking
17. Anaheim; its name, in German, means "home on the Ana [river]."
18. Iowa, which had a lot of Czech immigrants
19. Milwaukee, Wisconsin
20. France; they were nobles fleeing the guillotine during the French Revolution.
21. Delaware, whose original 1638 settlement was Fort Christina, built by Swedes under Minuit's direction
22. Swedes
23. Alaska, built in Sitka in 1848

the American map—full of Indian names from Massachusetts to Kalamazoo to Utah.

By the way, the name *Indian* stuck because poor Christopher Columbus thought he'd landed in India. He was a better sailor than a geographer.

1. Which two Great Lakes are named for Indian tribes?
2. What Indian item was usually made with ten or more bison skins and twenty or more cedar poles?
3. What Indian tribe, found mostly in New Mexico and Arizona, is the nation's largest, with about 200,000 people?
4. What white settlement did Pocahontas save from an Indian attack?
5. In what southwestern state do Indian tribes own more acreage than in any other state?
6. In what appropriately named North Carolina town could you find the Museum of the Cherokee Indian?
7. What famous island was bought from Indians for twenty-four-dollars' worth of beads and trinkets?
8. What future U.S. president gained fame putting down an Indian uprising in Alabama?
9. What state's name means "land of Indians"?
10. Indian City USA is an authentic reconstruction of Indian villages. What state is it in?
11. What was the fate of the Seminole Indians who fought white settlers in the Seminole War of 1835–42?
12. What fictional Indian hero is commemorated by a fifty-two-foot fiberglass statue in Ironwood, Michigan?
13. Early Virginia settlers were told by the Indians of a fabled land west of the mountains. What was it called?
14. If you wished to see Powhatan Indians making pottery and carving tools from deer antlers, where would you go?

Going Native: The American Indians *(answers)*

1. Huron and Erie
2. A teepee
3. The Navajo
4. Jamestown, the first settlement in Virginia
5. Arizona, which has twenty-three reservations
6. Cherokee (Surprise!)
7. Manhattan
8. Andrew Jackson, whom the Indians referred to as "Sharp Knife"
9. Indiana, naturally
10. Oklahoma, near the town of Anadarko
11. They were sent to lands west of the Mississippi River. A few remained behind in Florida's Everglades.
12. Hiawatha, made famous in Henry Wadsworth Longfellow's poem *The Song of Hiawatha*
13. Kentucky; later pioneers discovered that the legend was true—once they found a way through the Appalachian Mountains.
14. To Jamestown Settlement in Virginia, which has a re-created Indian village

15. What famous Virginia national park has an Indian name meaning "daughter of the stars"?
16. The Colorado River Indian Tribes Museum is in what southwestern state?
17. What national forest in Arizona shares its name with a fictional Indian of TV fame?
18. What Indian items attract visitors to Mesa Verde National Park?
19. What sad event is commemorated by Missouri's Trail of Tears State Park?
20. What southwestern Indian tribe takes its name from the Spanish word for "village"?
21. The area that eventually became Oklahoma was divided among the Cherokee, Creek, Chickasaw, Choctaw, and Seminole tribes. What was their collective name?
22. What infamous Shawnee Indian chief organized an intertribal alliance to fend off white settlement during the War of 1812?
23. What was the first American Indian tribe with its own written language and its own constitution?
24. The Shoshone-Bannock Indian Festival, a major Indian festival in the U.S., is held in what northwestern state? (Hint: potato)
25. Minnesota's pipestone was used by the Indians for making what objects?
26. The Museum of the Plains Indian focuses on the Blackfoot and other Plains tribes. What large state is it in?
27. What creature in Indian myth causes thunder and lightning? (Hint: Ford)
28. The northern Indians who wrapped their legs and feet in dark buffalo leather were known by what name?
29. What illiterate frontiersman had more knowledge of the Indians than any other white man?

15. Shenandoah
16. Arizona
17. Tonto, famous as the sidekick of the Lone Ranger
18. Cliff dwellings, many of them more than eight hundred years old
19. The forced removal of the Cherokee Indians to Oklahoma
20. The Pueblo
21. They were known as the Five Civilized Tribes.
22. Tecumseh
23. The Cherokee; their alphabet (which enabled them to have a written language, obviously) was invented by the remarkable Sequoyah.
24. Idaho
25. Pipes, what else? Specifically, the reddish stone was used for ceremonial pipes (peace pipes, that is).
26. Montana, near the town of Browning
27. The thunderbird, of course
28. The Blackfeet
29. Christopher "Kit" Carson, who helped negotiate numerous treaties with the Indians

30. In what war did notorious "white renegade" Simon Girty lead Indian raids against Americans?
31. What southwestern Indian tribe are the "people of peace"?
32. What state celebrates Indian Day in September and Will Rogers Day in November?
33. What Florida Indian tribe did not sign a peace treaty with the U.S. until 1975?
34. The Smithsonian Institution's National Museum of the American Indian is not in D.C. but in what metropolis?
35. What religious colonizer left Massachusetts and bought land from the Narragansett Indians in 1636?
36. In what condition was John Colter when Blackfoot Indians released him in the wilderness in 1808?
37. What did the Pawnee Indians sacrifice during their five-day Morning Star ceremony?
38. Prior to befriending the Pilgrims, what Indian had been sold into slavery in Spain?

☆ Melting Pot: A Nation of Immigrants (Part 2)

1. What midwestern metropolis formerly had more German-speakers than English-speakers? (Hint: brew)
2. What tragic 1840 event in Ireland sent many Irish off to America?
3. If you were visiting Louisiana's Acadiana region, what sort of people would you be hoping to meet with?
4. New Brunswick, New Jersey, has a museum devoted to what eastern European immigrant group? (Hint: goulash)
5. What nationality were the Pennsylvania Dutch? (Hint: *not* Dutch)
6. Nisei Week is a Los Angeles festival honoring which ethnic community?

30. The Revolutionary War; Girty, who had been reared by Indians, was noted for his cruelty.
31. The Hopi
32. Oklahoma
33. The Seminoles
34. New York
35. Roger Williams, founder of the Rhode Island colony
36. Stark naked; they intended to hunt him down and kill him, but the gutsy Colter somehow made a three-hundred-mile, eleven-day journey to an American fort. The worst part of being stripped bare there in the wilds was that he had no shoes—ouch!
37. A human being, usually one captured from another tribe
38. Squanto

Melting Pot: A Nation of Immigrants (Part 2)
(answers)

1. Milwaukee, Wisconsin
2. The potato famine, causing widespread starvation
3. The Cajuns, descendants of the French who had originally settled the area after being expelled from Acadia (in Canada) by the English
4. The Hungarians
5. German; the name they used for themselves was the German word *Deutsch*, meaning "German." Eventually they came to be called "Dutch"—an ethnic error we've all learned to live with.
6. The Japanese

7. Miami's biggest event is the Carnaval Miami Festival. What ethnic group is at the center of this?

8. *La Petite Roche,* named by early French explorers, is now what southern state capital?

9. The colony of New Amsterdam was founded by the Dutch in 1625. What colony (and state) did it later become?

10. The Wurstfest in New Braunfels, Texas, celebrates what European heritage?

11. Which New England state had been part of the old French colony of Acadia?

12. New Ulm, Minnesota, has the Fasching, the traditional winter festival of what immigrant group?

13. What New York ethnic section, centered on Mulberry Street, has an annual San Gennaro festival?

14. The Temple Beside the River in Oroville, California, belongs to what Asian ethnic community?

15. Towanda, Pennsylvania, has a refuge built for a very famous queen of France. Who?

16. Who were the German troops employed as British mercenaries during the Revolutionary War?

17. What European nationality founded the pretty California town of Solvang? (Hint: pastry)

18. Sugarcreek, Ohio, is known as a center for what distinctive type of cheese? (Hint: holes)

19. Due to French influence, what southern state has parishes instead of counties?

20. English explorer Henry Hudson, who sailed into New York in 1609, was sailing on behalf of what country?

21. Alabama's first permanent settlement was Mobile, settled in 1702. What European country made the settlement?

22. Ole Bull, a world-famous Norwegian violinist, tried (and failed) to start a New Norway colony in what eastern state?

23. What New York metropolis took its name from a mis-pronunciation of *beau fleuve,* French for "beautiful river"?

7. The Cubans
8. Little Rock, which is what the French name means; it is Arkansas's capital.
9. New York
10. German; the town was settled by spunky German immigrants. A Wurstfest is a sausage festival.
11. Maine; Acadia included parts of Maine and the future Canadian provinces of Nova Scotia and New Brunswick.
12. Germans; New Ulm is named for *old* Ulm, in Germany.
13. Little Italy
14. The Chinese; it is all that remains of that city's Chinatown.
15. Marie Antoinette; *La Grande Maison* was built in 1793 for the queen in case she needed to flee the French Revolution. She never made it, since she lost her head (literally) over the revolution.
16. The Hessians, from the small German state of (you guessed it) Hesse
17. The Danish; every fall the town holds its Danish Days Festival.
18. Swiss; the town hosts the Ohio Swiss Festival.
19. Louisiana
20. The Netherlands; the Dutch became the first European settlers of what later became New York.
21. France; Mobile is a sister city to New Orleans, also settled by the French.
22. Pennsylvania; there is now a state park named for him.
23. Buffalo; the river was the nearby Niagara.

PART FIFTEEN

Ten for Fifty(Plus One):
Ten Questions
about Each State

☆ Alabama, the Cotton State

1. What large state college is located in Auburn?
2. What praline ingredient is the official state nut?
3. In what city would you see a huge iron statue of the naked god Vulcan holding a torch?
4. Horseshoe Bend Military Park commemorates the victory of a future U.S. president over the Creek Indians. Who? (Hint: Old Hickory)
5. The Big Seam helped make the city of Birmingham a major industrial town. What was found in the Big Seam?
6. The site of the University of Alabama was named for a Choctaw Indian chief who led a raid against invading Spaniards. What was his (and the city's) name?
7. Sylacauga is noted as a marble mining center. What notable D.C. building was constructed from Sylacauga marble? (Hint: justice)
8. The city of Enterprise, Alabama, has a monument to the boll weevil, an insect known for destroying cotton plants. Why was the monument built?
9. If you were looking for the address 1 Tranquility Base, what world-famous museum in Huntsville would you be looking for?
10. Dauphin Island, off the Alabama coast, was named for what royal person of Europe?

☆ Alaska, Land of the Midnight Sun

1. What valuable substance was discovered near Prudhoe Bay in 1968? (Hint: *not* gold)
2. The Russians established Alaska settlements in the 1780s. What local item were the Russians interested in?
3. What species of bear, the world's largest, lives in Alaska?
4. What objectionable animal's fur is sometimes marketed as "Alaska sable"?

Alabama, the Cotton State *(answers)*

1. Auburn University (Did anyone actually miss this question?)
2. The pecan; you can't get more southern than a pecan praline. A praline is a type of candy, in case you Yankees didn't know.
3. Birmingham, Alabama, known (formerly) as a steel production town; Vulcan was the Roman god of metalworking. (He isn't *completely* naked in the statue—he's wearing a workman's apron.)
4. Andrew Jackson; the Indians called him "Sharp Knife."
5. Iron ore; the discovery helped propel Alabama into the industrial age.
6. Tuscaloosa; the name means "Black Warrior," which is the name of the nearby river.
7. The Supreme Court building
8. Because of the weevil's destruction of cotton crops, area farmers had to learn to diversify with other crops. (You might say it's a monument to "diversity.")
9. The U.S. Space and Rocket Center; Huntsville is the site of a NASA installation.
10. The eldest son of the king of France; he had the title Dauphin just as the eldest son of the ruler of Britain is known as the Prince of Wales.

Alaska, Land of the Midnight Sun *(answers)*

1. Oil
2. Furs
3. The Kodiak bear
4. The skunk, which actually makes a nice fur

5. What independence-loving political party is extremely popular here? (Hint: *not* Republican or Democrat)
6. What was remarkable about the man who designed Alaska's flag in 1927?
7. What types of towns are found along the Richardson Highway?
8. What Asian nation occupied some of Alaska's islands during World War II?
9. What notorious oil tanker spilled ten million gallons of oil into Prince William Sound in 1989?
10. America's highest mountain is in Alaska, a 20,320-foot peak named for a U.S. president. Who?

☆ Arizona, Land of the Sun Devils

1. What historic Old West town calls itself "the town too tough to die"? (Hint: a brand of pizza)
2. Arizona has a national park with 93,000 acres of trees permanently hardened by volcanic ash. What is the park's name?
3. What national monument features Arizona's state flower?
4. The Madonna of the Trail does not honor the Virgin Mary but, rather, a certain type of woman. What type?
5. What near-legendary gunfight took place at Tombstone in 1881?
6. What source of wealth did German-born Henry Wickenburg discover when he threw a rock at a stubborn donkey in Arizona?
7. What name is given to the glass-enclosed, three-acre earth model in Tucson?
8. What notorious Old West cemetery is in Tombstone?
9. The San Carlos Indian Reservation belongs to what formerly warlike tribe?
10. Tombstone has the largest flowering bush of this type in the world. What type?

5. The Libertarians
6. He wasn't *quite* a man—he was a thirteen-year-old schoolboy.
7. Ghost towns, left over from the gold rush days
8. Japan
9. The *Exxon Valdez;* this was the worst oil spill in U.S. history.
10. McKinley, which now often goes under its pre-U.S. name, Denali

Arizona, Land of the Sun Devils *(answers)*

1. Tombstone
2. Petrified Forest National Park
3. Saguaro National Monument; the saguaro cactus, which may live to be two hundred years old, has lovely night-blooming flowers that are the state emblem.
4. Pioneer women who trekked west
5. The O.K. Corral shoot-out between the Earps and the Clantons
6. The Vulture Mine, Arizona's richest gold find
7. The Biosphere
8. Boot Hill, noted for its unusual epitaphs
9. The Apaches
10. A rose bush, spreading over eight thousand square feet

☆ Arkansas, the Razorback State

1. The capitol in Little Rock is a replica of what famous D.C. building?
2. The Hammond Museum in Eureka Springs is devoted to what type of noise-making item?
3. What is the claim to fame of Arkansas's Judge Isaac Parker?
4. What theme park in Arkansas is named for a place in the comic strip "Li'l Abner"?
5. What yellow spring flower is honored with a festival at Old Washington State Park?
6. If you visit the Toad Suck Ferry Dam, where are you?
7. A festival in Mena honors what comedy duo of radio fame?
8. What city is named for a flamboyant Confederate cavalry general?
9. What curious material is Benton, Arkansas's Gann Museum made of?
10. The Buffalo National River is in what beautiful mountain chain?

☆ California, Never-Never Land

1. If you are riding on BART, where are you?
2. What famous church in Garden Grove (seen often on TV) resembles a four-pointed glass star?
3. Max Factor's Museum of Beauty is in what city?
4. What is California's most celebrity-filled cemetery?
5. The country's most stunning Easter sunrise service is held at what huge amphitheater?
6. What famous British ocean liner can be toured at Long Beach?
7. In the famous "Stack" in Los Angeles, what is it that's stacked four deep?

Arkansas, the Razorback State *(answers)*

1. The U.S. Capitol; Little Rock's is smaller, appropriately.
2. Bells
3. During the wildest days of Fort Smith, Parker, known as "the hanging judge," had more than seventy-nine men hanged during his twenty-one years as judge.
4. Dogpatch USA, near the town of Harrison
5. Jonquils; some of the flowers were planted by the town's original settlers. They aren't all yellow, either, since there are also white and pink varieties.
6. Conway, Arkansas, which hosts the Toad Suck Daze every May
7. Lum and Abner
8. Forrest City, named for a Tennessean, Nathan Bedford Forrest, a noted cavalry leader
9. Bauxite, the metal ore from which aluminum is made; it is the only known bauxite building in the world.
10. The Ozarks

California, Never-Never Land *(answers)*

1. In California's San Francisco–Oakland area. BART is Bay Area Rapid Transit.
2. Robert Schuller's Crystal Cathedral; it is all glass, except for the frames.
3. Hollywood, where else?
4. The Hollywood Memorial Park Cemetery Mortuary, with Rudolph Valentino, Nelson Eddy, Cecil B. DeMille, Tyrone Power, and many others
5. The Hollywood Bowl
6. The *Queen Mary,* which also functions as a hotel
7. Freeways—specifically the Hollywood, Harbor, Santa Ana, San Bernardino, and Pasadena Freeways, which at some points are four deep

8. What popular comic strip characters walk the paths of Knott's Berry Farm? (Hint: Aaargh!)
9. What fertile farming valley is often called "the Garden of the Sun"?
10. What sport is associated with the resort city of Palm Springs?

☆ Colorado, the Mountain Empire

1. What winter sport has its hall of fame in Colorado Springs?
2. What sport do the Colorado Rockies play at Coors Field?
3. If you wanted to attend Donkey Derby Days, where would you go?
4. Where could you see wax figures of all the U.S. presidents?
5. Before Aspen was the nation's best-known ski center, what metal attracted people to the area?
6. If you are looking at the Kissing Camels and the Balanced Rock, where are you?
7. What rare (and radioactive) element heats the natural springs in Colorado's Idaho Springs?
8. Estes Park is the gateway to what much-visited national park?
9. The city of Golden has a museum honoring one of the West's most colorful characters, a sharpshooter. Who?
10. What city was named for the east coast newspaper editor who uttered the famous advice, "Go west, young man"?

☆ Connecticut, the Nutmeg State

1. What popular cable sports network has its headquarters in Bristol?
2. What world-renowned circus entrepreneur has a museum in Bridgeport?

8. The "Peanuts" characters
9. San Joaquin, with the greatest agricultural production in the U.S.
10. Golf, of course; with seventy courses around the city, Palm Springs is known as the Winter Golf Capital of the World.

Colorado, the Mountain Empire *(answers)*

1. Figure skating
2. Baseball
3. To Cripple Creek, Colorado; it's held in June.
4. In Colorado Springs's Hall of Presidents
5. Silver; seven great silver mines made the town boom in the 1880s.
6. The Garden of the Gods, famous for its odd rock formations
7. Radium
8. Rocky Mountain National Park
9. "Buffalo Bill" Cody, who is buried there
10. Greeley, named for Horace Greeley

Connecticut, the Nutmeg State *(answers)*

1. ESPN
2. P. T. Barnum

3. What new type of telephone was first installed in Hartford in 1899?
4. The official state hero is what patriot hanged by the British?
5. Milford has a summer festival celebrating what edible shellfish?
6. What lovely seaside town takes its name from the Indian word *Mistuket*?
7. What jangly item (usually connected with Christmas) was a key product of New Britain in the 1800s?
8. What Ivy League school did not become coeducational until 1969?
9. On what appropriately named river is New London located?
10. What kinds of animal tracks are preserved in a museum in Wethersfield?

☆ Delaware, the Diamond State

1. What fruit tree's blossom is the state flower? (Hint: fuzz)
2. Lord De La Warr, whom the state is named for, was governor of what other colony?
3. For what two nations did the state supply troops from 1861 to 1865?
4. What Scandinavian group was the state's first group of permanent settlers?
5. What nearby colony was Delaware originally part of?
6. What painful form of public punishment was Delaware the last state to abolish?
7. The oldest active Protestant church in the nation was started by what denomination?
8. Dover, the state capital, has a museum devoted to what early form of home entertainment? (Hint: His Master's Voice)

3. A pay phone (This was *long* before the days of calling cards.)
4. Nathan Hale, famous for "I only regret that I have but one life to give for my country."
5. Oysters
6. Mystic
7. Sleigh bells
8. Yale, in New Haven
9. The Thames—same as the *old* London, in England
10. Dinosaur tracks, discovered while laying the foundation for a building

Delaware, the Diamond State *(answers)*

1. The peach
2. Virginia
3. The U.S. and the Confederacy; as a slave state, Delaware had many Confederate sympathizers.
4. Swedes, who settled in 1638
5. Pennsylvania
6. The whipping post, last used in 1952 and outlawed in 1972
7. Lutheran; it is the Holy Trinity (Old Swedes) Church, built by Swedish Lutherans in 1698. It is now owned by Episcopalians.
8. The Victrola, the early form of record player

9. Politician Pierre du Pont is better known by what name?
10. What flighty form of recreation has its own festival in Lewes?

☆ Florida, Vacation Paradise

1. What sunny gulf coast city (with lots of retired folks) is named for a cold and cloudy city in Russia?
2. What noted parade is held in Miami on New Year's Eve?
3. What large (and rare) sea mammal lends its name to a Florida county?
4. To hear country music stars at the Ocean Opry, what gulf coast city would you visit?
5. The Sunshine Skyway spans what large bay on the gulf coast?
6. Where can you see live mermaids performing water ballet?
7. What coastal town, named for a game fish, is noted for its Greek sponge divers?
8. Tampa Stadium is the site of what New Year's Day bowl game?
9. What tourist attraction is known worldwide for its glass-bottom boats and crystal-clear waters?
10. In the Black Hills Passion Play, who is the key character?

☆ Georgia, Empire State of the South

1. If you are riding on MARTA, where are you?
2. What valuable substance covers the dome of the state capitol building in Atlanta?
3. The figures of what three Confederate heroes are carved on Stone Mountain?

9. Pete; he's one of the famous (and wealthy) du Ponts of Delaware, best known for the chemical company.
10. Kite flying; the Kite Festival is held every Good Friday. *Lewes* is pronounced the same as *Lewis*, by the way.

Florida, Vacation Paradise *(answers)*

1. St. Petersburg
2. The King Orange Jamboree
3. The manatee, or sea cow; Manatee County is on the gulf coast.
4. Panama City
5. Tampa Bay; it's a long toll bridge beginning in St. Petersburg.
6. In Weeki Wachee; the mermaids are actually women divers, of course.
7. Tarpon Springs
8. The Hall of Fame Bowl
9. Silver Springs
10. Jesus; the outdoor play depicts the last seven days in the life of Christ. The play is held in Lake Wales.

Georgia, Empire State of the South *(answers)*

1. In Atlanta; MARTA is the Metropolitan Atlanta Rapid Transit Authority.
2. Gold, mined in northern Georgia
3. Jefferson Davis, president of the Confederacy, and Generals Robert E. Lee and Thomas "Stonewall" Jackson

4. Georgians refer to their favorite river as "The Hooch." What is its full name?
5. Atlanta's Cyclorama museum commemorates which American war?
6. The Great American Scream Machine at Six Flags Over Georgia is what sort of ride?
7. The impressive and historic Fort Pulaski lies near what seaport?
8. What large but movable item was stolen by Union spies at Kennesaw in 1862?
9. What world-famous botanical gardens are found at Pine Mountain?
10. Cartoonist Walt Kelly set his comic strip "Pogo" in what region?

☆ Hawaii, Pacific Paradise

1. Diamond Head and Waikiki beaches are in what city?
2. Mauna Loa, at 13,679 feet, is what type of mountain?
3. Belgian missionary François de Veuster founded a leper colony on the island of Molokai. By what name is he better known?
4. What was Captain Cook's earlier name for the islands? (Hint: sounds edible)
5. What nation was Sanford Dole president of?
6. What Christian group taught the Hawaiian natives to read and write?
7. Luther and Charlotte Gulick of Hawaii founded what organization for girls?
8. What author of massive historical novels wrote *Hawaii*?
9. Captain James Cook, the first white man to visit the islands, was from what country?
10. After Oahu, which is the most visited of the islands?

4. The Chattahoochee, made famous in Alan Jackson's song (and video) "Way Down Yonder on the Chattahoochee."
5. The Civil War; specifically, the Cyclorama is a multimedia reenactment of the Battle of Atlanta during the war. If you ever saw *Gone with the Wind*, you'll recall that Atlanta had an unpleasant time in the Civil War.
6. A roller coaster
7. Savannah
8. A locomotive; it was the *General*, and it belonged to the Confederacy. The theft was the subject of the Disney movie *The Great Locomotive Chase* and also a hilarious silent movie *The General*, with Buster Keaton.
9. The beautiful Callaway Gardens, noted for their enclosed butterfly and hummingbird center
10. The Okefenokee Swamp

Hawaii, Pacific Paradise *(answers)*

1. Honolulu
2. A volcano
3. Father Damien, sometimes called "the Leper Priest."
4. The Sandwich Islands
5. The short-lived Republic of Hawaii, which ended when the U.S. annexed the islands in 1898
6. Congregationalist missionaries
7. The Camp Fire Girls
8. James Michener; the book tells of the islands' first contacts with Europeans.
9. England; he was killed in Hawaii in 1779 (eaten by natives, to be specific).
10. Maui (rhymes with "zowie")

☆ Idaho, the Spud State

1. The U.S.'s deepest canyon is not the Grand Canyon but what Idaho canyon? (Hint: named for a *very* hot place)
2. U.S. Highway 12 is named for what two explorers of the early 1800s?
3. Idaho's tallest point, Borah Peak, is in a county named for what ill-fated Indian fighter? (Hint: last stand)
4. Boise has an international center devoted to conserving what types of birds?
5. What special type of poetry has its own festival in St. Anthony?
6. What large city gets some of its home heating energy from underground springs?
7. What folk instrument has its own hall of fame in Weiser?
8. What colorful European immigrant group has its own museum in Idaho?
9. Where could you see a volcanic landscape resembling the moon's surface?
10. Arco was the first U.S. town to be lighted by what energy source?

☆ Illinois, the Prairie State

1. In 1921, what chewing gum company stuck its thirty-story headquarters on Chicago's Michigan Avenue?
2. What theme park, part of the Six Flags chain, is in Gurnee, north of Chicago?
3. The Farm Implement Capital of America is what city?
4. Chicago's Finest refers to what group of public employees?
5. If you wanted to see more than seven thousand sea creatures, where would you go?
6. The University of Chicago was built with money from what multimillionaire?

Idaho, the Spud State *(answers)*

1. Hell's Canyon, 7,913 feet deep
2. Lewis and Clark
3. General George Custer
4. Birds of prey (that is, hawks, eagles, falcons, and so on); the center started as a program to protect the peregrine falcon.
5. Cowboy poetry
6. Boise; some local hot springs have temperatures up to 170 degrees.
7. Fiddles; actually, the hall of fame honors fiddlers. (By the way, Weiser is pronounced WEE-zer.)
8. The Basques, a group that immigrated from Spain in the early 1900s
9. Craters of the Moon National Monument
10. Atomic energy

Illinois, the Prairie State *(answers)*

1. Wrigley
2. Six Flags Great America
3. Moline, home of the John Deere company
4. The police; people who have dealt with them personally have called them other names. . . .
5. The famous Shedd Aquarium in Chicago
6. John D. Rockefeller

7. If you are watching the Cubs play a home game, what stadium are you in?
8. Jacksonville has the only U.S. factory for making what large fairground ride?
9. What kitchen-type nickname did early settlers give to the state's rich soil? (Hint: Cajun cookin')
10. What famous gangland massacre occurred on February 14, 1929?

☆ Indiana, Crossroads of America

1. Mount Baldy is a giant sand dune on the shores of what lake? (Hint: named for another state)
2. French Lick was named for the presence of what grainy substance?
3. Gary is the site of the main plant of what important metal company?
4. What giant pharmaceutical company is headquartered in Indianapolis?
5. Wabash was the first town to be lighted by what form of energy?
6. Muncie is home to what college named for a canning jar manufacturer?
7. A museum in Nashville traces the career of what gangster, Public Enemy Number One?
8. South Bend has a museum devoted to what make of autos (which are no longer produced)?
9. The Indianapolis 500 Festival features a tournament for what popular card game?
10. Corydon was the state's only battle site during what important war of the 1800s?

7. Wrigley Field
8. Ferris wheels
9. Gumbo
10. The St. Valentine's Day Massacre in Chicago

Indiana, Crossroads of America *(answers)*

1. Lake Michigan; it is in the Indiana Dunes National Lakeshore.
2. Salt; a salt lick in the area attracted wild animals in need of salt.
3. U.S. Steel
4. Eli Lilly
5. Electricity; this happened in 1880, when electric light radiated from the courthouse dome.
6. The Ball Corporation; the college is Ball State University.
7. John Dillinger
8. Studebakers, which ceased production in 1963
9. Gin rummy
10. The Civil War; the town suffered an invasion by Confederate raiders in 1863.

☆ Iowa, America's Heartland

1. What world-famous farm implement company can be toured in Waterloo? (Hint: antlers)
2. What religious group left Iowa en masse and moved on to Utah?
3. The fascinating Vesterheim museum in Decorah honors what ethnic group?
4. Cedar Rapids, Iowa, has a large museum devoted to what men's fraternal group?
5. What industrial center was begun by a German Christian group called the Inspirationists?
6. Burlington's Snake Alley is a street with what distinction?
7. If you ride the Dragon, the Tornado, and the Raging River, where are you?
8. What simple-living Christian group is the focus of the Kalona Historical Village?
9. What European immigrant group (much in the news in the 1990s) has an annual festival in Centerville?
10. What religious story is displayed in the Grotto of the Redemption?

☆ Kansas, the Jayhawk State

1. The town of Liberal has an annual race involving running while flipping what edible breakfast item?
2. What town is named for a fictional Indian hero? (Hint: Longfellow)
3. What town had such notable sheriffs as Bat Masterson and Wyatt Earp? (Hint: *Gunsmoke*)
4. What type of building is the Old Calaboose in Council Grove?
5. What city's tourist spots include the Eisenhower Center and the Greyhound Hall of Fame?

Iowa, America's Heartland *(answers)*

1. John Deere ("Nothing runs like a Deere.")
2. The Mormons
3. The Norwegians
4. The Masons
5. Amana, famed for its refrigerators, microwave ovens, and other products; the Inspirationists were a Lutheran offshoot, formed in the 1700s.
6. Supposedly it is the crookedest street in the world.
7. Adventureland, a theme park near Des Moines
8. The Amish
9. The Croatians
10. The Fall and redemption of man by Christ; the grotto covers an entire city block in West Bend, Iowa.

Kansas, the Jayhawk State *(answers)*

1. Pancakes; the International Pancake Race involves a 415-yard course.
2. Hiawatha, subject of Henry Wadsworth Longfellow's famous poem *The Song of Hiawatha*
3. Dodge City
4. A jail; *calaboose* is an old word for jail.
5. Abilene

6. What longtime Republican senator ran for president in 1996?
7. What much used cattle trail ran from San Antonio, Texas, to Abilene, Kansas?
8. What famous woman aviator's birthplace is in Atchison?
9. What men are displayed in the Hall of Generals in Abilene?
10. Independence has a Neewollah festival in October. What holiday is being celebrated?

☆ Kentucky, the Horse Kingdom

1. What city is infected with Derby Fever each May?
2. What Kentucky-born Confederate leader's birthday is celebrated on the first Sunday in September?
3. Rev. Elijah Craig was noted for inventing what drinkable substance?
4. In what national park can you take a boat ride on the underground Echo River?
5. Kentucky Wonders are what type of vegetable?
6. Cane Ridge was the site of what amazing Christian phenomenon of the 1800s?
7. What great American songwriter (who also wrote the state song of Florida) gave Kentucky its state song?
8. The John Conti Museum in Louisville honors what popular beverage? (Hint: grind)
9. A festival in Barbourville honors what near-legendary frontiersman?
10. The state capitol building was modeled after the tomb of what notable French leader?

6. Bob Dole
7. The Chisholm Trail (Yippi-yi-yippi-yay)
8. Amelia Earhart
9. Generals who had served under local boy Dwight Eisenhower; they're wax figures, by the way.
10. Halloween—which, spelled backwards, is Neewollah

Kentucky, the Horse Kingdom *(answers)*

1. Louisville, site of the Kentucky Derby
2. Confederate president Jefferson Davis's, who was born in Kentucky—as was his opponent, Abraham Lincoln
3. Bourbon whiskey; it's named for the state's Bourbon County, by the way.
4. Mammoth Cave
5. Beans
6. The camp meeting, which was not only a spiritual meeting but a major social gathering in frontier areas
7. Stephen Foster, who wrote "My Old Kentucky Home"; he was a Pennsylvanian who had spent practically no time in Kentucky.
8. Coffee
9. Daniel Boone
10. Napoleon Bonaparte

☆ Louisiana, the Bayou State

1. If you are strolling through the Crescent City, where are you?
2. A live Bengal tiger is kept as the mascot of what large university, famous for its football team?
3. What renowned French rogue had the nickname of "the Gentleman Pirate"?
4. What world-famous American artist lived in Louisiana while working on his famous collection of paintings, *Birds of America*?
5. What type of money used in Louisiana may have given a name to the entire South?
6. On what lake can you drive on a road across twenty-four miles of open water?
7. What feature of New Orleans cemeteries attracts tourists to them?
8. What hearty sandwich, made with meat and thick slices of French bread, originated in Louisiana?
9. What food sweetener, developed in Louisiana in the 1700s, changed the eating habits of people around the world?
10. What world-famous part of New Orleans culture first began in 1857?

☆ Maine, Home of Down-Easters

1. The islands near Acadia National Park are named for what popular holiday fruit? (Hint: Thanksgiving)
2. What official lives in the Blaine House in Augusta, the state capital?
3. What important objects were produced by the Bath Iron Works?
4. Until 1819, what New England state was Maine a part of?

Louisiana, the Bayou State *(answers)*

1. New Orleans; the nickname refers to the city's layout on a crescent-shaped stretch of the Mississippi River.
2. Louisiana State University (LSU) in Baton Rouge, whose team is (of course) the Tigers
3. The colorful Jean Lafitte
4. John James Audubon, who has a New Orleans park named in his honor
5. Ten-dollar bills, known as "Dixies" from the French word *dix* ("ten") printed on them
6. Lake Pontchartrain, north of New Orleans
7. They're built with the tombs *above ground,* due to the lowness of the soil and the likelihood of an underground grave being filled with water. Many of the above-ground tombs are stunningly beautiful.
8. The po'boy, similar to a submarine sandwich
9. Granulated sugar; sugar cane was, and is, widely grown in the state.
10. The Mardi Gras parade

Maine, Home of Down-Easters *(answers)*

1. Cranberries; there are five of the Cranberry Isles.
2. The state's governor
3. Ships, including destroyers, cruisers, battleships, and even pleasure craft
4. Massachusetts

5. Portland has the boyhood home of what poet, famed for *Hiawatha* and *Evangeline*?
6. What popular food fish is raised in pens in the waters off Eastport? (Hint: croquettes)
7. The St. Croix River separates Maine from what nation?
8. What Maine city was named for a tune the original settler hummed?
9. What is the distinction of Maine's seaside Cadillac Mountain?
10. The seaport of Kittery has a memorial to what famed American seaman of the Revolutionary War?

☆ Maryland, the Free State

1. What crop was often used in place of money in colonial Maryland? (Hint: puff)
2. What religious group was Maryland designed to serve as a refuge? (Hint: Mary-land)
3. What war's bloodiest single-day battle occurred at Antietam?
4. What federal political body met in Annapolis in 1783 and 1784?
5. At Ocean City's annual wood-carving festival, what creatures are carved?
6. If you are skinning hides at Cambridge's annual February festival, what web-footed, buck-toothed animal are you skinning?
7. What very old college is noted for not having majors?
8. What warship, built in the 1700s, can be toured in Baltimore's Inner Harbor?
9. Pimlico in Baltimore has a hall of fame for what diminutive sportsmen?
10. The town of Crisfield has a festival honoring what edible Chesapeake Bay resident?

5. Henry Wadsworth Longfellow
6. Salmon—millions of them
7. Canada
8. Bangor; when Rev. Seth Noble, the original settler, went to register the town's name, he was whistling the tune "Bangor," the name he gave in reply to the registrar's question about the town's name.
9. It is the highest point on the Atlantic coast.
10. John Paul Jones, famous for "I have not yet begun to fight."

Maryland, the Free State *(answers)*

1. Tobacco, still a major crop in the state
2. English Catholics, who, in the 1600s when the colony began, were a persecuted group
3. The Civil War; it's sometimes known as the Battle of Sharpsburg. The grisly battle took place September 17, 1862.
4. The U.S. Congress
5. Waterfowl
6. Muskrats
7. St. John's College, established in 1696 in Annapolis; the curriculum centers on the liberal arts, and there are no majors per se.
8. The *Constellation,* which was involved in wars from the War of 1812 to World War II
9. Jockeys
10. The blue crab; Crisfield has the annual National Hard Crab Derby. (Yes, in case you were wondering, there are also *soft-shelled* crabs.)

☆ Massachusetts, the Old Colony

1. What world-famous annual athletic event is run from Hopkinton to downtown Boston?
2. What sea-centered industry dominated the historic town of Nantucket? (Hint: *Moby Dick*)
3. What famous settlers of the 1600s are portrayed in the Plymouth National Wax Museum?
4. What Massachusetts town has a witch museum?
5. What sports hall of fame would you find in Springfield?
6. What city contains the birthplace of the second and sixth presidents, both named Adams?
7. What island is the state's most noted seaside playground?
8. What famous Declaration of Independence signer was born in Quincy?
9. What national holiday in the fall is celebrated in a big way in Plymouth?
10. What famous painter was born in Lowell? (Hint: mother)

☆ Michigan, the Lake State

1. What unusual sort of shoes could you purchase at the DeKlomp factory in the town of Holland?
2. What did the huge Willow Run factory produce during World War II?
3. By what name is the former Pontiac Spring Wagon Works now known?
4. Grand Rapids has a college named for a key leader in the Protestant Reformation. Who?
5. The Warren Dunes on Lake Michigan are a popular site for what aerial sport?
6. Ishpeming is home to what winter sport hall of fame?
7. What national park on an island has five-thousand-year-old copper mines?
8. What automaker has a museum in Lansing?

Massachusetts, the Old Colony *(answers)*

1. The Boston Marathon
2. Whaling
3. The Pilgrims, naturally
4. Salem; it commemorates the notorious witchcraft trials of 1692.
5. The Basketball Hall of Fame; the game was invented in Springfield.
6. Quincy, birthplace of John Adams and his son John Quincy Adams
7. Martha's Vineyard
8. John Hancock, famous for his oversized signature
9. Thanksgiving, of course; Plymouth is the site of the original Pilgrims' Thanksgiving.
10. James Abbott McNeill Whistler; the birthplace is now the Whistler House Museum of Art.

Michigan, the Lake State *(answers)*

1. Wooden
2. Bombers; later the site became an airport.
3. General Motors
4. John Calvin; the city has Calvin College and Calvin Theological Seminary.
5. Hang gliding; the high dunes and the winds off the lake are perfect for the sport.
6. The National Ski Hall of Fame
7. Isle Royale, an island in Lake Superior
8. Oldsmobile; it is the R. E. Olds Museum, and it includes the first Olds, built in 1897.

9. Grand Rapids has a museum devoted to which Republican president of the 1970s?
10. What hockey team plays its home games at the Joe Louis Sports Arena?

☆ Minnesota, the Gopher State

1. Minnesota Mining and Manufacturing is better known by what corporate name? (Hint: adhesive tape)
2. What ice cream novelty was invented in Blue Earth, Minnesota? (Hint: chocolate and vanilla together)
3. What two fictional Indian characters have statues in a city park in Minneapolis? (Hint: Longfellow)
4. What icy sport is featured in an international competition in Hibbing each April?
5. What waterway links the far inland state of Minnesota with the ocean?
6. What is the meaning of the Indian name *Minnesota*?
7. What beautiful Minnesota lake is shared with Canada?
8. Northfield annually celebrates the defeat of what noted desperado?
9. What chilly (and violent) sport has its hall of fame in Eveleth, Minnesota?
10. According to folklore, the ten thousand lakes in Minnesota are the footprints of what giant?

☆ Mississippi, the Deep, Deep South

1. What *very* southern flower (which grows on a beautiful evergreen tree) is the state flower?
2. What attraction near the town of Floria is thirty-six million years old?
3. What Confederate leader represents the state in D.C.'s Statuary Hall?

9. Gerald Ford, a Michigan man
10. The Detroit Red Wings

Minnesota, the Gopher State *(answers)*

1. 3M, maker of Scotch tape
2. The ice-cream sandwich
3. Hiawatha and his wife, Minnehaha, famous in Longfellow's poem *The Song of Hiawatha*
4. Curling, roughly equivalent to bowling on ice
5. The St. Lawrence Seaway, linking Minnesota's Great Lakes ports with the Atlantic Ocean
6. "Sky-colored waters"
7. Lake of the Woods, more than two thousand square miles in area
8. Jesse James, whose gang was foiled in the attempt to rob the local bank in 1876
9. Hockey
10. Paul Bunyan, the lumberjack, and his blue ox, Babe

Mississippi, the Deep, Deep South *(answers)*

1. The magnolia blossom, y'all
2. The Mississippi Petrified Forest
3. Confederate president Jefferson Davis, who had been a senator from Mississippi before the Civil War

4. What was unique about the state college founded in Columbus in 1884?
5. Where would you find the Tomb of the Unknown Soldier of the Confederate States of America?
6. What major city was once a trading post called LeFleur's Bluff?
7. The best-known tour of southern antebellum homes is in what town?
8. In Vaughan you could find a museum devoted to America's most famous railroad man. Who?
9. Rev. Newitt Vicks's Methodist mission became what city?
10. Who lived in the historic home Beauvoir in Biloxi?

☆ Missouri, Truman- and Twain-land

1. What notorious outlaw's farm can be visited in Excelsior Springs?
2. What French king's forty-seven-foot statue stands outside the St. Louis Art Museum?
3. Where can you see the Adventures of Tom Sawyer Diorama Museum?
4. St. Louis has a hall of fame devoted to what popular indoor sport?
5. What city's pro hockey team is the Blades?
6. Kansas City's sports complex is named for what president?
7. Fulton, Missouri, was named for what inventor?
8. What pop singer's Branson, Missouri, theater is named the Moon River?
9. What is unique about the College of the Ozarks's tuition fees?
10. The wax museum in Sullivan, Missouri, is devoted to what outlaws?

4. It was the nation's first state college for women. Today it's Mississippi University for Women.
5. In Biloxi
6. The capital, Jackson
7. Natchez; the Natchez Pilgrimage is held in both spring and fall.
8. Casey Jones; the museum is near the site of the 1900 train crash in which he was killed.
9. Vicksburg, named for the reverend; it is one of the most historic towns in the South.
10. Confederate president Jefferson Davis, after the Civil War

Missouri, Truman- and Twain-land *(answers)*

1. Jesse James's
2. King Louis IX's, who was also St. Louis, known in his day for leading a Crusade
3. In author Mark Twain's hometown, Hannibal
4. Bowling
5. Kansas City's
6. Missouri-born Harry Truman
7. Steamboat inventor Robert Fulton
8. Andy Williams's, of course
9. The students work, rather than pay, for tuition.
10. Jesse James and his gang, plus several other outlaws of the Old West

☆ Montana, the Treasure State

1. What would you expect to see at the Crow Fair in Hardin?
2. What town is named for the warm winter winds that melt the snows?
3. What city, a mining center, claims it sits on "the richest hill on earth"?
4. What late newscaster developed the resort community of Big Sky? (Hint: "Good night, David.")
5. What town is named for a huge South American snake?
6. One of the biggest glaciers has an odd name, based on the millions of insects frozen in it. What is it called?
7. What city was a gold-rush town formerly called Last Chance?
8. Beartooth Highway was called America's most beautiful roadway by what roving news reporter?
9. What pacifist Christian group operates some of Montana's largest cattle ranches?
10. What type of gem mine can be visited in Hamilton, Montana?

☆ Nebraska, Land of the Platte

1. What farm animal is celebrated in an annual festival in Wayne? (Hint: pluck)
2. Where would you see the famous *He Ain't Heavy, He's My Brother* statue?
3. What well-known insurance company has a glass-domed (and underground) building in Omaha?
4. Whose statue is atop the capitol dome in Lincoln?
5. What historic communications station could you visit in Gothenburg?
6. What majestic birds are observed in an annual Wings over the Platte festival?

Montana, the Treasure State *(answers)*

1. Not birds, but Crow Indians; they hold a large all-Indian rodeo at the fair.
2. Chinook
3. Butte, a center for copper, gold, silver, and many other metals
4. Chet Huntley
5. Anaconda
6. Grasshopper Glacier
7. The capital, Helena
8. Charles Kuralt, now retired, but formerly "On the Road" each week
9. The Hutterites, Germans who found religious refuge in Russia, then later in America
10. Sapphire

Nebraska, Land of the Platte *(answers)*

1. Chickens; the Chicken Show each July includes omelet cook-offs, egg games, a chicken art show, and a chicken parade.
2. In Boys Town; the statue commemorates a boy carrying an injured friend.
3. Mutual of Omaha, naturally
4. A sower, pointing to the state's agricultural heritage
5. A pony express station
6. The large sandhill cranes, which stop each spring on the Platte River on their migration north

7. Lincoln has the national festival for what eastern European immigrants?
8. What religious group has a pioneer cemetery in Omaha?
9. What is the Indian meaning of "Nebraska"?
10. Indian chief Mahpiua Luta was better known by what name? (Hint: weather)

☆ Nevada, the Sagebrush State

1. What world-famous resort city's name means "the meadows"?
2. What notable dam created Lake Mead in Nevada?
3. What famous TV house could you visit in Incline Village? (Hint: Hoss and Little Joe)
4. Las Vegas has a museum devoted to what flamboyant pianist?
5. What town calls itself "the Biggest Little City in the World"?
6. What famous mine made Virginia City into a boom town?
7. What name is given to Las Vegas's gaudy row of casinos, hotels, and nightclubs?
8. What precious metal tops the dome of the Nevada state capitol?
9. If you wished to see the Circus Maximus, what famous Las Vegas hotel would you visit?
10. The formations in the Valley of Fire are made of what?

☆ New Hampshire, Mother of Rivers

1. The world record for wind speed (231 mph) was recorded on what famous mountain?
2. New Hampshire was the first state to use what new method of fighting forest fires?

7. The Czechs; the colorful Czech Festival is held each August.
8. The Mormons
9. "Flat water"
10. Red Cloud

Nevada, the Sagebrush State *(answers)*

1. Las Vegas
2. The Hoover Dam
3. The Cartwrights' home in the series *Bonanza;* it is part of the Ponderosa Ranch and Western Theme Park.
4. Liberace; it has several of his pianos, and pieces from his notorious wardrobe.
5. Reno
6. The Comstock Lode, which yielded both silver and gold
7. The Strip
8. Silver; Nevada is the Silver State as well as the Sagebrush State.
9. Caesar's Palace
10. Red sandstone

New Hampshire, Mother of Rivers *(answers)*

1. Mount Washington, noted for its violent weather
2. Artificial rain, first used in 1947

3. The Sea Shell on New Hampshire's coast is what sort of structure?
4. What appropriate name is given to the mountain range that includes Mount Washington, Mount Adams, and Mount Jackson?
5. What is distinctive about the state's eighteen-mile coastline?
6. Where could you see America's Stonehenge, dating around 2000 B.C.?
7. The beautiful Cathedral of the Pines is a nondenominational shrine honoring whom?
8. What famous orator of the U.S. Senate in the 1800s was born in Franklin?
9. What is distinctive about this small state's legislature?
10. What lofty mountain has such treacherous weather that the annual average temperature is below freezing?

☆ New Jersey, Mid-Atlantic Eden

1. The game of Monopoly is based on the streets of what seaside resort city?
2. The Religious Research Center is connected with what prestigious college?
3. What type of gem are the Cape May diamonds?
4. What oversized household item tops the Edison Memorial Tower?
5. Which Six Flags theme park would you find in Jackson, New Jersey?
6. What city has the same name as a province of Canada?
7. What crustaceans are raced in an annual pageant in Ocean City?
8. What noted colonial preacher died shortly after becoming president of Princeton?
9. What teetotaling resort town is near (but very different from) Atlantic City?

3. A band shell, used for summer concerts
4. The Presidential Range
5. It's the shortest oceanfront of any state (excepting states that have *no* coast, of course).
6. It's in North Salem and, like Stonehenge in England, has stones set up to form a sort of astronomical calendar.
7. All American war dead
8. Daniel Webster; his birthplace can be visited there.
9. It's the largest in the country, with more than four hundred seats.
10. Mount Washington

New Jersey, Mid-Atlantic Eden *(answers)*

1. Atlantic City
2. Princeton; it is also connected with the famous Gallup organization.
3. Pure quartz, found on the Delaware Bay shores
4. A thirteen-foot electric light bulb
5. Six Flags Great Adventure
6. New Brunswick
7. Hermit crabs
8. Jonathan Edwards, who is buried in Princeton
9. Ocean City, founded by three devout Methodist ministers

10. What two New Jersey toll roads are two of the country's busiest highways?

☆ New Mexico, Land of Lobos and Aggies

1. What fictional animal has his own museum in Ruidoso? (Hint: forest fires)
2. What famous Western trail ended at Santa Fe?
3. What state park is named for an infamous Mexican outlaw?
4. Mesilla was briefly the capital of New Mexico—under what nation?
5. What large New Mexico city is known as the Hot Air Balloon Capital of the World?
6. What town is named for an Indian tribe usually associated with southern Mexico?
7. Abo Elementary School in Artesia has what curious location?
8. Santa Rosa has a museum devoted to what notorious young gunslinger?
9. Whose names are carved on Inscription Rock?
10. What New Mexico city is alphabetically first among the top fifty cities in population?

☆ New York, the Excelsior State

1. What world-famous magazine and book company is headquartered in Pleasantville? (Hint: condense)
2. What famous New York skyscraper opened in May 1931?
3. Who opened his first five-and-dime store in Utica in 1879?
4. Big as New York City is, only one president has been born there. Who? (Hint: glasses and a *very* wide grin)

10. The Garden State Parkway and the New Jersey Turnpike

New Mexico, Land of Lobos and Aggies *(answers)*

1. Smokey the Bear, the national symbol of forest fire prevention
2. The Santa Fe Trail (surprise!); the city has a marker for the trail's end.
3. Pancho Villa, who killed several Americans in a 1916 raid
4. The Confederate States of America
5. Albuquerque
6. Aztec; some early settlers mistook local Pueblo ruins for Aztec ruins.
7. Underground, built there out of fear of nuclear fallout
8. Billy the Kid
9. Several of the Spanish conquistadors who passed through the area in the 1500s; the inscriptions have been helpful to historians.
10. Albuquerque

New York, the Excelsior State *(answers)*

1. The Reader's Digest
2. The Empire State Building
3. F. W. Woolworth
4. Theodore Roosevelt

5. What explorer in 1609 sailed up the New York river that now bears his name?
6. What pro football team plays its home games in Rich Stadium?
7. What great canal was originally known as "the big ditch"?
8. What feat did New York saloonkeeper Steve Brodie claim to have done in 1886?
9. What notorious prison in Ossining was built with convict labor in 1825?
10. What great short-story author is buried in Sleepy Hollow Cemetery?

☆ North Carolina, the Old North State

1. Duke University in Durham received much of its endowment from what crop? (Hint: puff)
2. If you're shaking hands with Yogi Bear and Fred Flintstone, what theme park near Charlotte are you in?
3. Mount Airy was the hometown of what actor famous as a TV sheriff?
4. Snow falls up, rather than down, at what site?
5. What town is home to more than 125 furniture factories?
6. What picturesque mountain near Linville is named for its resemblance to a bearded old man?
7. What persecuted group of Italian Christians settled the town of Valdese?
8. The state capital was named for what famous English soldier and author?
9. *Worthy Is the Lamb,* an outdoor drama on the coast, concerns what historical figure?
10. Evangelist Billy Graham's birthplace in Charlotte is now occupied by what corporate giant?

5. Henry Hudson
6. The Buffalo Bills
7. The Erie Canal, opened in 1825
8. Jumped off the Brooklyn Bridge (and lived to tell about it)
9. Sing Sing
10. Washington Irving, author of "Rip Van Winkle" and "The Legend of Sleepy Hollow."

North Carolina, the Old North State *(answers)*

1. Tobacco; the Dukes were wealthy tobacco farmers.
2. Carowinds
3. Andy Griffith, who played Sheriff Taylor on *The Andy Griffith Show* for many years
4. Blowing Rock; it is a large stone formation over the John's River Gorge. Air currents often blow objects, including snow, upward from the gorge.
5. High Point
6. Grandfather Mountain
7. The Waldensians, who practiced Protestant beliefs several centuries before the Protestant Reformation
8. Sir Walter Raleigh, famous in the court of Queen Elizabeth I in the 1500s
9. Jesus, called "the Lamb of God" in the New Testament
10. IBM, which thoughtfully erected a plaque mentioning the connection with Graham

☆ North Dakota, the Flickertail State

1. What "champagne musicmaker" was a North Dakota native?
2. What grain is the state's leading crop? (Hint: bread)
3. The state is sometimes called the Flickertail State. What are flickertails?
4. What game, legalized in 1981, turned the state into a gamblers' destination?
5. What city, the state's largest, is named for a famous cargo and security company?
6. Where could you attend the Potato Bowl?
7. What is "the Skyscraper of the Prairies"?
8. What outdoorsy president, born in New York, is connected with North Dakota?
9. Bismarck has a statue of what noted Indian woman?
10. The state's only national park is named for what president?

☆ Ohio, Birthplace of Presidents

1. At what college were four students shot by the National Guard on May 4, 1970?
2. Milan has the birthplace of one of America's greatest inventors. Who? (Hint: light bulbs)
3. At what theme park can you ride the Beast and shake hands with Huckleberry Hound?
4. What city was named for a fraternity of Revolutionary War veterans?
5. What TV evangelist broadcasts his *Cathedral of Tomorrow* from Akron?
6. What meat-cooking contest spices the air of Cleveland every September?

North Dakota, the Flickertail State *(answers)*

1. Lawrence Welk, who else? ("A-one, and a-two . . .")
2. Wheat; it leads the U.S. in wheat production.
3. Ground squirrels, similar to chipmunks
4. Blackjack
5. Fargo, named for William Fargo of the Wells Fargo Company
6. In Grand Forks in September; a Potato Queen is crowned.
7. The eighteen-story capitol building in Bismarck
8. Theodore Roosevelt, who pursued his hairy-chested hobby of hunting and ranching in North Dakota
9. Sacajawea, who aided the Lewis and Clark expedition
10. Again, Theodore Roosevelt; the park contains land that was part of his ranch.

Ohio, Birthplace of Presidents *(answers)*

1. Kent State
2. Thomas Edison, who spent his first seven years there
3. King's Island
4. Cincinnati, named for the Society of the Cincinnati
5. Rex Humbard
6. The Plain Dealer Barbecue Ribs Burnoff

7. What ingredient—normally used in desserts—is a distinctive part of Cincinnati chili?
8. What city is so extremely *normal* that fast-food marketers have named it "Test Market, U.S.A."?
9. *The Living Word* outdoor drama in Cambridge, Ohio, depicts the life of what important person?
10. In what portrait museum in Canton would you see portraits of Martin Luther, David Livingstone, and Billy Sunday?

☆ Oklahoma, Oil and Cowboys and Prairie Dogs

1. What ever-popular musical by Rodgers and Hammerstein is presented continuously at Tulsa's Discoveryland Theatre?
2. What large city is headquarters of the U.S. Jaycees?
3. Lake Texoma lies on the border with what state?
4. What ancient sport has its hall of fame in Stillwater? (Hint: no equipment needed)
5. What large-beaked water bird is honored by a festival in Grand Lake?
6. Bartlesville is home to what corporate petroleum giant?
7. What was the sad name given to the eastern Indians' trek to their new home in Oklahoma?
8. What name was given to parts of Oklahoma where topsoil completely dried out in the 1930s?
9. What movie "King of the Cowboys" days has a museum in Bartlesville?
10. What does the McClellan-Kerr Navigation System provide for the landlocked state?

7. Chocolate
8. Columbus
9. Jesus
10. The Christian Hall of Fame, a museum operated by the Canton Baptist Temple

Oklahoma, Oil and Cowboys and Prairie Dogs
(answers)

1. *Oklahoma!*—what else?
2. Tulsa
3. Texas, naturally; the lake's name blends TEXas and OklahOMA.
4. Wrestling—*real* wrestling, not the theatrical knockabouts that charge admission
5. The white pelican; the Pelican Festival is held every September, when the huge birds pass through on their migration south.
6. Phillips Petroleum (of Phillips 66 fame); the founder's mansion is in the town.
7. The Trail of Tears; many Indians died en route.
8. The Dust Bowl
9. Tom Mix, who was king in the silent movie era (pre–John Wayne, that is)
10. A direct water route to the Mississippi River and Gulf of Mexico

☆ Oregon, the Christmas Tree Empire

1. What major city's twenty-four-day Rose Festival attracts visitors from around the world?
2. At 1,932 feet, what lake is the deepest lake in the U.S.?
3. What Portland college is named for two of America's most famous explorers?
4. Lincoln City calls itself the world capital of what flighty pastime?
5. The beautiful 620-foot Multnomah Falls are near what metropolis?
6. What large-hoofed animal is barbecued at the Jedediah Smith Mountain Man Rendezvous?
7. The "62" Day Celebration commemorates what great discovery in 1862?
8. What noted English explorer saw the coast of Oregon in the 1700s?
9. The World Championship Timber Carnival is held where?
10. What town was the site of gold mining among beach sands?

☆ Pennsylvania, the Quaker State

1. What patriot's funeral in 1790 drew a crowd of twenty thousand mourners in Philadelphia?
2. What metal do we associate with Bethlehem?
3. What chocolate company created the town that surrounds it?
4. The National Civil War Wax Museum is near what famous battle site?
5. What famous potato chip company could you tour in Hanover?
6. If you wished to see the Promised Land, where would you go?

Oregon, the Christmas Tree Empire *(answers)*
1. Portland's
2. Crater Lake, sitting in the basin of a dormant volcano
3. Lewis and Clark
4. Kite flying
5. Portland
6. Buffalo
7. Gold, of course
8. Captain James Cook, more commonly associated with South Sea islands
9. Near the town of Albany
10. The aptly named town Gold Beach

Pennsylvania, the Quaker State *(answers)*
1. Benjamin Franklin's
2. Steel, since the town is home to Bethlehem Steel, known the world over
3. Hershey, which created Hershey, Pennsylvania
4. Gettysburg
5. Utz
6. Promised Land State Park, near the town of Hawley

7. The annual Bark Peeler's Convention is for what type of workers?
8. What Bible passage was supposed to be the basis of the colony of Pennsylvania?
9. Lancaster is the heart of what colorful and much-traveled area?
10. Pittsburgh's Alcoa Building is constructed of what metal?

☆ Rhode Island, the Ocean State

1. The International Tennis Hall of Fame is in what posh resort town?
2. The popular Jazz Festival in Newport is named for what Japanese electronics firm?
3. What tree, noted for its blaze of color in fall, is the state tree?
4. What artist, noted for portraits of George Washington, was a Rhode Island native?
5. What prestigious college was originally named Rhode Island College?
6. The stunning Blithewold Gardens mansion overlooks what bay?
7. What religious group settled here before settling Pennsylvania?
8. What is the largest city *on* Rhode Island?
9. Providence has a memorial to what colonial pastor?
10. What celebrated yacht race was first held in Newport in 1930?

☆ South Carolina, Palms and Plantations

1. If you are gazing at the Atlantic and walking the Battery, in what old city are you?
2. What drastic step did the state take in 1860?

7. Lumberjacks
8. The Sermon on the Mount, according to the deeply religious founder, William Penn
9. The Pennsylvania Dutch region
10. Aluminum

Rhode Island, the Ocean State *(answers)*

1. Newport
2. JVC
3. The red maple
4. Gilbert Stuart
5. Brown University, in Providence
6. Narragansett Bay
7. The Quakers, who in both places were seeking religious freedom
8. Newport, which is on the actual island named Rhode Island
9. Its founder, Roger Williams
10. America's Cup

South Carolina, Palms and Plantations *(answers)*

1. Charleston
2. Seceding from the U.S.; it was the first state to do so, and thus the first state of the Confederacy.

3. What U.S. president has a state park named for him near Lancaster?
4. The sixty-mile-long Atlantic beach strip is called what?
5. The state has a huge lake named for its longtime senator. Who?
6. What nation attempted—unsuccessfully—to settle here in the 1500s?
7. What 1989 disaster caused $6 billion in property damage?
8. What infamous Yankee general set fire to Columbia in February 1865?
9. The renowned Spoleto Festival was founded by what composer?
10. What oriental grain was the basis of the colony's economy?

☆ South Dakota, Land of Mount Rushmore

1. What noted Wild West gunslingers are buried in Mount Moriah cemetery in Deadwood?
2. The world's largest statue, 563 feet high, is of what Sioux Indian chief?
3. What handicraft is the center of a museum in Custer?
4. If you ride the train with Fred, Wilma, and Dino, where are you?
5. In what national park can you see bison, pronghorn antelope, and bighorn sheep?
6. The world-famous Black Hills Roundup is held where?
7. According to western folklore, the Black Hills of South Dakota are a burial mound over what mythical animal?
8. What were the bullwhackers of the frontier days?
9. The Enchanted World Museum features what kind of toys?
10. What famous western character was shot in Deadwood's Saloon #10?

3. Andrew Jackson, who was born in the area
4. The Grand Strand
5. Republican senator Strom Thurmond, who at age 93 was elected to another term in 1996
6. France; the French Huguenot settlement at Port Royal did not last.
7. Hurricane Hugo
8. William T. Sherman, still excited (apparently) after his notorious March to the Sea
9. Gian Carlo Menotti, best-known for his Christmas opera, *Amahl and the Night Visitors*
10. Rice

South Dakota, Land of Mount Rushmore *(answers)*

1. Wild Bill Hickok and Calamity Jane
2. Crazy Horse, noted for defeating George Custer
3. Wood-carving
4. Flintstones Bedrock City, near the town of Custer
5. Badlands
6. Near the town of Belle Fourche
7. Babe, the blue ox belonging to lumberjack Paul Bunyan
8. Wagon drivers
9. Dolls—more than four thousand of them, in scenes from fairy tales and other stories
10. Wild Bill Hickok

☆ Tennessee, Music and Mountaineers

1. Dollywood is a theme park owned by what bigger-than-life country singer and actress?
2. Smyrna is the home of what Japanese automaker's plant?
3. Christus Gardens in Gatlinburg depicts scenes from the life of what person?
4. Nashville's Union Gospel Tabernacle became what country music palace?
5. The French Broad and the Holston Rivers converge to form what major river? (Hint: named for a state)
6. The American Museum of Science and Energy is in what city?
7. What type of pilots are trained at the aviation school in Elizabethton?
8. The Hermitage is the home and burial place of what president?
9. What snack cake company, named for a little girl, is in Collegedale?
10. Where is the Gospel Music Hall of Fame?

☆ Texas, Land of Longhorns

1. What enormous stadium would you find in Houston's Astrodomain?
2. On January 1, where can you see the Cotton Bowl?
3. What rock and roll pioneer is honored with a statue in Lubbock? (Hint: Peggy Sue)
4. By what more famous name do we know the Mission San Antonio de Valero?
5. What bank-robbing couple was shot down by Texas Rangers in 1934?
6. Sweetwater, Texas, has a roundup of what fearsome fanged creatures?

Tennessee, Music and Mountaineers *(answers)*

1. Dolly Parton
2. Nissan's
3. Jesus Christ
4. The Grand Ole Opry; the building was originally built by wealthy Tom Ryman to house the crowds coming to hear revival preachers. After Ryman's death, the building was renamed the Ryman Auditorium.
5. The Tennessee
6. Oak Ridge
7. Missionaries; they receive specialized training, since they often fly to very remote areas.
8. Andrew Jackson; his wife, Rachel, is also buried there.
9. Little Debbie
10. Nashville, very near the Country Music Hall of Fame

Texas, Land of Longhorns *(answers)*

1. The Astrodome, naturally
2. Dallas
3. Buddy Holly, a Texas native
4. The Alamo
5. Clyde Barrow and Bonnie Parker, better known as Bonnie and Clyde
6. Rattlesnakes; more accurately, it hosts the Rattlesnake Roundup every March.

7. What Texas city was named for the Huaco Indians?
8. The world's largest marine park is in what historic metropolis?
9. "Old Sparky" in the Texas Prison Museum is what sort of apparatus?
10. What is the distinction of the King ranch in Texas?

☆ Utah, the Mormon State

1. What is the Mormon Temple in Salt Lake City used for?
2. The world's largest genealogical library is where?
3. What southern crop did Mormons try (and fail) to grow in southern Utah?
4. What large city was named for French fur trapper Etienne Provost?
5. Moab, Utah, has a museum honoring what important part of the movie industry?
6. What valuable radioactive mineral was discovered in Moab, Utah?
7. What site has yielded more dinosaur skeletons than any other archaeological dig in the world?
8. Golden Spike National Historic Site commemorates what important 1869 event?
9. For the Mormon settlers, a gentile was what sort of person?
10. Beaver, Utah, was the birthplace of what noted outlaw? (Hint: Paul Newman)

☆ Vermont, Ethan Allen Land

1. What is the meaning of Vermont's name?
2. What "sweet-natured" tree is the state tree of Vermont?
3. What famed English author of children's tales lived in Vermont in the 1890s? (Hint: *The Jungle Book*)
4. Middlebury College has a cabin that belonged to what great New England poet?

7. Waco; the Spanish *Huaco* is pronounced (almost) the same as Waco.
8. San Antonio; it's Sea World of Texas.
9. An electric chair
10. With 825,000 acres, it is the world's largest privately owned ranch.

Utah, the Mormon State *(answers)*

1. The church "ordinances," such as baptisms and marriages; unlike the Mormon Tabernacle, it's not open to non-Mormons.
2. Salt Lake City; it is the Mormons' Family History Library.
3. Cotton
4. Provo, which is the pronunciation of the French name *Provost*
5. Stuntmen; the Hollywood Stuntmen's Hall of Fame is a popular tourist attraction.
6. Uranium
7. Dinosaur National Monument
8. The completing of the first transcontinental railroad; a real golden spike was used at the opening ceremony. It's in Brigham.
9. A non-Mormon
10. Butch Cassidy, born in Beaver in 1866

Vermont, Ethan Allen Land *(answers)*

1. The same as its nickname—"green mountain"; the French is *vert mont*.
2. The sugar maple
3. Rudyard Kipling, author of *The Jungle Book*, *Kim*, and other classics; he and his wife, a Vermont woman, lived in Brattleboro.
4. Robert Frost

5. What distinction does state capital Montpelier—population eight thousand—hold?
6. What type of fishing is the focus of a museum in Manchester?
7. Burlington, Vermont's largest city, lies on what large lake (named for a French settler)?
8. Rock of Ages is what sort of place?
9. Brandon has the birthplace of what noted political opponent of Abraham Lincoln?
10. What U.S. president was born near the tiny town of Bardoville?

☆ Virginia, the Cavalier State

1. What historic college lies at the west end of colonial Williamsburg? (Hint: named for a king and queen of England)
2. The scenic Skyline Drive is in what national park?
3. The nation's largest naval base is in what historic port city?
4. What famous Confederate war figure was imprisoned in Fort Lee after the war?
5. The battlefield museum at Yorktown commemorates the end of what war?
6. What college, with a campus designed by Thomas Jefferson, is found in Charlottesville?
7. What renowned Confederate general's home can you tour in Lexington?
8. The famous Smithfield hams come from hogs fed on what distinctive diet? (Hint: Peter Pan)
9. Arlington Cemetery was built on the estate of what noted Confederate general?
10. What cable network, headquartered in Virginia Beach, was launched by Christian broadcaster Pat Robertson?

5. It's the nation's smallest state capital.
6. Fly fishing
7. Lake Champlain
8. A quarry (surprise!); it's also a center for stone cutting and monument design.
9. Stephen Douglas, famed for the Lincoln-Douglas debates
10. Chester Arthur (If you missed this, well, Arthur was *not* the best-known of U.S. presidents.)

Virginia, the Cavalier State *(answers)*

1. The College of William and Mary
2. Shenandoah
3. Norfolk
4. Confederate president Jefferson Davis; his cell can still be visited there.
5. The American Revolution; George Washington accepted the surrender of British forces there in 1781.
6. The University of Virginia
7. Thomas "Stonewall" Jackson's; he was a professor at Virginia Military Institute, also in Lexington.
8. Peanuts
9. Robert E. Lee; the house was confiscated by the federal government shortly after the war began.
10. The Family Channel, spun off from Robertson's Christian Broadcasting Network; both are based in Virginia Beach.

☆ Washington, the Chinook State

1. The San Juan Islands have a museum devoted to what enormous sea creature?
2. What tall leftover from the 1962 World's Fair dominates Seattle's skyline?
3. What fruit is normally associated with the state?
4. Washington is represented in D.C.'s Statuary Hall by Marcus Whitman. What was his claim to fame?
5. What gold rush (much further north) turned Seattle into a boomtown?
6. The state's highest mountain is the center of what national park?
7. What noted aircraft manufacturer is based in Washington?
8. What fur-bearing creatures first attracted settlers?
9. Where did the state get its name?
10. What famous English sea captain sighted the area in 1579?

☆ West Virginia, Miners and Mountaineers

1. From about 1873 to 1890, the famous feud between what two mountain families was at its worst?
2. What major American river (named for a state) forms the state's border with Ohio?
3. Jackson's Mill Museum is the boyhood home of what renowned Confederate general?
4. What future president was in West Virginia in the Civil War, fighting Confederate guerrillas?
5. The state's longtime senator is from what wealthy New York family?
6. Charles Town was the site of one of the nineteenth century's most important executions. What antislavery radical was hanged there in 1859?

Washington, the Chinook State *(answers)*

1. Whales; the Whale Museum also gives some attention to porpoises.
2. The Space Needle
3. Apples, naturally
4. He and his wife were missionaries to the Indians; those Indians killed the Whitmans in 1847.
5. The Klondike Rush of 1897, which sent prospectors scurrying north, using Seattle as a supply town
6. Mount Rainier
7. Boeing ("If it's not Boeing, I'm not going.")
8. Sea otters
9. From George Washington (Did anyone actually miss this?)
10. Sir Francis Drake, on his noted voyage around the world

West Virginia, Miners and Mountaineers *(answers)*

1. The Hatfields and McCoys
2. The Ohio, appropriately enough
3. Thomas "Stonewall" Jackson
4. William McKinley, a Union army officer long before he was president
5. The Rockefellers
6. John Brown, who had led the fanatical raid on Harpers Ferry

7. According to the state motto, what type of people are always free?
8. What covers 75 percent of the state?
9. When the Civil War began, what did West Virginia *not* have that Virginia had?
10. In what census year did the state's population peak?

☆ Wisconsin, America's Dairyland

1. What is the smallest pro football town in the U.S.?
2. Baraboo has a museum devoted to what colorful type of entertainment? (Hint: three rings)
3. What famous pen manufacturer has its offices in Janesville?
4. What room in the average home has a connection to the town of Kohler?
5. If you wished to visit Paul Bunyan's camp, where would you go?
6. Couderay has The Hideout. What famous Chicago gangster used it as his real hideout?
7. The Burlington Liars' Club promotes what type of entertainment?
8. What gleeful singing organization has its headquarters in Harmony Hall in Kenosha?
9. What native of Appleton went on to become the world's most famous escape artist?
10. What important (but not attractive) metal led waves of settlers to the Wisconsin wilderness?

☆ Wyoming, the Equality State

1. What famous western trail led thousands of immigrants through Wyoming?
2. What is the appropriate team name for the University of Wyoming?

7. Mountain people; the Latin motto is *Montani semper liberi*—mountaineers are always free.
8. Forests; it is one of the most heavily forested states.
9. Slaves—or it had relatively few, anyway; slaves were only about 4 percent of the population. This was a key factor in separating from the state of Virginia.
10. In 1950, at about 2.5 million; it has gone down while most states' populations have increased.

Wisconsin, America's Dairyland *(answers)*

1. Green Bay, the only one with less than 100,000 population; but no city is more loyal to its team than Green Bay.
2. Circuses; it is the Circus World Museum, built in the former Ringling Brothers quarters.
3. Parker
4. The bathroom; the town has the Kohler Co., noted for making bathroom fixtures.
5. Eau Claire; it is a re-created 1890s logging camp—not the home of the fictional lumberjack.
6. Al Capone
7. Telling tall tales
8. The SPEBSQSA—Society for the Preservation and Encouragement of Barber Shop Quartet Singing in America
9. Harry Houdini
10. Lead, called simply "mineral" by the early settlers

Wyoming, the Equality State *(answers)*

1. The Oregon Trail
2. The Cowboys, naturally; Wyoming is also nicknamed "the Cowboy State."

tence here.

3. What national park's name means "large bosom"?
4. What near-legendary mountain man is buried in Cody?
5. The National First Day Covers Museum is devoted to what hobby?
6. What material composes the ceilings of the Senate and House chambers in the capitol?
7. What huge state did Wyoming surpass in having the smallest population?
8. What is distinctive about the Accidental oil well in Newcastle?
9. What famous Indian guide is buried at Fort Washakie?
10. What town was founded by the famous Buffalo Bill Cody?

☆ The District of Columbia, Federal Town

1. What famous trees bloom along the Tidal Basin in April?
2. What famous building has a statue of Justice outside it?
3. What name is given to the nineteen-foot statue atop the U.S. Capitol?
4. The Library of Congress's concert hall is named for which nontalkative president?
5. What federal agency prints money and postage stamps?
6. What warrior president's statue is in Lafayette Square?
7. The Museum of the Third Dimension is devoted to what type of photography?
8. The Folger Library is devoted to what noted English author?
9. What was the original name for the White House?
10. Whose gun could you see on display at Ford's Theatre?

3. Grand Teton—the original name being French
4. Jeremiah Johnson, subject of a movie with Robert Redford
5. Stamp collecting
6. Stained glass
7. Alaska, which was traditionally the largest state with the smallest population; that changed with the 1990 census.
8. It is the nation's only producing oil well dug entirely by hand.
9. Sacajawea, who aided the Lewis and Clark expedition
10. Cody, appropriately enough; it is now one of the key gateways to Yellowstone Park.

The District of Columbia, Federal Town *(answers)*

1. The Japanese cherry trees
2. The Supreme Court building
3. *Freedom*
4. Calvin Coolidge, known as "Silent Cal"
5. The Bureau of Engraving and Printing
6. Andrew Jackson's
7. Holography
8. William Shakespeare
9. The President's House (how original); it wasn't white at the beginning.
10. John Wilkes Booth's; it is the gun he used to assassinate Lincoln at the theater.